"I'll teach you about trains, William,
and you teach me about life."

Father *for* Life

Father
for Life

A Journey of Joy, Challenge, and Change

Armin A. Brott

Best-selling author of *The Expectant Father*

ABBEVILLE PRESS PUBLISHERS
NEW YORK   LONDON

To Dad and Mom for making me a son. To Tirzah and Talya for making me a dad. And to Lizzie and the Z, for helping me do it again.

EDITOR: Susan Costello
CONSULTANT: Jacqueline Decter
COPYEDITOR: Miranda Ottewell
DESIGNER: Celia Fuller
PRODUCTION MANAGER: Louise Kurtz

First edition
10 9 8 7 6 5 4 3 2 1

For cartoon credits see page 320

Library of Congress Cataloging-in-Publication Data
Brott, Armin A.
  Father for life : a journey of joy, challenge, and change / Armin A. Brott.
    p. cm.
  Includes bibliographical references and index.
  ISBN 0-7892-0784-2 (alk. paper)
    I. Fatherhood. 2. Father and Child. I. Title
HQ756. B764 2003
306.874'2-dc21   200304178

Contents

Introduction

Ask any father you know, and he'll say the same thing: he's a very different person today than he would have been if he hadn't had children. He'll probably tell you about the bad back he developed from being used for years as a living piece of playground equipment, about the lack of sex or having less disposable income because it's all been spent on tuition, or about the minivan he'd have never, ever set foot into a few years ago. But if you push a little more, he'll tell you that what's *really* changed him is his children. It's the act—actually the ongoing process—of being a father that's made him the man he is today and has forever altered his behavior, his priorities, his choices, his attitudes about the world and his place in it, and even where and how he lives. In short, being a father changes *everything*.

Really and truly, the idea that fatherhood transforms men isn't all that surprising. It's one of those "well, duh" kinds of things. But what *is* surprising is how little we really know about how parents—and fathers in particular—evolve over their lifetimes. We know a lot about child development and how parents influence their children. And every year dozens of books and thousands of magazine articles give us more insights into how we can raise happy, healthy, successful kids. We also know a fair amount about how adults develop over their life spans. But almost nothing has been written on how *parents* change and grow over time or how children impact their *parents'* lives. What little information there is focuses almost exclusively on mothers.

It's tempting to put the blame for this on the anthropologist Margaret Mead, who once said that fathers are a biological necessity but a social accident, a comment that still pretty well reflects our society's attitudes about fathers. For years, researchers studying families and children basically ignored fathers, never even bothering to include them in studies or to consider that they might play an important role in their children's lives. Fortunately, not everyone took that tack, and some even focused their energies on fathers. In 1975 one of those trend-bucking researchers, Michael Lamb, wrote that far from being "social accidents," fathers were actually the "forgotten contributors to child development."

In the decades since Lamb opened the door and brought fathers out of the closet, we've discovered just how important fathers are. Children whose fathers are involved in their lives are healthier and happier than kids whose dads aren't involved. They also do better in school, are more likely to go to college, earn more, and are less likely to abuse drugs or alcohol, have behavioral problems, go to jail, or become teen parents. As it turns out, fathers are no less important to their children than mothers are.

But back to father development. Fathers don't usually do their parenting in a vacuum. Like mothers, fathers play a variety of roles. Besides being dads, they're husbands, brothers, uncles, sons, nephews, employees, employers, coaches, and much more. So from a scientific perspective, it's hard to prove that being a father—as opposed to any other factor, such as being married or rich or living in Montana—is responsible for anything in particular.

But, as is often the case, people intuitively know things that scientific research simply can't prove. Take the differences between boys and girls, for example. No matter how politically correct it is to insist that boys and girls are the same, just about every parent who has at least one of each will tell you that despite the most gender-neutral upbringing, the two genders are just plain different. The same goes for father development. Just about everyone agrees that fathers are, in a way, the product of their children, growing with—and often in response to—them. Perhaps that's what William Wordsworth meant when he wrote, "The child is father of the man," in his 1802 poem "My Heart Leaps Up."

Father for Life is the first book ever to look specifically at how fathers develop over their entire life span. It's written for men—and women—who want to understand the symbiotic relationship between fathers and children and how each affects the other's growth and development.

I've been fascinated with this topic for quite some time, and started writing about it in *The Expectant Father: Facts, Tips, and Advice for Dads-to-Be*. The idea seemed simple enough: a man who's just found out that his partner is expecting is clearly very different from the kind of man he'll be when he first holds his newborn in his arms. And, as you might guess, that brand-new dad will have grown tremendously by the time his baby speaks his first words, and he'll keep changing and developing as that same child takes his first steps, gets potty-trained, and starts preschool. I explored this progression in the next two books, *The New Father: A Dad's Guide to the First Year* and *The New Father: A Dad's Guide to the Toddler Years*.

The process doesn't end there—in fact, it never does. To paraphrase Therese Benedek, one of the first researchers to study parent development, fatherhood is a process that ends only with the death of the father. Fathers continue to change every day, as their children hit puberty, learn to drive, move out, have kids of their own, move back home, and perhaps eventually reverse the roles and care for the father himself. But no matter how old his children are or where they live, a father is always a father.

So how do dads change over the course of their lifelong fatherhood? Many dads say that being a dad has given their life new meaning and direction. Others say that having children, interacting with them, getting to know them, teaching them, guiding them, being an active part of their lives, and generally dealing with the joys and frustrations of parenthood has made them:

- More patient, understanding, and empathetic.
- More aware of their own strengths and flaws and more tolerant of others' weaknesses.
- More flexible and better able to prepare contingency plans.
- More concerned about making the world a better place.
- Better able to see and appreciate things from others' perspective.
- A better husband, friend, employee, employer, and person in general.
- Emotionally deeper, able to experience and express unconditional love as well as many other emotions they'd rarely or never felt.
- Restructure their priorities, placing family and children above work and personal advancement.
- Proud—of their children's accomplishments and of their own role in helping their children achieve them.
- Slow down, enjoy life, and have more fun.
- Healthier and less likely to engage in risky or dangerous behavior.
- Smarter—you can go back and learn all those things you didn't get to when you were a kid.

"During the next stage of my development, Dad, I'll be drawing closer to my mother—I'll get back to you in my teens."

Father for Life is the product of years of ongoing research, starting with my own experience as a father of three. I've also spoken extensively with dozens of leading experts and studied literally hundreds of books and scientific articles about human development, parental development, parents, men in general, and fathers in particular.

But without a doubt, the most important sources of information were the hundreds of fathers I've interviewed over the years about their experiences and feelings. Besides reviewing my interview notes, I also did a more in-depth study—specifically for this book—of several dozen fathers (including brand-new dads, dads of toddlers, dads of school-age kids, dads of teens, dads whose kids are adults, grandfathers, adoptive dads, stepdads, and single dads). These men were kind enough to share their thoughts on how becoming and being a father had changed their life, which shed a lot of light on the overall pattern of the growth and development of fathers over time.

As you'll see over the course of this book, the stages of father (and parent) development are fairly predictable, just like the stages of child development.

Of course it's not quite as exact, but still, fathers who have kids of the same age seem to have something in common—worries, joys, a way of looking at things, concerns for their children and themselves.

Some of the major themes in this book are revisited from time to time, and that's only natural. Issues such as expectation vs. reality, coping with separation, adapting to changing relationships, learning to let go, independence, power struggles, and mortality crop up again and again over our lifetimes, often with varying degrees of intensity. Some people spend more or less time dealing with these issues before moving on.

How This Book Is Structured

Because fatherhood is a progression, I've structured this book chronologically. There are seven chapters in all, covering the stages of development from expectant fatherhood all the way through grandfatherhood. Throughout, I've tried to address the concerns of many different types of fathers: biological, adoptive, first-timers, experienced, the very young, those who started the process later in life, divorced, never married, and those who have kids with special needs or disabilities.

Chapter 1 discusses the issues that expectant fathers face—from the struggle to connect in the early months of the pregnancy and how-can-we-afford-this to the amazement of feeling the first kick and worries about being left out. Besides chronicling fathers' dramatic changes over the course of nine short months, we'll chart the growth and development of the fetus and check in with the expectant mom to see how she's doing. (Having a basic understanding of what the woman is going through is critical to understanding the expectant father's experience. After all, if she weren't pregnant, he wouldn't be having the experience at all.)

Chapter 2 starts with the birth of the baby and, in a sense, the birth of the new father. We'll see how the baby's growth and development over the first twelve months—from the blobby stage to those first wobbly steps—parallels the father's own evolution. We'll deal with the growth of skills and confidence and changes in attitude toward work, family, and community. We'll also introduce an issue that will come up over and over throughout the book: the difference between expectations of parenthood and reality.

Chapter 3 covers the preschool years, the period from the child's first birthday through the end of his fifth year. As the child grows and moves out into the world, so does the father, as he deals with separation, power struggles, reexamining what it means to be a father, and changing friendships and other relationships. We'll also take a look at the costs incurred in being an involved father and the benefits received by those who make that choice.

Chapter 4 focuses on the school years, from ages six to twelve. As the child becomes more independent and steps into the larger community, the father begins to take a greater interest in making that community—and the world—a better place for his children. We'll talk here about the evolution of fathers' ethics and spirituality, as well as the growth in their responsibilities, interest in teaching, mentoring, and tolerance of others.

Chapter 5 covers perhaps the toughest stage of parenthood—the adolescent years, ages thirteen through nineteen—which isn't much easier on the kids than it is on the father. Important issues include coping with the child's separation from family, going away to college, divorce, having to give up control in the parent-child relationship, jealousy of the child's (especially a son's) youth and vigor, facing mortality, caring for children and aging parents at the same time, and of course such explosive issues as drugs, sex, driving, and risk-taking.

Chapter 6 deals with a period of time some call "the launching years"— when adult children are from twenty to about thirty-five. Sometimes "emerging adults" move out and start their own lives. Others either stay or come back home, continuing their adolescence for a few more years. The father's role must change from parent to adviser, and he must learn to offer advice, not impose it. He has to think more flexibly and figure out ways to help his adult children when they need it without undermining their independence. At the same time he has to deal with a potential midlife crisis, aging, the empty nest, his changing relationship with his spouse, and the early stages of becoming a grandfather.

Chapter 7 shows that a father's growth and development continues even into his final years. Here, the now-elderly dad reviews his life, looking for confirmation that he's been a good father and a good man, and preparing himself to pass the torch to the next generation. We cover the continually shifting roles and changes between the father and children and his partner, how an adult child's troubles impact parents, dealing with physical decline, the joys and struggles of creating relationships with grandchildren, dealing with the loss of friends and relatives, and even preparing for one's own inevitable death.

All of the chapters have more or less the same organization. Each includes four basic parts:

+ **What's going on with the child.** Briefly explains how the child (or fetus) is developing physically, mentally, and emotionally/socially. You need to know

"You will find that time passes."

this because a lot of how you develop as a father is related to how your child develops—in other words, you adapt your development to his needs.

♦ **What's going on with you.** This is the meat of the chapter and discusses in detail the kinds of change and development you're likely to be experiencing at any specific stage, as well as the concerns you may be dealing with. This section covers emotional, psychological, and, where applicable, physical development.

♦ **Why be involved?** Sadly, too few men—and even fewer women—realize just how important fathers are—to their children and their families. We'll talk here about the specific ways being an involved father benefits his children, their mother, the parents' relationship, and the father himself.

♦ **How to stay involved.** Now that you know how critical the father's role is, this section includes a short discussion of specific ways you can develop and deepen your relationships with your children. The chapter on grandfatherhood also includes a lot of information on the importance of grandfather-grandchild relationships and how granddads can stay involved.

A Note on Terminology:
He, She, Girl, Boy, Your Partner, Your Wife

In the not-so-distant past (and the present, really) parenting books, in which the
parent was assumed to be the mother, almost always referred to the child as "he."
There's certainly a good argument to be made that in grammatically proper
English, the male pronoun is sort of a generic term. Still, as the father of three
girls, I've always wanted to see at least an occasional "she," if for no other reason
than to let me know that what I was reading might actually apply to me too. But
as a writer, I absolutely hate "his or her," "he or she," and especially "s/he." They
also make for cumbersome reading and awkward sentences. So, to make things a
little easier on everyone, I've alternated between "he" and "she" a chapter at a
time. Except in very specific circumstances, whatever's being said about "him"
applies equally to "her" and vice versa.

In the same way that referring to all children as "he" discounts the experiences
of all the "shes" out there, calling all mothers "wives" essentially denies the existence
of the many other kinds of women who have (or care for) children: stepmothers,
girlfriends, lovers, fiancées, domestic partners, and so on. Whatever your feelings
about the sanctity (or not) of marriage the fact is that many men out there aren't
married to the biological mother of their children. So, in an attempt to keep
ruffled feathers to a minimum, I'm referring to the woman you're involved with
as "your partner," although sometimes an occasional "wife" will slip in.

I'D LOVE TO HEAR FROM YOU

I hope you'll share with me your experiences, feelings, comments, and
suggestions about anything you read in this book. You can reach me c/o
Abbeville Press (the address is on the copyright page) or by e-mail at
armin@mrdad. com. And please visit my Web site: (*www.mrdad.com*).

A DISCLAIMER...

I'm not a pediatrician, attorney, financial planner, or accountant, nor do I play
one on TV (although I do have a radio show). And even though the information
in this book is solidly based on extensive research as well as on many individuals'
experiences, every father's situation is unique. So please be sure to consult with
an appropriate professional about whether your plans are in your best interests
and those of your family.

The Expectant Father

1

THE FANTASY STAGE

Until fairly recently, there has been precious little research on expectant fathers' emotional and psychological experiences during pregnancy. The very title of one of the first articles to appear on the subject should give you some idea of the medical and psychiatric communities' attitude toward the impact of pregnancy on men. Written by William H. Wainwright, M.D., and published in the July 1966 issue of the *American Journal of Psychiatry,* it was called "Fatherhood as a Precipitant of Mental Illness."

As you'll soon discover for yourself, an expectant father's experience during the transition to fatherhood is not confined simply to excitement—or mental illness; if it were, this book would never have been written. The reality is that your emotional response to pregnancy is going to be no less varied than your partner's. During your partner's pregnancy you'll experience everything from relief to denial, fear to frustration, anger to joy, and everything in between. And if you're like a lot of men, you may even have some physical symptoms as well.

So why haven't men's experiences been discussed more? In my opinion it's because we, as a society, value motherhood more than fatherhood, and we automatically assume that issues of childbirth and child-rearing are women's issues. But as you'll learn—both from reading this book and from paying attention to your own experience—this simply isn't the case.

What's Going On with the Fetus

Month

1	Just because you can't feel anything doesn't mean that things aren't action packed. Only about two hours after you and your partner had sex, the egg is fertilized, and a day or so later you've got a tiny bundle of quickly dividing cells. By the end of the month the embryo will be about a quarter inch long and will sport a heart (but no brain), and some pretty stumpy little arm and leg buds.
2	This month your baby changes from embryo to fetus. By month's end, his or her (it's way too early to tell which) stubby little arms develop wrists (but no fingers yet), sealed-shut eyelids appear on the side of the face, along with ears, and a tiny, beating heart shows up (albeit on the outside of the body). Not exactly the bouncing baby one normally envisions. If you bumped into a six-foot-tall version of your baby in a dark alley, you'd run the other way.
3	By now, your little fetus looks pretty much like a tiny person—except that he or she (a really sharp ultrasound technician might be able to tell you which, but don't count on it) is only about two or three inches long, weighs less than an ounce, and has transparent skin. Teeth, fingernails, toenails, and hair are developing quite nicely, and the brain is not far behind. By the end of this month, the baby will be able to curl its toes, turn its head, and even frown.
4	By the end of month four, your baby will grow to about four or five inches long. The heart is now fully developed and will start pounding away at 120–160 beats per minute—about twice as fast as yours. In addition, the whole body is pretty much covered with smooth hair called *lanugo*. The fetus can swallow, suck his thumb, and kick like nobody's business. Your baby also knows when your partner is eating sweet things or sour things and may have a lot to say about it. He also reacts to light and dark at this stage. Shine a strong light on your partner's abdomen, and the baby will turn away.
5	Your baby's eyelids are still sealed, but the eyebrows and lashes are fully grown in, and you might be able to see the beginnings of a head of hair. By the end of this month your future darling is about nine inches long and weighs in at close to a pound. He kicks, punches, grabs at the umbilical cord, and has developed something of a regular sleep pattern—waking and dozing at regular intervals. Interim time will be spent doing somersaults and

eavesdropping on goings-on outside the womb. No kidding—he can hear at this point.

6 | Your baby's lean and mean and covered with *vernix,* a thick, waxy, protective coating. His eyes are starting to open, he coughs and hiccups, and you can see (if you were inside the uterus) his unique footprints and fingerprints. The movements of your now foot-long two-pounder are getting more controlled and stronger—especially when he starts responding to sounds from the outside world. He may even jump at the sound of a door slamming or car backfiring.

7 | Your baby has bulked up to three pounds or so, he's about fifteen inches long, and he sports red, wrinkly skin and two functional lungs. If he were born right now, he'd have a pretty good chance of survival. He'd probably like to be born right now anyway, since it's getting a little cramped inside— especially if he's bunking with a womb-mate. His eyes are fully open, and his irises react to light and dark. He can even dance, moving in time to music played outside the womb. His brain is developing incredibly quickly, but the surface of it is still fairly smooth, and he's not really capable of much rational thought. Given his living situation, that's probably a good thing.

8 | At this point, your baby's about eighteen inches long, weighs five pounds or so (a little less if he's sharing his quarters with a sibling), and his body now looks a little more like it belongs with that huge head. He'll probably have assumed the head-down, duck-and-cover position that he'll maintain for the rest of the pregnancy. With practically no room to maneuver, movements become less and less frequent but are often so powerful that you can tell which part of his body is doing the poking. His hearing is getting so good that he now responds differently to your and your partner's voices. Chances of survival outside the womb are excellent.

9 | During this final month, your baby grows like a maniac, putting on about half a pound a week. By the time he finally decides to leave the nice, warm uterus, he'll weigh six to nine pounds (less if he's a twin or triplet) and be about twenty inches long—so big that there will be hardly any room to kick or prod your partner anymore. His fingernails and toenails are frequently so long they have to be trimmed right after birth, and the lanugo and vernix that have been covering and protecting his little body are starting to slough off. And, despite the widespread myth that babies are born blind, his sight is just fine. If you shine a bright light (which you really shouldn't do) at his mother's abdomen, he'll blink.

Meanwhile, Back in Your Brain

THRILLED AND RELIEVED AND PROUD...

My wife and I had been trying to conceive for a few months, so the positive result on the pregnancy test wasn't much of a surprise. But that didn't make it any less thrilling. I'd always wanted to have children, and suddenly it seemed that all my dreams were finally going to come true. It was like hitting the million-dollar jackpot on the nickel slots. At the same time, I was filled with an incred-

---

The Shock Factor

I'm assuming that since you're reading this book, you have some interest in becoming a father. There are a ton of resources out there for expectant mothers, and even a few for expectant fathers. But what about resources for preconception? Practically none.

I know, the idea of preparing yourself to conceive sounds a little silly. After all, what do you really need besides a candlelit dinner and a nice bottle of wine? The truth is that preparing for parenthood—before conception—is very important. If the results of your partner's pregnancy test have come as something of a surprise to you, you're not alone; about half of all pregnancies in this country are unintended.

Thanks to modern contraception and legal abortion, women have a lot more control over whether they become parents than men do. We're limited to three options: condoms (which don't always work), abstention (which isn't very practical for most men), and vasectomies. Researchers Christine Bachrach and Freya Sonenstein speculate that "men's relative lack of control over their reproduction" may be one of the major reasons that fathers often feel less responsible for their children and are generally less involved with them than mothers.

Nine months of pregnancy might seem like enough time for most people to get used to the idea that they're going to be parents. But having a little extra time to get psychologically (and maybe financially) ready to have kids makes a huge difference. Overall, "the quality of parenting and child well-being are related to the extent to which births were wanted and planned," write Bachrach and Sonenstein. "When children are the unintended consequence of sexual activity...they begin life at a disadvantage."

If you're looking for some guidance in planning a future pregnancy, my favorite books are *Thinking Pregnant* by Megan Steelman, and *The Parenthood Decision* by Beverly Engel.

---

ible feeling of relief. Secretly, I'd always been afraid that I was sterile and that I'd have to be satisfied with taking someone else's kids to the circus or the baseball game. I also felt a surge of pride. After all, I was a man, a fully functional man—all right, a stud, even. And by getting my wife pregnant, I'd somehow lived up to my highest potential.

AND NOW FOR SOMETHING COMPLETELY IRRATIONAL

At some point after the initial excitement subsides, a surprising number of men find themselves experiencing an irrational fear that the child their partner is carrying is not theirs. Psychologist Jerrold Shapiro interviewed more than two hundred men whose partners were pregnant, and found that 60 percent "acknowledged fleeting thoughts, fantasies, or nagging doubts that they might not really be the biological father of the child." The majority of these men don't actually believe their partners are having affairs. Rather, Shapiro writes, these feelings are symptoms of a common type of insecurity: the feeling many men have that they simply aren't capable of doing anything as incredible as creating life, and that someone more potent must have done the job.

EASING INTO ACCEPTANCE

It shouldn't come as any big surprise that your partner will "connect" with the pregnancy sooner than you will. Even though she won't be able to feel the baby kicking until about the fourth month, she's well aware that something's going on inside her body.

For you—and most men—however, pregnancy in the first month or two is a pretty abstract concept. For me—as excited as I was—the idea that my wife was really pregnant was so hard to grasp that I actually forgot about it for several days at a time. Most expectant dads find that the process of completely accepting the pregnancy is a long one—with the baby becoming progressively more real over the course of the nine months. "It's like getting the measles," as one father put it. "You get exposed, but it takes a while before you realize that you've got it."

Starting in about the third month, the pregnancy should start feeling a little more tangible. By far the biggest reality booster for me was hearing the baby's heartbeat, even though it didn't sound anything like a real heart at all, more like a fast *hoosh-hoosh-hoosh*. Somehow, having the doctor tell us that what we were hearing was really a heartbeat—and a healthy one at that—was mighty reassuring.

It was also what set off a real conflict for me—one that would plague me for months. On the one hand, sometimes when I remembered we were expecting, I got so elated that I could barely contain myself; I had visions of walking with my child on the beach, playing, reading, and helping him or her with homework, and I wanted to stop strangers on the street and tell them I was going to be a father. On the other hand, I made a conscious effort to stifle my fantasies and to keep myself from getting attached to the idea of being pregnant. That way, if we had a miscarriage or something else went wrong, I wouldn't be devastated.

For most expectant dads, hearing a beating heart isn't enough to convince us that the pregnancy is real. We're in what Dr. Katharyn May calls the "moratorium phase" of pregnancy—intellectually we know she's pregnant, but we still don't have any "real" confirmation. So what about the positive pregnancy tests and all those pelvic exams and blood and urine tests. And so what that her breasts and belly are swelling and that she even has food cravings. Even with all that, I still had the lingering suspicion that the whole thing was an elaborate, *Mission: Impossible*-style fake.

That'll all change the day you go in for the first ultrasound. Somehow, seeing the baby's tiny heart pumping and watching those bandy little arms and legs squirm convinced me that we might really be pregnant after all. (If your partner had to have any early ultrasounds, you may have had this little jolt of reality a while ago.)

For some men, even seeing a ultrasound isn't enough to bring the whole thing home (after all, the technology to fake a sonogram must exist, right?). But when your partner grabs your hand, puts it on her belly, and you feel that first gentle kick, a lot of your doubts vanish. If that still doesn't convince you that there's a baby in there and that he's yours, don't worry. Researcher Pamela Jordan found that a few hard-core skeptics don't really experience their children as real until they meet them face-to-face at birth.

Your growing acceptance of the pregnancy may be reflected in your dreams as well. Researcher Luis Zayas has found that in expectant fathers' dreams in the early and middle stages of the pregnancy, "the child is not represented as a person. Instead, symbols of the child are present." But as the pregnancy advances to the final stage, expectant fathers—consciously and unconsciously—produce clearer images of their children.

OUT OF SYNCH

You and your partner are going to be on a very similar psychological journey while she's pregnant. You'll both experience a huge variety of feelings, emotions, worries, and joys, all of which follow a basic progression from beginning to end. Unfortunately, you won't be going through the same things at the same time. Men are generally one trimester behind. Here's a rough comparison of what each of you is going through as the pregnancy progresses.

TRIMESTER	YOUR PARTNER	YOU
1ST	Excited, distracted, has some apprehension about the future, some worries about miscarriage, concerns about the baby's health and safety.	Brief excitement, then not much for a while. It's all too abstract to grasp, and you may find yourself forgetting about it for a few days at a time.
2ND	Turning inward. Decreasing worries about things going wrong with the pregnancy, but more worries about how the pregnancy is changing her body. She's a little self-absorbed and more concerned about practical things: Is she going to be a good mother? Can you afford this? When will she go back to work? She may be looking for role models and could develop a deeper bond with her mother.	Excited, distracted, some apprehension about the future, worries about miscarriage, the baby's and your partner's health and safety, feeling left out and jealous of all the attention she's getting.
3RD	Focusing on you. More dependent on you, needs confirmation that you love her, that you find her attractive, that you're not going to abandon her, that you're going to be an involved dad.	Turning inward. Less worried about health and safety, more concerned with practical things: What kind of dad are you going to be? Where are you going to find role models? Can you afford this? How will this affect your life? How will you balance work and family?

FEELING LEFT OUT

Although everything both you and your partner are going through psychologically is normal, as you can see from the chart above, there are some potential conflicts—especially in the second and third trimesters. The biggest danger is that while your partner is turning inward or bonding with her own mother and the baby, you may end up feeling left out, rejected, or even pushed out of the way. This can be particularly painful, and the excitement you feel at this stage can be outweighed by bitterness. But no matter how much it hurts, resist the urge to "retaliate" by withdrawing from her. Fortunately, this period of turning inward won't last forever.

In a lot of cases, men's feelings of being excluded are aggravated by the way they're treated by their partner's doctors. Pamela Jordan found that most men feel that their presence at prenatal visits is perceived as "cute" or "novel," and many men complain that medical professionals have a tendency to treat them as mere onlookers or intruders and consider their partners the only ones worth interacting with. If they are talked to at all, it is only to discuss how to support their partners. The fact that fathers have very specific and important needs and concerns doesn't seem to occur to many doctors.

Fortunately, this wasn't my experience at all, and my interviews with new and expectant dads are indicating that this situation is changing, albeit slowly. My wife's OBs have all gone out of their way to include me in the process. They made a special point of looking at me when talking about what was happening with my wife and the baby, encouraged me to ask questions, and answered them thoroughly. Part of the reason for this, however, was that from the very beginning I made it clear that I wanted to be involved, and I asked a lot of questions, making it pretty well impossible for them to ignore me. I'd suggest that you do the same, especially if you have even the slightest suspicion that your partner's practitioner is ignoring you or not taking you seriously.

Several researchers have noted that a small number of expectant fathers have affairs during the late stages of their partners' pregnancies. But these "late pregnancy affairs" rarely happen for the reasons you might think. Jerrold Shapiro found that most men who have had a late-pregnancy extramarital affair share the following characteristics:

- They felt extremely attracted to their partners and were very interested in "affectionate sexual contact" with them.
- They felt particularly excluded from the pregnancy and birth process.
- The affair was with a close friend or relative of the woman. (This would indicate that the person with whom the man had the affair was also feeling excluded from the pregnant woman's life during the pregnancy.)

Expectant mothers also have affairs during their pregnancies. In fact, Dr. Shapiro suggests that women are just as likely to have affairs as men. Couples who suddenly find themselves with no sexual outlet—and are feeling pushed away or misunderstood by their partners—may be tempted to satisfy their needs elsewhere.

TURNING INWARD

Toward the end of the pregnancy, other conflicts may arise because you and your partner aren't in the same psychological place. Just as it was for your partner, your "turning inward" and thinking about fatherhood, finance, work and family, and everything else is perfectly normal. You've got a lot of stuff to think about, most of which you need to work thorough on your own. The problem is that while you're focusing on everything that's going on inside your head, your partner (who has been pretty focused on *herself* until now) is now turning her thoughts to you. She may be feeling insecure and need to be reassured that you aren't going to leave her. She may also be feeling emotionally needy and crave

A Note for Renewed Dads

Since expectant mothers and fathers are rarely in the same psychological place at the same time, there's lots of room for conflict. If your partner is excited, for example, she may expect you to feel the same way and may get upset if you don't. This is especially true if you're a "renewed" dad—someone who has kids from a previous relationship, gets into a new one, and becomes a new dad all over again. This brings up a potentially sticky problem: being an expectant dad isn't something new and exciting for you. Besides the natural, slower male pregnancy-acceptance pace, you've been through the whole thing before, and you know exactly what you're in for. But for your partner, it *is* new and exciting, and she won't be too happy about your lack of enthusiasm. It may make her feel that you don't love her as much as you loved the mother of your other kids, or it may make her afraid that you aren't going to be supportive or that you aren't interested in being a parent—at least not with her. I never advocate lying to your partner, but having been in exactly this position, I'd strongly suggest that if you're not absolutely thrilled, you make a serious effort to act a little more excited than you may be feeling.

Of course, not all renewed dads feel this way. Some I interviewed said that being expectant again after a long break was better than the first time—having done it before and being more secure financially and in their relationships took a lot of the pressure off and made it possible to enjoy the experience more fully.

confirmation of your love for her. Or she may be worried—just as you are—about her physical safety.

The combination of the pressure you're putting on yourself and the pressure your partner is putting on you can put you in a terrible spot. On the one hand, you have to pay close attention to her subtle (or not-so-subtle) hints and make sure she gets the attention she needs. If she doesn't, she may think you don't care. As Libby Lee and Arthur D. Colman, authors of *Pregnancy: The Psychological Experience*, write, "A man who ignores his partner's anxieties may find they escalate rather than abate with a condescending 'Everything is going to be all right, dear.'" On the other hand, just when you're feeling most vulnerable and least in control, your own needs are swept under the rug. And what's worse, the one person you most depend on for sympathy and understanding may be too absorbed in what's going on with herself and the baby to do much for you.

This results in what Luis Zayas calls an "imbalance in interdependence," which leaves you to satisfy your own emotional needs along with your partner's. In many cases this imbalance becomes a kind of vicious circle: the less response you get to your dependency needs, the more dependent you feel. It can be extremely tempting in this kind of situation to try to get away from the external pressures by distancing yourself from your partner. You can't, of course, get away from your internal pressures. If you are feeling trapped or pressured or dependent, it's important to let your partner know in a gentle, nonconfrontational way.

TAKING A GREATER INTEREST IN FATHERHOOD

After the initial excitement of that first kick has passed, you may find yourself consumed with the question of whether or not you're ready to be a father. When this happened to me, I still wanted children—nothing had changed there—but I

Expectation vs. Reality, Round One

One of the biggest issues you'll have to deal with over the many, many years you'll be a father is the conflict between your expectations and reality. How you deal with this conflict and how well you accept the frequent disconnects will have a lot to do with your overall level of satisfaction with being a father. You probably already had some experience with this: Did your partner get pregnant when you expected her to, and did you react the way you—or she—expected? Is being an expectant father affecting you, and is it changing your relationship with your partner the way you thought it would? And so on. After your baby is born, there'll be

a lot more: you'll have to reconcile your expectations for your partner's labor and delivery with how they actually went. Later, you'll have to find a balance between how you expected fatherhood to be, how you expected your child to be, and the way things actually are. The process never ends.

At this point, though, one of the most troublesome expectation-vs.-reality battles you may be dealing with is over the gender of your future child. In case you hadn't noticed, our society is absolutely fixated on gender. So it's not surprising that most parents (if they don't already know) eventually—or constantly—speculate about the sex of their unborn baby. A lot of this is based on common stereotypes and prejudices that almost all of us have about gender, and it starts long before our kids are even born. Take the baby's kicks, for example. Expectant mothers who know they're carrying boys often describe the babies' movements as "vigorous," "earthquakelike," or even just "very strong." They describe girls' kicks as "very gentle," "not terribly active," or "lively but not excessively energetic." In reality, says Carole Beal, author of *Boys and Girls: The Development of Gender Roles,* there aren't any significant differences between boys' and girls' fetal activity levels.

Preconceived (so to speak) notions such as these may also have an influence

(continued on following page)

(continued from previous page)

on your preferences. "Parents usually say they don't care what gender their child is as long as it's healthy," says Beal. "But the truth is that couples have a definite preference for the sex of their child." That preference is usually for a boy, and it's expressed by both men and women. Generally speaking, dads prefer boys because they feel more comfortable with them, or because they feel that a boy would carry on the family name. Mothers may prefer boys because they know—instinctively or otherwise—how much it means to their husbands.

Some guys are actually afraid of getting a child of the "wrong" gender, feeling that if they do, they won't be able to have the parenting experience they'd imagined. For many men, their images of themselves as parents are closely linked to the gender of their children. As boys, we spent a great deal of our childhood running, jumping, wrestling, playing football, and doing other physically active things. So it's natural to imagine ourselves doing the same things with our own children. But some men feel uncomfortable with the idea of wrestling with their daughters, believing that playing physically with girls would somehow be inappropriate. Wrong. Not only is it safe and appropriate to play physically with girls, it's quite beneficial for them in some unexpected ways (we'll talk about these and other benefits at the end of every chapter).

Your preferences may have a major impact on a lot of other people too. According to Beal, boys tend to bring fathers into the family more: fathers of newborn boys actually visit the nursery more often and stay there longer than fathers of girls. In addition, couples who have girls first often have more children, trying to have a boy. But those who have boys first often end up with smaller families. Some experts speculate that this is at least in part due to the perception that boys are more "difficult." Even stranger, Carole Beal found that divorce rates are lowest for couples who have only boys, and highest when they have only girls.

The moral of the story is that if you find yourself preferring one gender over the other—particularly if you're hoping for a boy—try to stop. If you can't, do yourself and everyone else a favor and keep it to yourself. If your child turns out to be the "wrong" gender, chances are he or she will eventually find out about it (probably from an unthinking friend or relative whom you once told in complete confidence). Besides the problems I just raised in the previous paragraphs, the feeling of being inadequate, of "letting you down," and even of being secretly rejected or loved less may haunt your child for many years, especially in adolescence, when self-confidence is often at a low.

suddenly realized that in only four or five months I'd be facing the biggest challenge of my life, and I didn't know a thing about what I was getting into. I felt as though I were about to attempt a triple back flip from a trapeze—without ever having had any lessons, and without a safety net.

I had already done a lot of reading about pregnancy and childbirth, but I still didn't feel confident that I knew what fathers are really supposed to do and how they're supposed to do it. Doesn't it seem a little strange—scary, really—that you need a license to sell hot dogs on the street or to be a beautician, but there are absolutely no prerequisites for the far more important job of being a father?

Feeling the baby's first kicks may make you much more interested in reading about pregnancy, if you haven't been doing so already. You may also find yourself wanting to spend more time with friends or relatives who have small kids, asking questions, or just watching how other men interact with their children. You'll probably notice that younger dads (those under about twenty-five) spend a little less time with their kids—playing, teaching, reading—than older dads (those over thirty-two).

WHAT, ME WORRY? OBSESSING ABOUT MONEY

American society values men's financial contribution to their families much more than it does their emotional contribution. And expressing strong feelings, anxiety, or even fear is not what men are expected to do—especially when their wives are pregnant. So as the pregnancy progresses, most expectant fathers fall back on the more traditionally masculine way of expressing their concern for the well-being of their wives and little fetuses: they worry about money. Not surprisingly, though, expectant fathers in their early and mid-twenties feel more financial pressures than dads-to-be who are over thirty-two. These "older" fathers tend to be more settled in their careers and have greater income than the young bucks.

You may express your financial worries—if you have them at all—by becoming obsessed with your job, your salary, the size of your home, the Dow, NASDAQ, and even the rise and fall of interest rates. Expectant fathers frequently work overtime or take on a second job; others become tempted by lottery tickets or get-rich-quick schemes. Watch out for insurance agents and financial advisers who try to pressure you into buying insurance policies you don't need or making investments you and your family can't afford. Clearly, a new baby (and the decrease in household income while the mother is off work) can have a significant impact on your finances. But as real as that impact is, your financial worries may "get out of proportion to the actual needs of the family," write the Colmans. "They become the focus because they are something the man can be

J. DATOR

expected to handle. The activity may hide deeper worry about competence and security." So calm down.

TRYING TO UNDERSTAND WHAT'S GOING ON WITH YOUR BETTER, SOMETIMES MORE MISERABLE, AND CRABBIER HALF

At this point most of your fatherhood experience is going to be a reaction to what's going on with your wife. Here's a brief look at how the pregnancy is affecting *her.* Understanding what she's going through, physically as well as emotionally, will make you a lot more sympathetic—and appreciative.

MONTH	PHYSICALLY	EMOTIONALLY
1	◆ Morning sickness (nausea, heartburn, vomiting). ◆ Food cravings or aversions. ◆ Dizziness, irritability, headaches. ◆ Fatigue. ◆ Breast changes: tenderness, enlargement.	◆ Thrilled, stunned, apprehensive, or even a little frightened about the coming nine months and what's in store. ◆ A heightened closeness to you. ◆ Mood swings and sudden, unexplained crying.

MONTH	PHYSICALLY	EMOTIONALLY
2	• Ongoing fatigue. • Ongoing morning sickness. • Frequent urination. • Tingly fingers and toes. • Breast tenderness and darkening nipples.	• Continued elation, which can alternate with ambivalence about being pregnant. • Inability to concentrate on her work. • Fear you won't find her attractive anymore. • Continuing moodiness. • Fear of an early miscarriage.
3	• Fatigue, morning sickness, breast tenderness, and other early pregnancy symptoms begin to disappear. • But moodiness continues. • Waistline thickens.	• Heightened sense of reality about the pregnancy once she hears the baby's heartbeat. • Though her bond with the baby grows, her ambivalence about the pregnancy may continue. • Frustration and/or excitement over thickening of waistline. • Turning inward—beginning to focus on what's happening inside her.
4	• Nipples darkening; freckles and moles might get darker and more obvious (a normal side effect from her increasing skin pigmentation). • Increasing appetite as morning sickness begins to wane. • Clumsiness—dropping and spilling things. • She may be able to feel some slight movements (although she probably won't associate them with the baby unless she's already had a child).	• Great excitement when she sees the sonogram. • Worries about miscarriage are beginning to fade. • Concern about what it really means to be a mother. • Continuing forgetfulness and mood swings. • She may get very depressed when her regular clothes stop fitting her and may become obsessed with her appearance.

MONTH	PHYSICALLY	EMOTIONALLY
4 *(continued)*	• She may notice some strange changes in her vision. If she wears contacts, they may be bothering her. • She may get gingivitis (swollen, bleeding gums)—60 to 75 percent of pregnant women do.	
5	• Can feel the baby's movements—and knows what they are. • May have occasional painless tightening of the uterus called Braxton-Hicks contractions or "false labor." The difference between false and real labor is that during real labor, the cervix begins to open. In false labor, it doesn't. • Continuing darkening of nipples; appearance of dark line from belly button down the abdomen. • Her breasts are getting larger and may "leak" a little when she's sexually excited. • Hormones are running wild; she's forgetful, her fingernails may be brittle, and her skin may be splotchy. But her hair probably never looked better (pregnant women tend to not lose as much hair as nonpregnant women, and this makes her locks thicker and silkier).	• Very reassured by the baby's movements and less worried about miscarriage. • Developing feeling of bonding with the baby. • Increasing sensitivity about her changing figure. • Increase in sexual desire. • Increasingly dependent on you—needs to know you'll be there for her, that you still love her.

MONTH	PHYSICALLY	EMOTIONALLY
6	• Period of greatest weight gain begins. • Increased sweating. • Increased blood supply gives her that pregnant "glow", it may also be giving her some sciatica or even carpal tunnel syndrome as all that extra blood compresses some of her nerves. • Swelling of the hands and feet. • Fatigue, dizziness, and a runny nose are not uncommon. • A pretty serious backache—especially if she's carrying twins or more. • Some incredibly bizarre food cravings (see below for more).	• Moodiness is decreasing. • Continued forgetfulness and even some short-term memory loss (see below for more). • Feeling that the pregnancy will never end. • Increased bonding with the baby. • Even more dependent on you, damn it.
7	• Increasing general physical discomfort (cramps, dizziness, abdominal achiness, heartburn, gas, constipation, and so forth). • Itchy belly. • Some increasing clumsiness and decreasing stamina. • Her hip joints are expanding, and she's having to learn to walk in a new, awkward way, which may explain why she's a little more susceptible to muscle pulls. • Some thick, white vaginal discharge (it's called leukorrhea, and is completely normal). • Increased Braxton-Hicks (false labor) contractions.	• Decreased moodiness. • Dreaming/fantasizing about the baby. • Concerned about work—not sure she'll have the energy to go back, and concerned about how to balance roles of mother, wife, employee . . . • Fear about the labor and delivery.

MONTH	PHYSICALLY	EMOTIONALLY
8	• Even stronger fetal activity. • Heavier vaginal discharge. • General discomfort getting more severe. • Frequent urination. • Sleeplessness—can that really be a surprise? • Increased fatigue. • Shortness of breath as the baby takes up more room and presses against her internal organs. • Water retention, and swelling of the hands, feet, and ankles. • More frequent Braxton-Hicks contractions.	• Feeling special—people are giving her their seats on buses or in crowded rooms, store clerks go out of their way to help her. • Feeling a bond with others, like a member of a secret club (strangers keep coming up to tell her about their own pregnancy experiences or to touch her belly). She might also be scared by all those horror stories or angry at all those unsolicited touches. • Feeling exceptionally attractive—then ugly. • Worried about whether the baby will be normal, whether she'll be able to cope with the responsibilities of motherhood, and whether her body will ever get back to normal again. • Afraid her water will break in public.
9	• Increased sleeplessness and fatigue. • A renewed sense of energy when the baby's head "drops" into the pelvis and takes some of the pressure off. • She may have stopped gaining weight, but she's still just plain miserable, with increased cramping, constipation, backache, water retention, and	• More dependent on you than ever—afraid you won't love her after the baby is born (after all, she's not the same woman you married). • Impatient: can't wait for pregnancy to be over. • Short-tempered: tired of answering "So when's the baby coming?" questions—especially if she's overdue.

MONTH	PHYSICALLY	EMOTIONALLY
9 *(continued)*	swelling of the feet, ankles, and face. ♦ If her bellybutton was an innie before, it may have become an outie (the change isn't permanent, though). ♦ Absolutely no interest in sex.	♦ May be afraid she won't have enough love to go around—what with loving you, and all. ♦ Increasing preoccupation with the baby and, perhaps, a sudden and unexplained interest in Martha Stewart and interior decorating. ♦ Fear she won't be ready for labor when it comes.
	♦ Birth birth birth birth.	♦ Birth birth birth birth.

DADDY, THE PROTECTOR

As if worrying about finances weren't enough, many expectant fathers find themselves preoccupied with the physical health and safety of the other members of their growing family (but not their own—studies have shown that men go to the doctor much less frequently than usual when their partners are pregnant). Some men's health and safety concerns take on a rather bizarre twist. Psychiatrist Martin Greenberg, for example, found that "more than a few men purchase weapons during a pregnancy." Fortunately, most of them sell their arsenals after the baby is born.

In my case, I quizzed my wife about how much protein she was eating; I reminded her to go to the gym for her workouts; I even worried about the position she slept in. All in all, I was a real pain. (I was right about the sleeping position stuff, though. Sleeping on the back is a bad idea; the baby-filled uterus presses on the intestines, back, and a major vein—the inferior vena cava—and could cause hemorrhoids or even cut off the flow of oxygen or blood to both your partner and the fetus. It's rare, but it could happen.)

The sad fact—especially for pessimists like me—is that miscarriages happen fairly frequently. Some experts estimate that as many as one pregnancy out of five ends in miscarriage. In fact, almost every sexually active woman will have one at some point in her life. (In most cases the miscarriage happens before the woman ever knows she's pregnant—whatever there was of the tiny embryo is swept away with her regular menstrual flow.)

In most cases, miscarriages—most of which happen within the first three months of the pregnancy—are a blessing in disguise, the body's way of eliminating a fetus or embryo that would be better off not surviving. If your partner has a miscarriage, neither of you is likely to find that particularly reassuring. But remember that over 90 percent of couples who experience a single miscarriage are able to conceive again and have a healthy baby later.

Many expectant dads also worry about birth defects—this seems to be especially common among guys whose partners are over thirty-five, when all those prenatal tests are constant reminders about the possibility. If one of those tests indicates that your baby will be born deformed or with any kind of serious disorder, you and your partner have some serious discussions ahead of you. You and your partner have two basic options: keep the baby or terminate the pregnancy. Fortunately, you won't have to make either of these decisions on your own; every hospital that administers diagnostic tests has specially trained genetic counselors who will help you sort through the options.

If your partner is carrying three or more fetuses, you may have to deal with the question of "selective reduction." Basically, the more fetuses in the uterus, the greater the risk of premature birth, low birth weight, and other potential health hazards. Simply—and gruesomely—put, all these risks can be reduced by reducing the number of fetuses. It's an agonizing decision that only you and your partner can make.

Whether you and your partner chose to terminate your pregnancy or reduce the number of fetuses, or whether the pregnancy ended in miscarriage, the emotional toll can be devastating, and don't make the mistake of thinking it won't affect you. You won't have to endure any of the physical pain or discomfort, but your emotional pain can be just as severe as your partner's. You shared the same hopes and dreams about your unborn child, and you'll probably feel a profound sense of grief if those hopes and dreams were dashed. And many men, just like their partners, feel tremendous guilt and inadequacy when a pregnancy ends prematurely.

Almost all the studies done on how people grieve at the loss of a fetus have dealt only with women's reactions. The ones that have included fathers' feelings generally conclude that men and women grieve in different ways. Dr. Kristen Goldbach found that "women are more likely to express their grief openly, while men tend to be much less expressive, frequently coping with their grief in a more stoical manner." This doesn't mean that men don't express their grief at all. Instead, it simply highlights the fact that in our society, men don't have a lot of opportunity to express their feelings.

It's critical that you and your partner get as much emotional support as possible, anywhere you can get it. Many men who attend support groups say that until they joined the group, no one had ever asked how they felt about their loss. The group setting may also give you the chance to stop being strong for your partner for a few minutes and grieve for yourself. If you'd like to find a support group, your doctor or the genetic counselors can refer you to the closest one—or the one that might be most sympathetic to men's concerns. Some men, however, are not at all interested in getting together with a large group of people who have little in common but tragedy. If you feel this way, be sure to explain your feelings tactfully to your partner—she may feel quite strongly that you should be there with her and might feel rejected if you aren't. If you ultimately decide not to join a support group, don't try to handle things alone—talk to your partner, your doctor, your cleric, or a sympathetic friend. Keeping your grief bottled up will only hinder the healing process.

Me, Fall Apart When She's in Labor, Ha!

Men are supposed to be strong, right? Especially while their wives are pregnant. And any sign of weakness could be taken as an indication of, well, weakness. Perhaps it's those old societal pressures that make most men dread labor—not only because they aren't looking forward to seeing their partners in pain, but because they're afraid that they'll simply fall apart. And everybody knows that real men don't crack under pressure. Fortunately, this rarely ever happens. The best cure for this fear is to take a childbirth class. The more you know about what to expect during the labor and delivery, the less likely you are to worry that you won't be able to handle things. You should also let your partner know how you feel. The more supported and understood you feel, the less likely you'll be to feel as though you need to do everything absolutely perfectly. And finally, talk to some other dads who've been through it. Most fathers who have will say it was some combination of tiring, exhilarating, amazing, boring, scary, exciting, bloody, annoying, and just about any other positive or negative feeling you can come up with. They'll also tell you they wouldn't have missed it for the world.

Your Changing Sex Life

Your sex life is constantly in flux, changing and reacting to whatever's going on in your life. But at no other time are changes happening so fast, or are they so contradictory. For a lot of couples, sex in the first trimester is better than ever. You might be reveling in the recent confirmation of your masculinity, and she might be excited by the confirmation of her femininity and by the awe at what

Adoption Validation

If you're adopting, the time between your decision to adopt and the actual arrival of your child could be considered a "psychological pregnancy." Unlike with a biological pregnancy, you won't in most cases know exactly how long it's going to take from beginning to end. But what's interesting is that most expectant adoptive parents go through an emotional progression that's pretty similar to the one expectant biological parents experience, according to adoption educator Carol Hallenbeck. The first step is what Hallenbeck calls "adoption validation," which basically means coming to terms with the idea you're going to become a parent through adoption instead of by "normal" means.

This might seem pretty simple, but it's usually not. For many parents, adoption is a second choice, a decision reached only after years of unsuccessfully trying to conceive on their own, years of disappointments and intrusive, expensive medical procedures, says researcher Rachel Levy-Shiff. Infertility can make you question your self-image, undermine your sense of masculinity (how can I be a man if I can't even get my partner pregnant?), force you to confront your shattered dreams, and take a terrible toll on your relationship. If you're having trouble coping with accepting that you won't be having biologically related children, I urge you to talk to some other people about what you're feeling. Your partner certainly has a right to know—and she might be feeling a lot of similar things. In addition, the agency you're working with will probably have a list of support resources for adoptive fathers. Give them a try.

her body is doing. The two of you might be feeling closer to one another, or maybe it's the freedom of not having to worry about birth control. Whatever the reason, sex in the early months of the pregnancy is frequently wilder and more passionate than before.

Other expectant couples experience a drop in their sex life. Your partner may be exhausted and nauseated, neither of which makes for a terribly romantic evening. You may be turned off by your partner's changing figure. One or both of you may be afraid of hurting the baby (a nearly impossible task at this stage of the game). And some people feel that there's no sense in having sex anymore now that they're pregnant. Whatever your feelings—about sex, or anything else for that matter—try to talk them over with your partner. Chances are she's feeling—or soon will be—something very similar.

A lot of other factors will affect your sex life as the pregnancy progresses. After about the third month, your partner's nausea and fatigue are probably gone, which will make sex more appealing for both of you. You may find her pregnant body (with its larger breasts and fuller curves) erotic. She may be proud of her more ample figure and may be feeling sexier. She may also be aroused by how much she's arousing you. The increased blood flow to her pelvic area may make your partners' orgasms more powerful and easier to reach. (If that were happening to you, you'd want to have sex more often too.) And if you experienced a miscarriage in an earlier pregnancy, you may have been holding off on having sex for the first trimester. Now that it's safely behind you, all that pent-up desire may have gotten you both to the point where you're about ready to explode.

Again, on the downside, about 25 percent of women in their second trimester feel too uncomfortable or too awkward to want to have sex. She may even find it painful. Either or both of you may be having a tough time reconciling the reality that you're about to become parents with the idea that parents aren't supposed to be sexual. (Even though we are all living proof that our parents had sex at least once, it's somehow hard to imagine the two of them, in bed, naked.)

Your partner might think that you don't find her attractive and don't want to have sex with her, and you may not, in fact, be attracted to a woman whose body has been transformed from fun to functional. Or you may be thinking that she isn't feeling attractive and wouldn't be interested in sex anyway. If this is what you're thinking, you're probably wrong. According to psychologists Wendy Miller and Steven Friedman, expectant fathers generally underestimate how attractive their partners feel, and expectant mothers consistently underestimate how attractive their partners find them. (The bottom line is that most men find their pregnant partners' bodies erotic, and most pregnant women feel quite attractive. Neither men nor women manage to convey this to their partners, though.)

If you're afraid that sex will hurt your baby or your partner, you can stop worrying. The baby is safely cushioned by its amniotic fluid-filled sac, and unless your partner has cramps or bleeds during sex or her doctor feels there are special circumstances, sex during pregnancy is no more dangerous for your partner than at any other time. You (and she) may find this information reassuring. If you do, great; if not, now may be the time to talk about and try some different sexual positions (lying on your sides or with your partner on top, for example) and different ways of bringing each other to orgasm (oral sex, vibrators, and so on). Often simply making a few such changes can go a long way toward alleviating your fears.

While the first two trimesters can be a time of either increased or decreased sexual desire and activity, during the third trimester both head in the same direction: down. The most common reasons for this are a mutual fear of hurting the baby or your partner, fear that your partner's orgasm might trigger premature labor, her physical discomfort, and the fact that her larger body makes the "usual" sexual positions uncomfortable. Again, unless your partner's doctor has told you otherwise, sex still poses no physical risk to the baby or to your partner. But if you're both still interested in sex, this is the perfect time to try out some new and different positions.

Perhaps the biggest sex-related conflicts during pregnancy are the result of the man and the woman not being on the same sexual wavelength. So what do you do if she feels like having sex just when you're feeling put off by her Rubenesque figure, or if you want to have sex at a time when she's simply not interested? To start with, talk. As Arthur and Libby Colman so wisely write, "Unless the couple can talk about their sex life, their entire relationship may suffer, and that in turn will compound their sexual problems." After that, try some nonsexual affection, such as snuggling, touching, or just hugging each other. And say up front that that is what you're interested in doing, because it isn't as easy as it sounds. Researchers Carolyn and Philip Cowan have found that many couples need practice finding sensual ways to please each other short of intercourse. And both men and women hesitate to make affectionate overtures if they aren't sure they're ready to progress to intercourse and are worried they'll be misinterpreted. And finally, be nice to each other. Being critical of her figure will make her feel self-conscious, less attractive, and less interested in sex.

PANIC, ABSOLUTE PANIC

Just about six weeks before our first daughter was born, I suddenly had a great epiphany: our childless days were about to be over. It wasn't that I was worried about becoming a father—I already felt confident and prepared for my new role. What had struck me was much more superficial: once the baby came, it would be a long time before we'd be able to go to movies, plays, or concerts (or just about anyplace where you might have to be quiet), or even stay out late with our friends.

As it turned out, my wife was feeling the same thing at about the same time, so during the last two months of the first pregnancy, we ate out more often, went to more movies, saw more plays, and spent more late evenings with friends than in the next three years combined. A lot of expectant dads I've spoken with who are worried about the impending loss of their social lives have said they find themselves looking up and visiting old friends they haven't seen for years.

In addition to trying to pack a lot of fun activities into the last few months of the pregnancy, you might want to consider cramming in a few practical things as well: when you (or your partner) are preparing food, try to double or even triple the recipes and freeze what's left over in two-person servings. Believe me, during that first postpartum week, defrosting a bag of frozen spaghetti sauce is a lot easier than making a new batch from scratch.

NESTING, FULL THROTTLE

After morning sickness and 2 A.M. cravings for pickles, perhaps the most famous stereotype about pregnancy is a woman's "nesting instinct." Most women, at some point in their pregnancies, become obsessed (often unconsciously) with preparing the house for the new arrival: closets and cupboards are cleaned, and furniture that hasn't been budged for years suddenly has to be swept under.

Although much has been made of the woman's instinct, a variety of studies have shown that almost all expectant fathers experience some sort of nesting instinct themselves. Besides worrying about finances, many men spend a lot of time assembling—or even building from scratch—cribs, changing tables, and other baby furniture; shopping for baby supplies; painting and preparing the baby's room; rearranging furniture in the rest of the house; and even trying to find a larger living space for their growing families.

For some men, these activities are a way to keep busy and to avoid feeling left out. But for others, they represent something much more fundamental. As Pamela Jordan writes, "These nesting tasks may be the first opportunity the father has to do something for the baby rather than his pregnant mate."

A FEW ACHES AND PAINS AND HORMONE CHANGES OF YOUR OWN

Although most of what you'll be going through during your pregnancy will be psychological, don't be surprised if you start developing some physical symptoms as well. As many as 90 percent of expectant American fathers experience *couvade syndrome* (from the French word meaning "to hatch"), or "sympathetic pregnancy." Couvade symptoms are typically the same as those traditionally associated with pregnant women—weight gain, nausea, mood swings, food cravings—as well as some not associated with pregnant women: headaches, toothaches, itching, and even cysts. Symptoms—if you're going to have them at all—usually appear in about the third month of pregnancy, decrease for a few months, then pick up again in the month or two before the baby is born. In almost every case, though, the symptoms "mysteriously" disappear at the birth.

"My wife works, and I sit on the eggs. Want to make something of it?"

Interestingly, couvade symptoms aren't limited to biological expectant dads. In fact, according to adoption educator Patricia Irwin Johnson, sympathetic symptoms of pregnancy are fairly common among couples who are adopting. "One or both partners may experience repeated, and even predictably scheduled, episodes of nausea," says Johnson. "Food cravings and significant weight gain are not unusual. One or both may complain of sleep disturbances or emotional peaks and valleys."

So why do men have physical symptoms when their partners are pregnant? Well, there are several possible explanations. First, men have traditionally been socialized to bite the bullet when it comes to pain and discomfort. And when our loved ones are suffering, and we can't do anything to stop it, our natural (and slightly irrational) instinct is to try to take their pain away—to make it ours instead of theirs. This is especially true if we have even the slightest feeling—no matter how irrational—that we're responsible for the pain in the first place. If your partner has been suffering from morning sickness or has had any other pregnancy-related difficulties, you may feel responsible and guilty. And if her symptoms have been particularly rough, she might even reinforce your subconscious guilt by reminding you that you're the one who "got her into all this" in the first place.

Second, some men who develop couvade symptoms are jealous and are subconsciously trying to shift at least some of the focus of the pregnancy to themselves. My father, who was pacing the waiting room while my mother was in labor with me, suddenly got a gushing nosebleed. Within seconds the delivery room was empty—except for my mother—as three nurses and two doctors raced out to take care of my poor, bleeding father. I'm sure he didn't do it on purpose, but for one brief moment during the delivery, Dad was the complete center of attention. The same, of course, holds true during the pregnancy.

Third, some psychologists speculate that men's physical symptoms could be a kind of public way of asserting their paternity. Others say that expectant dads' physical couvade symptoms could be a chemically driven way of showing their partners just how committed they truly are. After all, you could be lying when you tell her you love her and that you're excited about being a dad. But it's a lot harder to fake a nosebleed or a backache or a weight gain. In short, your physical symptoms may be nature's way of giving your partner a way of evaluating your true feelings about her and the baby as well as your reliability as a partner and fellow parent.

Even stranger than couvades is the recent discovery that an expectant dad's hormones change along with his partner's. No, I haven't got that backward. While she's pregnant, several of your partner's hormone levels gradually rise. These include prolactin, which helps get her breasts ready to lactate (produce milk), and cortisol, which seems to be associated with parent-child bonding. It used to be that everyone thought these hormone changes were triggered by the developing fetus. But in a fascinating study, researcher Anne Storey and her colleagues found something that may change some minds. Storey took blood samples from expectant mothers and fathers at various points during the pregnancy and found that expectant dads' levels of cortisol and prolactin (which you wouldn't think guys would even have) paralleled their partners'. "The differences for mums were much more drastic, but the patterns were similar," she said. Fortunately, this doesn't mean that you'll be developing breasts any time soon. Like your partner, your hormone levels will return to normal not long after your baby is born, and your manliness will remain intact.

Couvade and male hormone changes may be related. Storey found that the men in her study who had experienced tiredness, weight gain, changes in appetite, or any other physical couvade symptoms had higher-than-average levels of prolactin and lower-than-average levels of testosterone compared to expectant dads who didn't have those physical couvade symptoms. In addition, studies have shown that the stronger an expectant dad's couvade symptoms, the better he'll care for his newborn. That may explain why it is that so many expectant dads develop an increased interest in children during their partner's pregnancy—it could be the body's way of preparing the expectant dad for his changing responsibilities.

REEXAMINING YOUR RELATIONSHIP WITH YOUR FATHER

As the reality of your prospective fatherhood unfolds, you'll probably find yourself contemplating how you'll juggle the various roles—parent, provider, husband, employee, friend—that will make up your paternal identity. You may already be spending more time reading about childhood and watching how your male friends, family members, or even strangers do it. But eventually you'll realize that your own father—whether you know it or not—has already had a profound influence on the kind of father you'll be. You also may find yourself nearly overcome with forgotten images of childhood—especially ones involving your father. Just walking down the street, I'd suddenly remember the times we went camping or to the theater, how he taught me to throw a baseball in the park, and the hot summer afternoon he, my sisters, and I stripped down to our underwear in the backyard and painted each other with watercolors. There's nothing like impending paternity to bring back all the memories and emotions of what it was like to be fathered as a child.

Your childhood memories may not all be positive. Some men's images of their fathers are dominated by fear, pain, loneliness, or longing. Either way, don't be surprised if you find yourself seriously reexamining your relationship with your dad. Was he the kind of man you'll want to use as your role model? Was he the perfect example of the kind of father you don't want to be like? Or was he somewhere in between? Many men, particularly those who had rocky, or nonexistent, relationships with their fathers, find that the prospect of becoming a father themselves enables them to let go of some of the anger they've felt for so long.

Don't be surprised if you start having a lot of dreams about your father. Dream researcher Luis Zayas found that an expectant father's uncertainty about his identity as father, his actual role, and his changed relationship with his wife and family are "among the psychic threads of fatherhood" that are fundamentally related to the man's relationship with his own father and are frequently present in his dreams.

So, whether you're awake or asleep, as you're thinking about your father, remember that what's really going on is that you're worried about what kind of a father you will be when your baby arrives. And remember that the kind of

father you become is completely up to you—despite all those silly expressions like "the acorn never falls far from the tree," and those sillier myths that we're doomed to be just like our parents. If you work at it, you can be the father *you* want to be, rather than the one that you might think fate planned.

A NEW SENSE OF MORTALITY

Although I've always been more than just a little fascinated by death, it wasn't until I became an expectant father the first time that death became more than a mere abstraction. Suddenly it occurred to me that my own death could have a serious impact on other people.

This realization had some interesting and fairly immediate results. The first thing that happened was that I became a much better driver—or at least a safer one. Overnight, yellow lights changed their meaning from "floor it" to "proceed with caution." I began to leave for appointments a few minutes earlier so I wouldn't have to hurry, I wove in and out of traffic less, and I found myself not quite so annoyed with people who cut me off in traffic. But besides becoming a better driver, I began to look back with horror at some of the risky things— parachuting, scuba diving—I'd done before I'd gotten married, and I began to reconsider some of the things I'd tentatively planned for the near future—

43

bungee jumping, hang gliding. Suddenly, there were people counting on me to stay alive.

My preoccupation with my own mortality had other interesting consequences as well. I found myself strangely drawn to my family's history; I wanted to learn more about our traditions, our history, our family rituals, the wacky relatives no one ever talked about. I even bought a family-tree computer program and began bugging my relatives about their birth dates. I didn't realize it at the time, but it's quite common for expectant fathers to experience a heightened sense of attachment to their relatives—both immediate and distant—even if they weren't particularly close before.

This really isn't so unusual, especially when you consider that one of the main reasons we have kids in the first place is so that a little piece of us will live on long after we're gone. I guess the hope is that one day seventy-five years from now, when my great-grandson is expecting a child, he'll start to explore his roots and want to get to know more about me.

FEELING HER PAIN

Especially in the last month or so of the pregnancy, many men begin to feel guilty about what they think they've been putting their partners through. Yes, you're the one who got her pregnant, and yes, she's uncomfortable as hell. But strange as it might seem to you, your partner does not blame you for what she's going through. She understands and accepts—as you should—that this was a joint idea, and that (at least short of surrogate motherhood or adoption) there's simply no way to have a baby without going through this.

There's no question about it: labor and childbirth are going to be painful for your partner (unless she has some drugs)—and for you. For her, the pain is largely physical. For you, it's psychological. As men, we're hardwired to want to protect our families. I couldn't possibly count the number of times—only in my dreams, thankfully—I've heroically defended my home and family from armies of murderers and thieves. But even when I'm awake, I know I wouldn't hesitate before diving in front of a speeding car if it meant being able to save my wife or my children. And I know I would submit to the most painful ordeal to keep any one of them from suffering. Unfortunately, there's little if anything we can do to take our partner's pain away.

But the good news is that the pain is finite; after a while it ends, and you get to leave the hospital with a lovely parting gift: your new baby. Ironically, though, your partner's pain probably won't last as long as yours. She'll be sore for a few weeks or so, but by the time the baby is six months old, the memories will have

*"Me carrying the baby and you having the cravings
is not my idea of shared responsibility!"*

faded. (If women could remember the pain, I can't imagine that any of them would have more than one child.) But six months, a year, even two years after our first daughter was born, the memories of my wife's screaming in pain remained fresh in *my* mind. And when we began planning our second pregnancy, the thought of her having to go through even a remotely similar experience scared the hell out of me.

Why Be Involved at This Stage at All?

Simple. Because the more involved you are in raising your children, the better a father you'll be. And the earlier you start (and what could be earlier than during pregnancy?), the easier it will be to get—and stay—involved when your child actually shows up. As we'll talk about throughout this book, being an involved father is good for everyone: your kids, your partner, and even yourself. Here are some of the specific benefits at this time. At this point the list is fairly short, but this is where it starts.

BENEFITS FOR YOUR CHILD

- Kids who grow up in families without a father or where the father is distant and uninvolved are more likely to drop out of school, start smoking, abuse drugs, become teen parents, have psychological and social problems, turn to

45

violence, and end up in jail. Being there from the start is no guarantee that your kids will never suffer any of these problems, but there's no question that your children will be happier, healthier, and more successful with you than without you.

• It could make your baby smarter. See "Chat with your baby" in the bulleted list on page 50.

BENEFITS FOR YOUR PARTNER

• She'll have an easier, healthier pregnancy if you're involved and supportive.
• Women whose husbands are there during delivery are more positive about the birth experience than women whose husbands aren't.
• Having you there may make her labor shorter, which, believe me, will make your partner very, very happy.
• The more involved you are, the happier your partner will be. And the happier she is, the better your relationship will be, and the longer it'll last.

BENEFITS FOR YOU

• You'll have a closer relationship with your baby right from the start, which will be the foundation for a lifelong close relationship.
• It expands your capacity to feel and express a wide variety of emotions—including plenty that you've never felt before.
• The more involved you are from the start, the more seriously your partner will take you, the more confident she'll be in your parenting, and the more supportive and encouraging she'll be of your relationship with your child. This is absolutely critical for you and your baby. As we'll discuss later in the book, men are as involved with their children as their wives will let them be. I know that sounds harsh, but it's absolutely true.

Staying Involved during Pregnancy

The best way to be involved at this stage is to learn everything you possibly can—about what your partner is going through, how your baby is developing, and what you're going through psychologically, emotionally, and physically. It's also essential that you support your partner every way you can. Here are some specific things you might do while your partner is pregnant:

◆ **Exercise with her.** Getting sufficient exercise is critical. It will help improve her circulation, which will ensure that the baby has an adequate blood supply, and it will keep her energy level high. Exercising during pregnancy may also help your partner keep her weight gain steady and reasonable, help her sleep better, improve her self-esteem, and reduce some of the normal pregnancy-related discomforts. It'll improve her strength and endurance, which will be helpful during labor and delivery, and may even lessen the chance that she'll deliver prematurely or need a cesarean section. If she was already working out regularly before the pregnancy, and if her doctor approves, she can probably continue her regular physical fitness routine. If she wasn't physically active before getting pregnant, this isn't the time for her to take up rock climbing. That doesn't mean, however, that she should spend the entire pregnancy on the sofa. Before starting any kind of workout program, discuss the details with your practitioner and get his or her approval. Running, swimming, cycling, tennis, golf, yoga, and low-impact aerobics are all good. Stay away from sports where she might take a hard fall, that require heavy lifting, or that are

extremely exhausting. If she can't carry on a normal conversation while exercising, she's working out too hard. Remind her to take plenty of breaks and drink lots of water before, during, and after the workout.

- **Help her eat right.** This is one of the best things you can do to ensure that you'll have a healthy, happy baby (and a healthy, happy partner), but don't be too hard on her. While she'd undoubtedly be better off eating nothing but healthy foods all the time, an *occasional* order of fries or a candy bar probably won't cause any serious problems. Be supportive. This means that you should try to eat as healthily as she does. If you absolutely must have a banana split, do it on your own time (and don't brag about it).

  If you're one of the many expectant adoptive parents who has met your future baby's birthmother, do whatever you can to support her pregnancy without being annoying. Encourage her to exercise, stop smoking, eat right, take her prenatal vitamins, go to her regularly scheduled medical appointments, and so on.

- **Go to all the ob/gyn appointments.** The general rule that women connect with the pregnancy sooner than men has an exception: men who get involved early on and stay involved until the end have been shown to be as connected with the baby as early as their partners. And a surefire way to get involved is to go to as many of your partner's ob/gyn appointments as pos-

"The amnio's fine, the sex is male, and the name is Wade."

sible. Most of the appointments involve your partner peeing in a cup and the following conversation: Doctor: "How're you feeling?" Your partner: "Pretty good." Doctor: "Great. We'll see you back in a month." Some of the time you'll be bored out of your mind, but overall it's a great opportunity to have your questions answered and to satisfy your curiosity about just what's going on inside your partner's womb. Besides that, going to the appointments has other advantages: first, you will become more of a participant in the pregnancy and less of a spectator. In other words, it will help make the pregnancy "yours." Second, it will demystify the process and make it more tangible. Hearing the baby's heartbeat for the first time (in about the third month) and seeing his or her tiny body squirm on an ultrasound screen (usually in the fourth or fifth month) bring home the reality of the pregnancy in a way that words on a page just can't do. Third, as the pregnancy progresses, your partner is going to be feeling more and more dependent on you, and she'll need more signs that you'll always be there for her. And while going to her doctor appointments may not seem quite as romantic as a moonlit cruise or a dozen roses, being there with her is an ideal way to remind her you love her and reassure her that she's not going to be alone. And finally, the more you're around, the more seriously the doctor and his or her staff will take you, and the more involved they'll let you be. If you're planning to go to your partner's checkups, you'd better break out your Palm pilot right now. Most women see their doctor at least once a month for the first seven months, twice in the eighth month, and once a week thereafter.

- **Get some time to yourself.** There may be times when you find the pressures of the pregnancy so overwhelming that you need just to get away from it for a while. If so, take advantage of the fact that you don't have a baby inside you, and give yourself some time off. Go someplace quiet where you can collect your thoughts or do something that will give you a break from the endless conversations about pregnant women and babies. Before you go, though, be sure to let your partner know where you're headed. And whatever you do, don't rub it in: she'd probably give anything to be able to take a breather from the pregnancy—even for a couple hours.
- **Get your finances in order.** Make a budget, put together a plan to pay off those pesky credit cards, check with your lawyer and accountant about doing a will or a trust, check with an insurance agent about what your new, post-baby life insurance requirements will be, and start checking out college savings plans. The best ones are the 529 plans (named for the IRS regulation). Depending on the state, you may be able to contribute as much as $150,000

over the lifetime of the plan, including $50,000 in one chunk if you don't make any additional contributions for five more years. In some states, your contributions may actually be deductible from your state tax. There are no income restrictions, and money you contribute grows tax-free—at least through 2010. You can find out more about 529s from the College Savings Plan Network at *http://www.collegesavings.org/yourstate.html*.

• **Show her you care, and care, and care.** In case you don't know how, here are some perennial favorites that are guaranteed to make you popular around the house (and make your wife the envy of all of her friends—pregnant and otherwise): give her foot massages; do some extra housework (without being asked); give her a hug (research shows that the more she is hugged, the more she'll hug the baby after he comes); shop and cook meals; do laundry; write love letters; go away for a romantic weekend (together, of course); tell her she's beautiful even if she's put on weight, and tell her again a few hours later; do something with her that she knows you absolutely hate to do, like go to the opera; smile and nod agreeably when she says, "You have no idea what it's like to be pregnant"; call her on the phone during the day—just to tell her you love her.

• **Chat with your baby.** Although the very idea may sound a bit nuts, fetuses are extremely responsive to sounds from the outside world. But why would a mature man want to spend time trying to communicate with a fetus when he could be out playing pool with his friends? Simple. It's fun. Plus, it may be able to help you establish a bond with your baby even before he's born. A good part of the natural connection babies have with their mothers may have to do with the mom's voice, which the baby hears every day. If you're worried about being left out, spending a little time "conversing" with your baby before he's born will get her used to your voice too. Some researchers believe that prenatal communication (which, by the way, doesn't have to be limited to words) stimulates babies' brains, triggering nerve cell development, helping them process information more efficiently. In other words, they believe it may make babies smarter. They also contend (though not everyone agrees) that prenatally stimulated babies tend to cry less at birth, have longer attention spans, sleep better, are less likely to develop learning disabilities, and turn out to be more creative and musical. If you're thinking about giving it a try, here are few things to consider:

  ◇ **Take it easy.** Your partner has a right to a little peace and quiet once in a while. But keep in mind that some researchers have found that women whose babies are stimulated before birth have shorter labors and a lower rate of C-sections. In addition, certain kinds of stimulation may reduce the risk of breech births (where the baby comes out feetfirst instead of headfirst).

◇ **Speak up.** So speak loudly enough so that someone across the room can hear you.

◇ **Keep it regular.** Put yourself on a schedule, so the baby will get to know that something's going to happen. Ease into it by patting your partner's belly before you start. And don't go overboard. Half an hour twice a day is plenty. Fetuses need plenty of time to rest, even more than newborns or kittens.

◇ **Mix it up.** Playing the same piece of music or reading the same haiku every day is great, but throw in some variety too. Fetuses get bored too.

◇ **Don't get your expectations too high.** There's no guarantee that anything you do will affect your baby in any way.

• **Have fun—while you still can.** Now's the time to take walks, go out for romantic dinners, see friends, go camping, travel, etc. Do it now, because it may be a while before you get another chance.

• **Get everything taken care of at work.** Are you taking time off after the baby is born? Are you eligible for family leave? Investigate your legal rights and your company's benefits. While you're at it, start putting together a plan for who's going to sit in for you while you're gone, how long you'll be gone, and so on. Do this well in advance, and there's a good chance your boss will be supportive.

• **Take a childbirth class.** Until the late 1960s, all you had to know to have a baby was where the hospital was located. And all that expectant parents did to prepare for the arrival of their baby was set up a nursery. Women checked into the hospital, labored alone in stark, sterile rooms, received general anesthesia, and woke up groggy and tender, not even knowing the sex of the child they'd delivered. Meanwhile, men were left to pace anxiously in hospital waiting rooms until a nurse came to give them the happy news. Today, however, it's hard to find a man who didn't already, or isn't planning to, attend the birth of his children (according to recent statistics, 90 percent of fathers-to-be are present at the birth). Although a lot of people use the terms *Lamaze* and *childbirth preparation class* interchangeably, there are really quite a few very different childbirth methods. Most focus on natural childbirth, but what distinguishes one from another is the approach each takes to dealing with pain. Your partner's practitioner or the hospital where she'll give birth will have information on a variety of classes. Whichever method you settle on, try to stay away from the word *coach*. It places waaaaay too much pressure on you by implying that you should be providing direction if things don't go quite the way they're supposed to during labor and birth. Does anyone seriously expect that after, maybe, twenty hours of classes and absolutely no medical training, you're going to know how to handle a true emergency?

- **Take a baby CPR class.**
- **Make a birth plan.** Your partner and you should put together a document laying out exactly the way you want the birth to go, including whether you want the doctor to offer drugs and whether you'll be able to catch the baby and snip the umbilical cord. Give the plan to the doctors as far in advance as you can.
- **Take care of the last-minute details.** Interview some pediatricians; plan out the best route to the hospital as well as a few alternatives; pack bags to take to the hospital; check into adding the baby to your insurance; read up on recognizing premature labor; get a car seat (the staff won't let you out of the

Keep Talking to Your Partner

When a couple becomes a family, "generally all the things that are good get better, and all the things that are bad get worse," writes Jerrold Shapiro. As the pregnancy continues, then, it's critical to learn to talk—and listen—to each other, and to find ways to help each other through this marvelous, but emotionally bumpy, experience.

As men, we've been conditioned to try to protect our partners from harm. And when our partners are pregnant, protecting them may include trying to minimize the levels of stress in their lives. One way men do this is by not talking about their own concerns. Carolyn and Philip Cowan write that men fear that mentioning their own worries may not only cause stress to their partners but also expose their own vulnerability at a time when they're expected to be strong for their wives.

The Cowans also found that this overprotective, macho attitude has some very negative side effects. First, because we never give ourselves the chance to talk about our fears, we never learn that what we're going through is normal and healthy. Second, our partners never get the chance to find out that we understand and share their feelings.

There's also some evidence that there are other benefits to talking about how you're feeling—and getting your partner's support for those feelings. Researcher Geraldine Deimer found that men who receive their partners' emotional support hospital without one); and make sure you've got a stroller, crib, and enough clothes, diapers, towels, and so on to last a while.

- **Be nice.** She's uncomfortable as hell—particularly if it's the summertime. Try to come home a little earlier, postpone out-of-town biz trips, call or e-mail a few times a day just to check in, and have those last-minute conversations: religion, education, circumcision, and so on.

- **Don't assume anything.** Now's the time—before it's too late—to discuss all the things you really should have but never got around to. Not all of the following issues are important to everybody, but in talking to couples around the country, I've been amazed at how many leave critical ideas undiscussed. Here are a few of the biggies:

  ◇ **Your involvement in the pregnancy.** Dr. Katharyn Antle May has found that expectant fathers have one of three basic styles. The *observer father* maintains a certain emotional distance and sees himself largely as a bystander; the *expressive father* is emotionally very involved and sees himself as a full partner; the *instrumental father* sees himself as the manager of

during pregnancy have better physical and emotional health and are better able to maintain good relationships with their spouses than men who don't get that kind of support.

Bottom line? Talk about your feelings—good, bad, or indifferent. Talk about your excitement about having a child, your dreams, your plans for the future, your fears, worries, and ambivalence, and how satisfied you are with your level of involvement during the pregnancy. But don't forget to ask your partner what she's feeling about the same things. Have these discussions regularly—what the two of you are thinking and feeling in the third month may be completely different from what you'll be thinking and feeling in the fourth, sixth, or ninth months. As difficult as it may seem, learning to communicate with each other now will help you for years to come.

The quality of your relationship can have a big impact on the quality of your parenting. One study found that couples who have discussed such mundane things as who does what with child care do better coping with the stress of parenthood. Also, expectant fathers whose marriages were rated as "satisfying" during the third trimester of their wives' pregnancy were more involved in care giving and play with their six-month-old infants, according to researcher Shirley Feldman and her colleagues.

the pregnancy and may feel a need to plan every medical appointment, every meal, and every trip to the gym. Whatever your style is, make sure to talk it over with your partner. After all, she's pregnant, too.

◇ **Your involvement in family tasks.** How much child care are you planning to do when the baby comes? How much is your partner expecting you to do? How much are you expecting her to do? Several studies have shown that to a great extent, women control their partners' involvement at home. If she wants her partner to take an active role in child care, he generally wants the same thing. But if she wants to keep these activities to herself, he usually expects to be less involved.

◇ **Religion.** Both you and your partner may never have given a thought to the religious education—if any—you plan to give your child. If you have thought about it, make sure you're both still thinking along the same lines. If you haven't, this might be a good time to start.

◇ **Discipline styles.** How do you feel about spanking your children? Never? Sometimes? How does she feel about it? How you were raised and whether your parents spanked you will have a great deal to do with how you raise your own children.

◇ **Sleeping arrangements.** It's never too early to give some thought to where you want the baby to sleep: in your bed? in a bassinet next to you? in a separate room?

◇ **Work and child-care expectations.** Is your partner planning to take some time off after the birth before going back to work? How much? Would you like to be able to take some more time off? How long? What types of child-care arrangements do you and she envision?

◇ **Finances.** Do you need two paychecks to pay the mortgage? If you can get by on one, whose will it be?

Birth and the First Year

2

REALITY NIBBLES... AND COOS AND GIGGLES

Going from *man* to *father* is one of the most dramatic changes you'll ever experience. It'll force you to rethink who you are, what you do, and what it means to be a man. Your relationships—with your partner, your parents, your friends, your coworkers—will change forever as you begin to reevaluate what's important to you and reorder your priorities. Some parts of the man-to-father transition are sudden: one day it's just you and your partner, the next day you've got a baby. Most fathers develop and change along fairly predictable lines. Of course, there are individual variations, but for everyone, it's a gradual, ever-changing process that will last your entire lifetime.

The first year may be the most important one in your development as a father. It's the time when the initial parent-child bonds are formed, the foundation of your lifelong relationship with each other. It's also especially interesting because the growth and development you experience during these first twelve months is kind of a condensed version of what you'll go through over the rest of your life as a parent.

What's Going On with Your Infant

1–3 MONTHS: PHYSICALLY

- In your baby's first week, she's pretty much a bundle of reflexes. She wants 7–8 feedings a day and takes the same number of naps, spending 80 percent of her time asleep. She can, however, focus her eyes for a few moments on an object 8–10 inches from her head.
- By the end of the first month she'll accidentally discover her hand and realize that sucking, even if it doesn't result in any milk, is . . . fun.
- During her second month most of these reflexes will disappear. She starts grasping for objects voluntarily (as opposed to reflexively) and will even hold on to some for a few minutes at a time. She can't hold her head up for more than a few seconds. Her vision gets better, and she'll track you with her eyes everywhere you go.
- By the end of the third month she'll have learned how to keep her hands open (before, she used to keep them clenched), her head is a lot steadier on her neck, and she'll uses those new grasping skills to bring objects in for a closer look.

1–3 MONTHS: MENTALLY

- Crying is her favorite means of communication, but she's very interested in exploring her new world and will stare at new objects for longer than ones she's seen before.
- In her first few weeks of life she prefers simple patterns to complex ones, and the borders of objects (such as your jaw or hairline) to the inner details (mouth and nose). She can't differentiate herself from the other objects in her world. When grasping your hand, for example, her little brain doesn't know whether it's yours or her own.
- In her second month she'll take to more complex patterns. Just a few weeks ago she'd try to suck on anything that touched her cheek. This month she's learned to tell the difference between nipples and other things (like your fingers). She has no sense of "object permanence," meaning that once something is out of sight, it doesn't exist for her anymore.
- At three months your baby can now make associations between certain things and the qualities associated with them; she may associate your partner

with food and you with play and react differently to each of you. She now uses her voice to communicate—you should be able to tell the difference between the "I'm hungry," "I'm tired," and "Change my diaper right this minute" cries.

1–3 MONTHS: EMOTIONALLY/SOCIALLY

• Even in her first month, your baby has a lot to say and is trying to say it. If she hears a noise, she'll often quiet down and focus, and she'll usually calm down if you pick her up. Her expression is fairly blank, so it won't always be entirely clear to you what she's thinking.

• She sleeps 16–20 hours a day and sometimes uses sleep as a defense mechanism, short-circuiting when she gets overstimulated.

• At two months she can smile for real (until now what you thought were smiles were probably just gas). She expresses excitement and distress, is stimulated more by touch than by social interaction, and will stay awake longer if there are people around to amuse her.

• At three months she already has strong likes and dislikes, crying or calming depending on who holds her. She'll also smile at familiar people and gawk at strangers.

4–6 MONTHS: PHYSICALLY

• Now she can coordinate the movement of her head and eyes to track moving objects just like you do. She still grasps at anything she can and tries to shove it into her mouth for further analysis. She's figured out that the two sides of her body are separate, and to prove it to you will pass objects back and between her hands. While on her tummy, she can raise her head and prop herself up on her forearms.

• In her fifth month she discovers her toes—every bit as exciting as the finger discovery of a few months ago. She may be able to roll from tummy to back and might even be able to lift herself up on hands and knees. She now manipulates objects in her hands to study them from all sides.

• By the end of the sixth month she probably sits by herself and might even right herself if she tips over. She can clap her hands and bang two objects together. Whatever's not being banged goes straight into her mouth. She moves to her hands and knees with ease and gets tremendous enjoyment from rocking back and forth.

4–6 MONTHS: MENTALLY

- At the grand old age of four months she's learning about cause and effect. If she kicks a toy and it squeaks, she may just try to kick it again, hoping to get the same reaction.

- She's trying to communicate. She may respond to your speech, and she may even initiate a "conversation" of her own. She also recognizes the difference between speech and other sounds.

- At five months, she does a lot of reaching, which reinforces her knowledge that she's separate from other objects.

- Handling and turning objects teaches her that even though things look different from different angles, their shape remains the same. As a result, she may get excited at seeing a corner of a familiar object. She knows about gravity, and if she drops something, she may look down for it. But if she can't find it in a few seconds, it ceases to exist for her.

- At six months, she still thinks she has absolute control over all she sees or touches. She'll endlessly drop toys, dishes, and food from her high chair and revels in the way she can make you pick them up.

- She kinda sorta understands and responds to her name, and she'll spend 15–20 minutes at a time testing out her newfound ability to make vowel sounds.

- She also cries for attention—whether she needs it or not—just to prove that she can get you to come. This all shows that she can formulate plans and anticipate consequences of her actions. Verbally, she's added consonants and makes single-syllable "words" like *ka, ma, la, pa, ba*.

4–6 MONTHS: EMOTIONALLY/SOCIALLY

- At four months your baby is a pretty happy kid, smiling regularly and spontaneously and anticipating pleasurable encounters by vigorously kicking her arms and legs. She's such a social animal at this point that she'll suppress other interests in order to play. Talk to her while she's eating, and she's glad to stop and chat for a half hour or so. She'll even try to extend her playtime by laughing or staring at a desired object, and may protest loudly if you stop doing what she wants you to.

- At five months she's expressing a broad spectrum of emotions: fear, anger, disgust, and satisfaction. She'll cry if you put her down and be calm if you pick her up. She has—and expresses—strong preferences for toys and people.

- If she feels you're not paying enough attention to her, she'll try to interrupt whatever you're doing with a yelp or a cry. If she does start crying, you can usually stop her tears just by talking to her.

◆ Before now your baby didn't really care who fed her, changed her, played with her, or hugged her—just so long as it got done. But at six months, 50–80 percent of babies start caring about *who's* doing the satisfying and have a definite A and B list of people who can get near them. This is the beginning of stranger anxiety.

7–9 MONTHS: PHYSICALLY

◆ A true expert at getting from tummy to sitting position, she now can sit on her own without support. And (sometimes unfortunately) she's figured out how to use her opposable thumb, which means she'll be yanking up even more stuff than before.

◆ In her eighth month she's a master of crawling and will follow you everywhere. She might even start trying to pull herself upright. But to get down she'll have to fall. Manual dexterity is excellent now, and she'll use her brand-spanking-new pincer grip to pick up ever tinier things. She's not too bad at feeding herself with her hands and may even be able to hold a bottle or cup.

◆ In her ninth month she won't learn many new tricks, preferring to spend her time perfecting what she knows. By the end of this month she crawls forward and backward and maybe up a flight of stairs (childproofing is essential now, if you haven' t done it already). She can even crawl and hold on to something at the same time. After pulling herself upright, she can now unlock her knees and sit down—sort of.

7–9 MONTHS: MENTALLY

◆ At seven months her ability to make associations is getting better. She recognizes the sounds of your footsteps and gets excited before you even come into her room. "Object permanence" (that things exist even when they can't be seen) is slowly dawning on her. If an object falls, she'll spend as much as 15–20 seconds looking for it. Helium balloons are endlessly amusing—and confusing.

◆ She's now making multisyllable words (*babababababababa*) and understands her name and a few other words.

◆ At eight months, her newfound mobility gives her a chance to explore objects she's seen only from afar. Crawling around the floor, she'll stop and examine (including taking bites to test texture) things from every possible angle. She now babbles using adult intonation and rhythm, and responds to familiar sounds like a car approaching, refrigerator opening, telephone ringing.

- By nine months she's starting to get that she's not all-powerful and may bring you a wind-up toy to wind. She's also beginning to shake her "if I can't see it, it doesn't exist" attitude. If she watches you hide a toy, she'll look for it. But if you hide the same toy somewhere else, she'll keep looking in the first place. In her mind, something out of sight may be able to exist, but only in one specific place. She's also learning more about actions and consequences. If she sees you put on a coat, she knows you're going outside and may start howling.

7–9 MONTHS: EMOTIONALLY/SOCIALLY

- At seven months the fascination with objects continues, but she much prefers the same one-on-one social activities that your dog does: namely chasing and fetching.
- She knows the difference between adults and members of her own species (other babies her own age) and may be interested in playing with (actually, alongside) them. She recognizes, and reacts differently to, positive and negative tones of voice and your happy or sad facial expressions.
- At eight months she's so busy with her physical development that she doesn't nap much during the day, leaving her cranky. But when she's in a good mood, she really wants to be included in socializing; she may crawl into the middle of a conversation, sit up, and chatter.
- At nine months, she may be able to get you to understand—by pointing, grunting, squealing, or bouncing up and down—that there's something specific on her mind. Preferences are more distinct, and she pushes away things (and people) she doesn't want.
- Frightened of the new world she's discovering, she clings to you more than ever, and cries if you leave her alone; it's the beginning of separation anxiety, which is different from the stranger anxiety of the past few months.

10–12 MONTHS: PHYSICALLY

- There are few major physical advances in the tenth month. Most important, she gets to a standing position easily and cruises sideways while holding onto something for support. She also shows a preference for one hand over the other, using one to manipulate things, the other to hold them.
- By the end of the eleventh month she gets to a standing position from a squat, and may stand unsupported for a few seconds before crashing down.

She gets up and down from chairs and couches with ease and loves wrestling and being held upside down.

- By her first birthday she may take a tentative step or two (although many babies won't for a few more months). Hand preference is more obvious. If you put an object into her "weak" hand she'll transfer it to the "strong" one.

10–12 MONTHS: MENTALLY

- At ten months her world is categorized into "things I can chew on" and "things that are too big to get into my mouth." This adds some predictability and control to her life. She also thinks symbolically (associating things she can see with things she can't.) A few months ago she cried when seeing a nurse at her doctor's office because she associated the nurse with shots. Now she recognizes the doctor's office from the street and will start crying as soon as you pull into the lot.
- In her eleventh month, she recognizes the symbolic use of words—she'll say "Yum" if you're talking about ice cream, or "Meow" if you point to a cat. She babbles in long paragraphs, tossing in a recognizable word once in a while.
- By her first birthday she knows for sure that objects exist even though she can't see them. She'll search—in more than one place if necessary—for objects she's seen but didn't see you hide. She uses trial and error to solve problems and overcome obstacles. She has a vocabulary of 6–8 words, as well as a few other sounds like "moo," "woof," or "boom."

10–12 MONTHS: EMOTIONALLY/SOCIALLY

- At ten months she's a real mimic, saying "brr" after getting out of the bath, and taking power calls on the phone just like you. She's sensitive to your emotions and expresses plenty of her own. If you're happy, she is too; if you scold her, she'll pout; if you do something she doesn't like, she shows real anger; and if you leave her alone for too long (only she knows how long that is), she might just "punish" you.
- At eleven months she shows genuine tenderness and affection for you—and her stuffed animals.
- She understands approval and disapproval, looking for your praise when she does something good, hanging her head sheepishly when she's misbehaved.
- Around her first birthday she gets less cooperative, regularly testing your limits and your patience.

◆ She's developing a sense of humor, especially for incongruities. Pretend to cry, tell her a dog says "moo," or crawl like a baby, and she'll laugh hysterically. She plays nicely around other kids at home, where she feels safest. But in less secure environments she's less sociable and may not leave your side.

What's Going On with You

AND NOW, THE MOMENT YOU'VE BEEN WAITING FOR...

Watching your partner go through labor and delivery is stressful. She's in pain and you can't do anything about it, and you worry about her and the baby. That may explain the adrenaline rush you'll probably feel. A team of Scandinavian researchers took fathers' pulses during the birth of their children and found that they went from an average of 72 beats per minute to 115 just before the birth.

Even though you'll probably be feeling somewhat helpless, being there for the birth of your baby is going to be one of the great moments in life. Interestingly, from the instant their children are born, fathers are just as caring, interested, and involved with their infants as mothers are, and they hold, touch, kiss, rock, and coo at their new babies at least as frequently as mothers do. If you're like most guys I've spoken with, you'll probably experience at least some of the following feelings immediately after the birth:

◆ love
◆ excitement, almost like being intoxicated
◆ the desire to hold and touch and rock and kiss the baby
◆ an even stronger desire to simply stare dumbfounded at the baby
◆ accomplishment, pride, and disbelief
◆ virility and self-worth
◆ a powerful connection to baby and mother
◆ the firm belief that your baby is absolutely gorgeous and perfect
◆ the need to count toes and fingers to make sure everything's where it's supposed to be
◆ curiosity about whether the baby looks more like you or your partner

Back in the 1970s, Dr. Martin Greenberg did a study of fathers who were present for their child's delivery (which was a lot less common then than it is

now). The men in his study had many of the above feelings, and Greenberg coined a term, *engrossment,* to describe "a father's sense of absorption, preoccupation, and interest in his baby." Greenberg and a number of other researcher found that what triggers engrossment in men is the same thing that prompts similar nurturing feelings in women: early infant contact.

EVEN GUYS GET THOSE POSTPARTUM BLUES

Although baby blues or postpartum depression is almost always associated with women, the fact is that many men also get it after their babies are born. Your blues, however, are not hormonally based like your partner's. Instead, the sadness, mood swings, and anxiety you may be experiencing are more likely the result of coming face-to-face with the reality of your changing life.

For the first few weeks after the baby is born, you're a celebrity—people pay a lot of attention to you, and the people at work probably cut you a little slack. But

C-section

Most childbirth preparation classes put a great deal of emphasis on natural, unmedicated deliveries, which puts a lot of pressure on a lot of women to deliver vaginally. If they don't—particularly after investing many hours in a painful labor—they may feel that they've "failed."

You'll have a very different take. Only 8 percent of men whose partners delivered by C-section objected to the operation, according to researcher Katharyn May. Ninety-two percent were "greatly relieved." Although I didn't participate in this study, it accurately reflects my own experience. It simply never occurred to me that my wife had failed. On the contrary, I remember feeling incredibly thankful that her suffering would finally end. And seeing how quickly and painlessly the baby was delivered made me wonder why she hadn't done it sooner.

Despite the relief you may feel, a C-section can be a trying experience for you. You were probably separated from your partner while she was being prepped for surgery, and you may have felt some combination of scared, helpless, and useless. Maybe that explains why fathers whose kids are delivered by C-section spend more time doing routine care for them when they're five months old than dads whose kids were delivered vaginally.

then reality hits. "You begin to notice that you're coming home every night to a demanding baby and a distraught wife, and the bills are piling up," writes S. Adams Sullivan, author of *The Father's Almanac*. "You look at your wife and . . . the healthy, radiant glow that made her beautiful while she was pregnant has disappeared, and you're tempted to agree with her when she gripes about her looks. . . . You're getting maybe four and a half hours of sleep, total, and that's broken up into hour-and-a-half naps, so that you're nodding off every day and work and falling behind."

Some psychologists estimate that as many as two-thirds of all new dads go through some kind of postpartum depression. If you do, take some refuge in knowing that eventually it will pass: you'll get caught up at work, the baby will settle into a routine, and you'll get more sleep, and with a little exercise your wife's body will somehow get back to looking pretty much the way it did before she got pregnant. In the meantime, try spending more time with your baby. According to psychiatrist Kyle Pruett, that's the best treatment for new dads' depressed moods.

BONDING, ATTACHMENT, AND VARIOUS OTHER STICKY SUBJECTS

As we discussed above, most dads feel *engrossment,* a profound sense of connection and interest, the moment they lay eyes on their newborns, and that's where the process of getting to know and "bonding" with the baby starts. Although bonding is certainly an important goal, you need to remember that for the first six to eight weeks it's pretty much a one-way street. You establish a relationship with the infant and don't get much back: she doesn't laugh, doesn't seem to react to you in any noticeable way, and doesn't even smile unless she has gas. In fact, just about all she does is cry.

Attachment, though, starts a little later and is much more of a two-way street, with you and the baby establishing relationships with each other. Still, things are a little lopsided. In our attachment relationships with adults (including our partners), both people have "relatively equal positions in providing an emotionally satisfying relationship with each other," write Philip and Barbara Newman. Obviously, your baby isn't going to be able to put as much into the relationship as you are. But there is a lot of give-and-take: your child needs something, you respond. She reacts positively, and you get the indescribable delight of being able to fulfill her needs. That makes you feel warm all over, which makes you want to do even more. "Loving and nurturing our children is a transforming process that builds our parental identity and devotion in a geometric crescendo," writes Elin Schoen. "And from this process emerges and reemerges the parental self, which . . . can radiate outward in many different directions, profoundly influencing the evolution of the person as a whole."

Dads who attend their babies' birth bond slightly faster than those who don't. But if you weren't able to be there for the birth, don't worry. "Early contact at birth is not a magic pill," writes Ellen Galinsky, author of *The Six Stages of Parenthood.* "It does not guarantee attachment. Neither does lack of contact prevent bonding." That should be good news to adoptive parents, who often worry that they won't be able to bond with their baby as much as if they had given birth to him. In reality, parents are able to establish very close relationships with their adopted children—even if the first parent-child meeting happens months after the birth, according to adoption expert David Brodzinsky.

Still, a lot of new dads feel a huge amount of pressure to bond with their babies instantly—and they feel horrible and inadequate if they don't. If you're feeling this way, lighten up a little. In a study by psychiatrists Kay Robson and Remesh Kumar, 25 to 40 percent of new parents—mothers and fathers—admitted that their first response to the baby was "indifference." This really makes more sense than the love-at-first-sight kind of bonding you hear so much about. And anyway, there's no evidence whatsoever that your relationship with or feelings for your child will be any less loving than if you'd fallen head over heels in love in the first second. So just take your time. Don't pressure yourself, and don't think for a second that you've failed as a father.

Parent-child bonding and attachment come as a result of physical closeness. So if you'd like to speed the process up, try carrying the baby every chance you get, taking her with you whenever you can, and taking care of as many of her basic needs as possible.

Like it or not, the type of attachment you establish with your baby will be influenced (not set in stone, just *influenced*) by your own attachment experience with your parents. So as you read this section, think a little about your own childhood. This might help you understand a few things about yourself and your parents. More important, it may help you avoid making some of the same mistakes with your own children that your parents made with you. Your attachment with your child may also be influenced by your relationship with your partner. Dozens of studies confirm that the better the couple relationship, the more secure the parent-child relationship.

REALITY VS. EXPECTATIONS: HOW YOU IMAGINED THE BIRTH WOULD GO VS. THE WAY IT ACTUALLY WENT

Let's face it: every expecting couple secretly (or not so secretly) hopes for a pain-free, twenty-minute labor, and nobody ever really plans for a horrible birth experience. Even in childbirth education classes, if the instructor talks at all about the unpleasant things that can happen, she usually refers to them as "contingencies," which makes it seem as though everything is still under control.

If your partner's labor and delivery went according to plan, chances are you're delighted with the way things turned out, and you're oooing and aahhhing over your baby. But if there were any problems—labor had to be induced, an emergency C-section, a threat to your partner's or your baby's life— your whole impression of the birth process may have changed. It's not unusual in these cases to actually blame or resent the baby for causing your partner so much physical pain and you so much psychological agony. It can happen easily, without your really being aware of it, and it can subtly interfere with your relationship. So try to stay away from even thinking things like (as I did), "The baby had jammed herself in there sideways and refused to come out."

As we discussed in the previous chapter, the conflict between reality and expectation is something you'll be dealing with for the rest of your life. And in the days and weeks and months that follow your baby's birth, you'll be encountering reality all over the place. How's being a dad so far—is it everything you expected? More? Less? Do you love your baby as much as you thought you thought you would—or as much as you thought you were *supposed* to?

THE BRIEF "IS THIS REALLY MY BABY?" PHASE

Like most fathers, the first thing I did after both my daughters were born was make sure they had two arms and legs, and ten fingers and toes. Once all limbs and extremities were accounted for, I quickly looked over both my daughters to see whether they had "my" nose or chin.

Later on, I felt a little guilty about that—after all, shouldn't I have been hugging and kissing my daughters instead of giving them a full-body inspection?

"He has your intense patriotic gaze."

Hey, This Isn't What I Expected

Babies hardly ever look exactly like you imagined they would before they were born. And being disappointed about a nose, a chin, or even some toes is something you'll get over soon enough—especially when you discover in a few weeks that the baby *does* have something of yours (they always do).

But what about when the baby has a penis or a vagina where you weren't expecting one? Two researchers in Sweden recently found that men are generally more satisfied with their role as fathers when their babies—boys or girls—are the gender they'd hoped for. But "when one's fantasy is not fulfilled, there is a period of regret for what might have been," writes Ellen Galinsky. "And this unhappiness can stand in the way of the parents' reaching out, accepting the baby." In fact, children who aren't the gender their parents wanted have worse relationships with their parents in childhood than preferred-gender kids. That seems to be especially true for kids whose parents had wanted a boy but got a girl.

Maybe, but it turns out that that's what almost all new fathers do within the first few minutes after the birth of their babies. "They immediately look for physical similarities to validate that the child was theirs," says Pamela Jordan. And this happens for a reason: for almost all new fathers—no matter how many of their partner's prenatal doctor appointments they went to, how many times they heard the baby's heartbeat or saw her squirm around on an ultrasound, and how many times they felt her kick—the baby isn't "real" until *after* the birth, when father and baby have a chance to meet face-to-face. "Seeing the infant emerge from his mate's body through vaginal or cesarean birth is a powerful experience for each father," writes Jordan. "Birth proved that this infant had been the growth within the mother's abdomen."

Now, Who Did You Say I Was? Piecing Together Your New Identity

Becoming a father can wreak havoc with your identity in a lot of ways. There's nothing quite like having a kid to make you realize that you're a grown-up. "The responsibilities of fatherhood—even more powerfully than marriage itself—can catapult a man into adulthood," writes Terry Eicher in *Fathers and Daughters*. It also makes you realize that besides being a son, you're also a father. Now that may sound like a painfully obvious thing to say, but you'd be surprised at how

Coping with a Handicapped Child

We all expect a perfect baby, but unfortunately not everyone gets one. In recent years, technology has made it easier for expectant parents to avoid having—or at least prepare themselves for—a disabled child.

But prepared or not, parents of disabled children still have plenty of adjusting to do. For some fathers, having a disabled child is similar to having a miscarriage—there's a mourning for the child who might have been. Some feel shock, anger, disbelief, or denial. They may blame themselves and see the child as a kind of punishment, or they may blame their wife. Others feel ambivalent and may even secretly wish that the child had died.

Having a handicapped child is especially hard on socially or intellectually talented couples who had extremely high expectations for their children, according to Jaipaul Roopnarine and Brent Miller. And researcher Michael Lamb has found that both mothers and fathers may resent the child for not being able to living up to expectations, or for being a drain on time and finance. But overall, fathers and mothers have very different experiences coping with a disabled child. Mothers are more concerned about the emotional strain of having to care for the child, and they wonder whether all the extra time required will interfere with being able to take care of the rest of the family, according to Roopnarine and Miller. Fathers are more concerned with the costs of providing care and with the baby's ability to be a leader and potential for academic success. Having a disabled child can undermine a father's feelings of masculinity and his confidence in himself.

According to Lamb, couples who are in better marriages and who have more social support tend to have an easier time coming to terms with their disabled child. He also found that the acceptance of the disabled child by the father's parents had a big influence on the father's acceptance of the child. Oddly, boys who are mentally retarded seem to have a more negative impact on marriages than girls. This may be a reflection of fathers' and mothers' greater expectations for their sons (or lower ones for their daughters).

many men have a hard time with the concept. After all, we've spent our whole lives looking at our fathers as fathers and at ourselves as sons.

At the same time, there's nothing like being a dad to put you back in touch with your own childhood and to release some of that childlike behavior you've been suppressing for most of your adult life. Having a child gives you that perfect excuse to coo and giggle and make faces and crawl around on the floor and say things like "poop" and "pee." In a way it's liberating.

In the first few months and years of fatherhood you'll probably be flooded with images—pleasant and unpleasant—from your own childhood. "To brew up an adult, it seems that some leftover childhood must be mixed in," writes Roger Gould, a pioneer researcher on adult development. "A little unfinished business from the past periodically intrudes on our adult life, confusing our relationships and disturbing our sense of self." Other researchers put a slightly more positive spin on things. "The father . . . repeats with each child, in a different way, the steps of his own development, and under fortunate circumstances achieves further resolution of his conflicts," writes psychiatrist and author Therese Benedek, one of the pioneers in parent development. What she means is that having kids gives us the chance to work through whatever stuff we didn't work through when we were kids, and that, in turn, will make us better people.

Strangely, not everyone you come across is going to include "father" in the list of nouns they'd use to describe you. I can't count the number of times that I've been out with my kids in the middle of the day, and someone says something like, "Hey! You baby-sitting today?" I've never met a father who hasn't had a similar experience. Too many people see only "man" and not "father."

Sometimes they won't even see "man"—you'll just be Mr. Baby's Father, the invisible guy who's holding the child. People love to come over and "talk" to babies who aren't nearly old enough to understand what they're hearing, let alone respond. They look the baby right in the eye and ask questions like "And how old are you?" and "What's your name, you little cutie?" and "Where did you get that darling little outfit you're wearing?" and on and on, in the same way that they might ask a cat whether it's hungry. And if you answer, they seem genuinely startled, as if they hadn't seen you at all.

Still other people—mostly single women—may see "father," but they also see "sensitive guy/potential mate." There's apparently something about a man playing happily with a child that a lot of women find very attractive. A man with a child and a dog is even better. If you're a single father, this may be kind of fun. If you're married or in a relationship and want to stay that way, watch out.

DEFINING "DADDY"

To fully integrate the *idea* of being a father into your self-identity, it'll help to understand exactly what being a father actually involves. One of the most consistent findings by researchers is that new fathers almost always feel unprepared for their new role. Personally, I would have been surprised if it were otherwise.

As writer David L. Giveans says, "It is both unfair and realistic to expect a man . . . to automatically 'father' when his life experiences have skillfully isolated him from learning how."

When most of our fathers were raising us, a "good father" was synonymous with "good provider." He supported his family financially, mowed the lawn, washed the car, and maintained discipline in the home. No one seemed to care whether he ever spent much time with his children; in fact, he was discouraged from doing so, and told to leave the kids to his wife, the "good mother."

Today, yesterday's "good father" has retroactively become an emotionally distant, uncaring villain. And today's "good father," besides still being the breadwinner, is expected to be a real presence—physically and emotionally—in his kids' lives. That, in a nutshell, is exactly what most new fathers want. Most of us have no intention of being wait-till-your-father-comes-home daddies and want to be more involved with our children than our own fathers were. The problem is, we just haven't had the training. The solution? Jump right in. The "maternal instinct" that women are supposedly born with is actually acquired on the job. And that's exactly where you're going to develop your "paternal instinct."

Another question you're going to have to ask yourself here is how being a father fits with your definition of being a man. There are two major reasons why so many of us would prefer to drive ten miles down the wrong road than to stop and ask for directions. First, from the time we were little boys, we've been socialized to associate knowledge with masculinity—in other words, real men know everything, and admitting to being lost is a sign of weakness (and, of course, a lack of masculinity). Second—and even worse—we've also been socialized to be strong, independent, and goal oriented, and to consider asking for help as a sign of weakness (and, again, a lack of masculinity).

Nothing in the world can bring these two factors into play faster that the birth of a baby. Because of the near-total absence of active, involved, nurturing male role models, most new fathers can't seriously claim that they know what to do with a new baby (although never having cooked before didn't prevent my father from insisting he could make the best blueberry pancakes we'd ever taste; and boy, was he wrong).

Getting help seems like the obvious solution to the ignorance problem, but most men don't want to seem helpless or expose their lack of knowledge by asking anyone. In addition, too many dads are aware of the prevailing attitude that a man who is actively involved with his children—especially if he's the primary caretaker—is not as masculine as his less-involved brothers.

It's easy to see how the whole experience of becoming a father can lead so many new fathers to wonder secretly (no one ever openly admits to having these thoughts) whether or not they've retained their masculinity. All too often, the result of this kind of thinking is that fathers leave all the child-rearing to their partners and leave their kids essentially without a father. As we'll discuss throughout this book, "children are at a particular disadvantage when they are deprived of constructive experiences with their fathers," writes psychologist Henry Biller. "Infants and young children are unlikely to be provided with other opportunities to form a relationship with a caring and readily available adult male if their father is not emotionally committed to them."

EASING INTO FATHERHOOD

Most men (and women) see the father's role as that of a teacher of values and skills. Apart from it being a little limiting, there's really nothing wrong with that attitude—except that it puts dads with infants in a tough spot. Teaching requires communicating and interacting, which is hard to do when the student is a baby who's completely helpless and essentially nonresponsive. The result is that since they can't teach, a lot of new dads don't feel particularly fatherly.

This should start to change by the time your baby is three or four months old. She turns her head when you call her and gets excited when you walk into

"According to this, everything we've done up to now is right."

the room, wrestle with her, build a tower together, or tickle her. And she gives you a smile that could melt steel—and it's only for you. Your baby's reactions and "praise" may not seem like much, but whether you realize it or not, they're building your confidence, making you feel that she needs you and that you're playing an important and influential role in her young life. Your feelings of helplessness at not being able to connect with your child will gradually fade, and you'll become more confident in your ability to recognize—and satisfy—her needs.

Obstacles to Being as Involved as You'd Like to Be

Sometimes, despite all your wonderful intentions, there's a disconnect between how involved you say you want to be and how involved you actually are. Here are the most common barriers mentioned by the men I interviewed for this book:

- **A partner who gatekeeps.** It's essential to communicate with her, let her know that you want to be there, and reassure her that you really know what you're doing. We'll talk about this throughout the book.
- **Money/work.** Family leave isn't paid, and employers aren't always as supportive as they should be of men who want to put family first. Besides that, a lot of men in their thirties and early forties are in a quandary: on one hand they want to spend time with their family, but on the other hand this is a time of life when men need to establish themselves in their careers—partly for their own satisfaction and feelings of accomplishment, partly so they can support their families. Unfortunately, this usually involves means spending more time at work, which means spending less time at home.
- **Lack of social support.** There are very few resources out there for fathers. In addition, the media usually portrays dads as either neglectful, uninterested, abusive, dangerous, deadbeats, or simply useless. The combination of all this makes fathers feel that they haven't got what it takes to be good parents, and they back off, leaving the parenting to their partners.
- **The courts.** Most divorced dads aren't able to see their kids as often as they'd like to. Sometimes the problem is an unfair custody ruling; sometimes it's an ex who interferes with father-child visits or who has moved away and taken the children.

Although these obstacles can be significant, you can't just sit around waiting for someone else to fix things. If you don't take the initiative yourself, you'll never be as involved as you want to be. And you won't have anyone to blame but yourself.

And then, one of these days, things that would have had you panicking a few months before will seem completely ordinary. You'll have learned to understand your baby's cues, predict the unpredictable, and those feelings of not being able to do things right will nearly be gone. You'll feel more connected and attached to your baby than ever before, and you'll find yourself thinking, Damn, I'm really getting a good handle on this dad stuff.

Congratulations—you've entered what some sociologists and psychologists refer to as the "honeymoon period" with your baby. The calmness and smoothness of this period can spill over into your marriage as well. It's a time when a lot of men say that their relationships with their partners has gotten easier, and that they feel a sense of being a family.

Hey! Who's in Charge around Here Anyway?

It's hard to admit, but like it or not, your baby's running your life. She cries, you pick her up. She's hungry, you feed her. She fills her diaper, you change it. She wants to play, you play. She needs a nap, you drive around the block twelve times until she falls asleep. She wakes up in the middle of the night, you're up too. The ancient rabbis of the Talmud described it quite well. The first stage of life, they said, "commences in the first year of human existence, when the infant lies like a king on a soft couch, with numerous attendants about him, all ready to serve him, and eager to testify their love and attachment by kisses and embraces." It's all happening on your baby's schedule, not yours.

Not being in control is hard for anyone, but it's especially discombobulating for men, who are supposed to know everything and be in control all the time. Before my oldest daughter was born, I was incredibly anal about time; I always showed up wherever I was supposed to be exactly when I was supposed to, and I demanded the same from others. But, as you now know, going on a simple trip to the store with baby in tow takes as much planning as an expedition to Mount Everest. And getting anywhere on time is just about impossible.

You may be a great salesman or negotiator or cult leader, but your ability to turn adults to your way of thinking won't work with a baby. Babies are, almost by definition, irrational and not at all interested in your timetables. In no time at all your baby will figure out what you're most rigid and impatient about, and she'll begin pushing your buttons. That leisurely walk in the park you planned might have to be cut short when the baby panics and won't stop crying after a friendly dog licks her face. Or you might end up having to stay a few extra hours at a friend's house so as not to wake the baby if she's sleeping, or if she's awake, upset her nap schedule by having her fall asleep in the car on the way home. And just when you think you've figured out her routines and the surefire tricks to comfort her or get her to sleep, she revamps everything.

So you've got a very Zen-like choice to make: you can either bend and learn to accept change, or you can break. It took a while, but I eventually learned that trying to be a father and Mr. Prompt at the same time just wasn't going to work. Most of the men I interviewed said basically the same thing: since becoming fathers, they've learned to be a lot more flexible and tolerant— not only of themselves and their limitations, but of other people's as well.

FEARS—AND MORE FEARS

The combination of the novelty of fatherhood and feeling unprepared can make the first year of fatherhood somewhat frightening. Whatever your fears, you need to start by admitting to yourself that they exist and remembering that *all* new fathers are terrified sometimes. Here are some of the most common ones I've heard about:

- **Fear of not being able to live up to your own expectations.**
- **Fear of not being able to protect your children from harm or shield them from the horrors of modern life: poverty, war, disease, the destruction of the environment...**
- **Fear of simply not being "ready" to assume the role of father.**
- **Fear of picking up the baby because you'll hurt her.**
- **Fear of your anger at the baby** (see page 79).
- **Fear of not being in control.**
- **Fear that if you discuss your fears with your partner, she'll misinterpret them and think you don't love her or the baby.** This can be cured (to a certain extent) by taking a deep breath and telling her what you feel. She's going through many of the same things you are and will be relieved to find that she's not alone. Guaranteed.
- **Fear of repeating the mistakes made by your own father.**
- **Fear of doing things wrong.** A lot of very new dads worry that they're not correctly reading their baby's signals and that they can't deal with even the most basic parenting responsibilities, like feeding, clothing, and minor illness. These feelings, of course, can be made worse by a baby who won't stop crying (a reflection of your fathering skills?) or who has a dissatisfied or seemingly hostile look on her face (a reproach that you've done something terribly wrong).

    Of course, if you're really sure you're making serious mistakes, ask for some help. But chances are you're doing fine, and spending too much time analyzing things and worrying can get you into serious trouble. According to psychiatrist Stanley Greenspan, excessive worrying can destroy your self-confidence and lead to doing nothing at all, or to adopting a hands-off attitude toward the baby. (That way, the twisted logic goes, at least you won't make any more mistakes.) This, of course, can have a decidedly negative effect on your baby's development. Perhaps the best way to overcome your worries is to spend more time with the baby. The more practice you get, the better you'll be at understanding the baby's "language," and the more confident you'll be in responding.

♦ **Fear that your life will never be the same again (it won't).** Before your child was born, everyone you knew probably pulled you aside and tried to warn you that your lives would change forever once you became parents. You probably heard all about how hard it is to shift from worrying only about yourselves to being responsible for the safety and well-being of a completely helpless little creature. And you heard about the lack of sleep and privacy, and that you'd better go to a lot of movies and read a bunch of books, because you might not have another chance for a while. Everything you heard was absolutely correct, but none of it really prepared you for the reality of parenthood, did it? Perhaps the best description I've heard of the difference between what you hear parenthood will be like and what it actually turns out to be came from a mother who said it was like the difference between "watching a tornado on TV and having one actually blow the roof off your house."

But for me, the true depth of the changes was reflected in the tiny details. Here's what I mean: when my kids were babies, they'd sometimes put some food into their mouth, chew it a little, take it out, and hand it to me. Most of the time, I'd take the offering and pop it into my mouth without a second thought. Even more bizarre, since I became a father I have actually had serious discussions with my friends about the color and consistency of the contents of our children's diapers.

♦ **Fear of sexual feelings.** This may very well be the most controversial section in this book. So before you continue, you've got to promise that you'll keep an open mind and read all the way to the end.

Imagine this: you're rolling around on the floor with your baby, having the time of your life, or you're standing by your sleeping child's bed, stroking her beautiful, perfect cheek. Then, without warning, you get, well, aroused. Now, before you throw this book down and report me to the police, keep in mind that the overwhelming majority of mental health professionals say that it is *perfectly normal* for a parent to experience brief sexual feelings toward his or her child. "Most parents feel physical pleasure toward their babies," writes Greenspan. "For some, these pleasures are translated into fleeting sexual feelings."

Normal or not, feeling sexual desire—even briefly—for a child can be especially terrifying for men. You might be afraid that someone will accuse you of being a child molester, or that you actually *are* one and won't be able to control your unnatural "urges." Or that you might have to be locked up to protect your children. Or that you're completely insane. Fortunately, despite everything we hear about the "epidemic of sexual abuse," well over 99 percent of parents never abuse anybody. So the odds are pretty slim that you'll do anything even remotely improper. Nevertheless, many men (and women as well) are so afraid and feel so guilty about their feelings that they withdraw from their children and stop playing with them, picking them up, or cuddling them.

If you find yourself reacting in this way, stop it right now. "If you withdraw your physical displays of affection," says clinical psychologist Aaron Hass, "your child may believe there is something wrong with being affectionate in that manner. And if you stop hugging your child, you will miss the opportunity to enhance, in a very primal way, the bond between the two of you."

Just by reading this, you have, without even being aware of it, taken a very important step toward understanding and dealing with your momentary sexual feelings. Simply being aware of how normal these feelings are, says Greenspan, can "inhibit you from acting inappropriately," and "keep your special relationship with your baby from being dominated by fear." Of course, if you're seriously worried that your feelings towards your child *are* inappropriate, and/or if you're having trouble managing them, get some professional help—quickly. And don't worry, telling your therapist about your feelings will not get you arrested.

EMOTIONAL CHANGES

One of the most commonly heard complaints about men is that we are out of touch with our feelings and emotions or that we suppress them. A few years ago I think I might have agreed with this contention. But since becoming a father, I strongly disagree. As a father—especially one who's actively involved with your children—you'll experience a tremendous range of feelings. Some will be new and unfamiliar, some may trigger pleasant or unpleasant memories, and some will be so intense that they'll make you uncomfortable. You'll also learn new ways to express those emotions. When it comes to expressing affection and love, for example, men are generally limited to kissing, hugging, holding hands, and sex. But having children gives you a chance to expand your repertoire. Kissing, hugging, and holding hands are still appropriate affectionate gestures, but so are tickling, hugging, rocking, tumbling, snuggling, and stroking.

Here's what you may be going through emotionally during your first year as a dad:

- **Empathy.** Learning to see the world from another person's perspective (in this case, your child's) is what empathy is all about. You're naturally going to be curious about your baby's feelings and needs and wants, and you'll want to help your baby learn to express those feelings. As you do this, you'll learn to better recognize—and express—your own as well.

- **Selflessness.** One of the major markers of maturity is the ability to take pleasure in doing something for someone else—without any expectation of repayment. In a sense, that's what parenting is going to be about for the next fifty years, so get used to it.

- **A new sense of purpose.** Just as feeling needed and appreciated by your boss and coworkers can give you a sense of self-worth and security at the office, feeling needed and appreciated as a father has the same result at home. In fact, nearly half the men in Bruce Drobeck's studies described fatherhood "as giving them more of a sense of fulfillment and/or purpose in their lives."

  For some, becoming a father was the achievement of their fondest dreams and long-term goals. One man said, "I finally feel like I'm where I want to be and doing what I want to be doing." In a few months, your partner, your friends, and your relatives will all be telling you what a great father you are. But there's one person whose opinion of your abilities will mean more to you than anyone else's: the baby. As a grown man, you'd think you wouldn't need to have your ego stroked by a baby. But there's nothing in the world that will ever make you feel better, more powerful, or more loved than the feeling of being needed by your own child. Those feelings—that you're irreplaceable and that your life has meaning because of your role as a parent—can do wonders for your self-esteem.

- **A different kind of love.** The love you feel for your partner, for example, is completely different from the love you feel for your parents, which is different from the love you feel for your siblings. And none of those is even remotely similar to the love you have for your child.

  There's a line in Maurice Sendak's classic children's book *Where the Wild Things Are* that precisely captures the way I feel about my daughters: "Please don't go—we'll eat you up—we love you so." Whether we're playing, reading a book, telling each other about our days, or even if I'm just gazing at their smooth, peaceful faces as they sleep, all of a sudden I'll be overcome with the desire to pick them up, mush them into tiny balls, and pop them into my mouth.

While I usually describe my love for my children in fairly happy terms, I periodically experience it in a completely different way—one that sometimes frightens me. Here's how it happens: I'm watching one of my daughters (either one will do) play in the park, and I'll suddenly begin to imagine how I'd feel if something terrible were to happen. What if she fell and broke her neck? What if she got hit by a truck? What if she got horribly sick and died? The loss is almost palpable, and just thinking about these things is enough to depress me for the rest of the day.

Sometimes my imagination goes a step further, and I wonder what I'd do if someone—anyone—tried to hurt, kidnap, or kill one of them. At the same instant as that thought pops into my head, my heart suddenly begins beating faster, so loud I can almost hear it, my breathing quickens, and my teeth and fists clench. I haven't hit another person outside a karate studio for probably thirty years. But it's during these brief moments when my imagination runs loose that I realize that I am perfectly capable of killing another human being with my bare hands—without a moment's hesitation.

◆ **Anger.** New dads find it incredibly easy to get all caught up in how wonderful it is to have a child, and how perfect and well-behaved our babies are. We'll spend all sorts of time telling everyone in sight how much we love our kids, how we'd never ever spank them, and how we'd throw ourselves in front of a steamroller for them. But what we almost never talk about is that every once in a while our kids drive us so nuts and we get so furious at them that we're tempted to throw *them* in front of the steamroller. Those feelings are immediately followed by feelings of guilt and shame at having let our emotions get away from us, and by feelings of failure as a father. After all, what kind of father could have such horrible thoughts about his own kids?

Well, the truth is that just about every father (and mother) sometimes feels intense anger at his children. (A number of fathers I interviewed admitted that they'd gone through the same pattern: anger at the baby followed by feelings of guilt and failure. I suspect that the guys who didn't admit it had had the same experience too.) It's no wonder that, in the words of psychologist Lawrence Kutner, "Anger—no fury—is among the 'dirty little secrets' of parenthood."

Besides the child's actual behavior, things like job pressures, financial difficulties, health problems, or even car trouble can be redirected and make us lash out at our kids. "The conflicts that trigger the most intense responses often tell us more about ourselves than about our children," says Kutner. "Our most dramatic reactions to our children's behavior often come when we're feeling hurt. The child most likely to set off that strong, emotional response is the one who is most like us—especially when that child reminds us of things we don't particularly like about ourselves." Whatever the reason for your anger, remember that there's nothing wrong with feeling it—even when it's directed against your kids. It's what you do with your anger that really matters. A lot of wonderful things have happened as a result of anger—someone gets so pissed about a given situation (take the civil rights movement of the 1960s, for example) that they decide to go out and fix it.

But when it comes to getting angry at a child, it's not so easy to fix. So if you can, try to change your perspective. Every once in a while she may do something to deliberately annoy you, but in the first year, many of her actions are really beyond her control. Keeping your sense of humor and taking regular breaks can keep minor annoyances from accumulating and boiling over. If none of that works, remove yourself from the situation and your child before you do something you'll regret for a long, long time.

If you lose control once, resist the urge to punish yourself too much. You're only human, so lighten up. But if you're worried that it might happen again, get some help immediately: call a friend, a therapist, your child's pediatrician, or even a local parental-stress hot line.

◆ **Feeling left out.** "The single emotion that can be the most destructive and disruptive to your experience of fatherhood is jealousy," writes Dr. Martin Greenberg in *The Birth of a Father.* There's certainly plenty to be jealous about, but the real question is, Whom (or what) are you jealous of? Your partner, for her close relationship with the baby and the extra time she gets to spend with her? The baby, for taking up more than her "fair share" of your partner's attention, and for having full access to her breasts while they may be "too tender" for you to touch? The baby-sitter, for being the recipient of the baby's daytime smiles and love—smiles and love you'd rather were directed at you? Or maybe it's the baby's carefree life. The answer, of course, is, All of the above.

One thing that sometimes makes new dads feel left out and jealous is breastfeeding. This isn't to say that dads don't support it—they do. Before their babies are born, nearly all expectant fathers feel that breastfeeding is the best way to feed a baby and that their partners should do so as long as possible. Even after the baby comes, new fathers still feel that breast milk is best, but they may also start feeling a little more ambivalent.

SIPRESS

Most new fathers feel that breastfeeding "perpetuates the exclusive relationship the mother and infant experienced during pregnancy," writes Pamela Jordan, one of the very few researchers ever to explore the effects of breastfeeding on men. "Feeding the infant is often perceived by parents as the most important aspect of infant care, the most meaningful interaction." If your partner is breastfeeding, there's no question that you're at a bit of a disadvantage when it comes to feeding the baby. As a result, you might end up feeling inadequate, as if you don't have an opportunity to develop a relationship with your child, as if nothing you can do will ever be able to compete with your partner's breasts, or as if the baby has come between you and your partner.

Whether or not you're experiencing these or any other less than completely positive feelings, there's a pretty good chance that your partner is having a few ambivalent feelings of her own about breastfeeding. She may be exhausted, she may resent the way nursing interferes with some of the other things she'd like to do, and despite the images of smiling, happy nursing mothers, she may not be enjoying the experience at all (which will probably make her feel guilty or inadequate.)

If either of you (especially your partner) is having trouble coping with breastfeeding, the La Leche League is a wonderful source of education, resources, and support. Their website, *www. lalecheleague. org,* has listings and links to chapters throughout the United States and the rest of the world.

Like most emotions, a little jealousy goes a long way, and it's critical to talk to your partner if you're feeling excluded. Jealousy's "potential for destruction," writes Greenberg, "lies not in having the feelings but in burying them." As a mother—particularly a breastfeeding one—your partner has a great deal of control over the whole parenting thing. She has the power to invite you in or to exclude you. Dozens of studies have shown that the mother's role as a gatekeeper is directly related to how involved her partner will be. "When she allows, encourages and supports the father's involvement with the baby, the father tends to assume more parental responsibility," writes researcher Roseanne Zapp. Pamela Jordan agrees. "Just as the father is viewed as the primary support of the mother-infant relationship, the mother is the primary support to the father-infant relationship," she says. "Supporting the father during breastfeeding may help improve his, and consequently, the mother's, satisfaction with breastfeeding, the duration of breastfeeding, and the adaptation of both parents to parenthood."

Home isn't the only place dads can feel left out. I remember back in the days when I'd take my kids to the park for hours at a time. There'd always be lots of other parents—almost all women—gathered in groups of four or five, chatting, sharing information, and learning from each other. Newcomers, as long as they were female, were quickly welcomed into these groups. But although I had developed nodding relationships with a few of the women, I always felt excluded.

In reality, two things were going on. First, I actually was being excluded. But second, I was also excluding myself. I could have marched over to one of the groups of women, introduced myself, and tried to join in. But I never did. And neither do most guys. Once in a while, another father would drop by the park with his child, and we'd nod, smile, or raise our eyebrows at each other. We probably had a lot in common as fathers, shared many of the same concerns, and could have learned a lot from each other. But we didn't. Instead, we sat ten yards apart; if we ever spoke, it was about football or something equally superficial. Each of us was afraid to approach the other for fear of seeming too needy, too ignorant, or not masculine enough. What a couple of idiots.

"Most fathers," says psychologist Bruce Linton, "turn to their wives, not to other men, to help them understand their feelings about fatherhood." Unfortunately, that approach is often less than completely satisfying. Even if their wives are supportive, most men report that "there's something they are not getting," says Linton. The result is that you, like a lot of new dads, may end up feeling isolated. You probably have all sorts of concerns, worries, and feelings you don't completely understand, and there's no one else you can share your experience with. Fatherhood, it seems, can be a pretty lonely business.

CHANGING RELATIONSHIPS

Considering how small and helpless babies are, it's really amazing that they can have such a powerful impact on the lives of the adults around them. Simply by being born, your baby has already transformed you and your partner from a "couple" into "parents" and your parents and in-laws into, gasp, "grandparents." Even more amazing is the impact that babies have on the preexisting relationships between the adults in their lives. They can bring a couple together, for example, or they can create a lot of stress (or at least magnify it). They can reunite families and mend old wounds, or they can open new ones. They can even change the nature of your friendships. Here are a few ways this might play out:

"You may not recognize Bobby.
He's turned into his father."

◆ Some of your friends might feel a little neglected, since you and your partner aren't going to be nearly as available for last-minute movies or double
dates, and you might not be quite as happy to have friends drop by
unannounced.

◆ Your new, less spontaneous lifestyle may affect your relationships with your
single male friends most of all. As Terry Eicher writes, "renouncing the easy
companionship of male friends is one of the sacrifices fathers may be asked
to make" when they have kids. Having a new baby probably means fewer
all-night poker games. Your buddies may stop calling you because they think
you're too busy or not interested in hanging out with them anymore. Or
you might stop calling them because seeing their relatively carefree and
obligation-free lives may make you jealous.

◆ You and your partner might find yourselves more interested (or at least more
interested than you were before) in spending time with people—especially
couples—your own age. You might find that you don't have quite as much
in common anymore with your single or childless friends, and they might
start feeling the same way too.

◆ Some of your friends who have children who are older than yours might
start getting on your nerves by insisting on telling you every single thing
they think you're doing wrong as a parent.

◆ Some of your friends may be disdainful or unsupportive of your taking an
active, involved role in your baby's life, falling back on the old stereotype
that men should leave the parenting stuff up to their wives or that putting
your family first could have a negative impact on your career.

◆ Your relationships with new and old friends may be subtly—or not so subtly—affected by competition. Let's face it: we all want our children to be the
biggest, smartest, fastest, cutest, and funniest, and it's only natural (especially
for guys) to get a little competitive. If your friend's baby crawls, walks, talks,
sings, says "da-da," or gets a modeling contract or an early-admissions
preschool acceptance letter before your baby does, you may find yourself
more than a little envious. But you know that your baby is the best one in
the world. Go ahead and let them delude themselves into thinking that
theirs is. Why burst their bubble?

The most important thing you can do at this point is simply learn to accept
change. It may seem harsh, but the fact is that you may lose some friends (and
they'll lose you) now that you're a parent. But you'll gain many new ones in the
process.

Your Changing Relationship with Your Wife

As we discussed earlier, having a child can make your relationship better, or it can strain it. One of the most common traps couples fall into is that they stop communicating or at least change the way they communicate. Nearly all the couples in Jay Belsky's exhaustive studies of new parents experienced a drop in the quality of their communication. Half the time it was permanent.

Why? Here are some factors Belsky and several other researchers have identified as contributing to a decline in couples' communication skills:

+ "A new child deprives a couple of many of the mechanisms they once used to manage differences," says Belsky. For example, when you used to have disagreements about who did what around the house, you might have solved the problem by getting a housekeeper. But with the arrival of a new baby, strained finances might not allow for a cleaning person, which means you'll have to deal with the once painless who-does-what disagreements.

+ The lack of spontaneity. Before your baby was born, if you wanted to go see a movie or even just sit around and talk, you could just do it. But now, as parents, you don't have that luxury. If you want to go out, you have to get a sitter a day or so in advance, make sure the baby is fed, and be back at a certain time.

+ Physical exhaustion. Even if you stay home together with your partner, there's a better than even chance you'll be too tired to stay awake for an entire conversation.

+ There's a general decline in intimacy-promoting activities such as sex, hanging out with friends, and so on.

+ With so much time, money, and energy focused on your baby, you and your partner don't have as many opportunities to pursue individual interests and activities outside the home. As a result, you might find that your communications skills have "rusted." You won't have nearly as many new things to talk about, and you may lose (partially, at least) the ability to hear and understand each other.

+ Expectations have changed. The time your partner spends with your baby is time she can't spend with you. She may be feeling pressured to be a fantastic mom, and you may be putting even more pressure on her by reminding her that she's not there to satisfy your emotional needs as much as she used to.

Examining Your Relationship with Your Father

As you continue to grow and develop as a father, you may find yourself spending a lot of time thinking about your own father. Was he the kind of father you'd like to use as a role model, or was he exactly the kind of father you don't want to be? Was he supportive and nurturing, or was he absent or abusive? Like it or not, the relationship you had with your father when you were young sets the tone for your relationship with your own children.

Now, depending on your perspective, this is either good news or bad news. If you are satisfied with your relationship with your dad and you'd like to be the kind of father he was, you don't have much to worry about. But if your relationship with your father was not everything it should have been, you may be afraid that you are somehow destined to repeat your father's mistakes. Fortunately, this actually almost never happens—all that stuff you've probably heard about how people who were abused as children end up abusing their own kids is absolutely false. Pioneering researcher John Snarey found that overall, new fathers seem to take the good from their fathers and throw away the bad. In fact, many new fathers use their less-than-perfect relationship with their fathers as motivation to change:

+ Having fathers who were distant or non-nurturing predicts that men will provide high levels of care for their children's social-emotional and intellectual-academic development in adolescence.
+ Having fathers who provided inconsistent or inadequate supervision predicts that men will provide high levels of care for their children's physical-athletic development in childhood.
+ Having fathers who used or threatened to use physical punishment that instilled fear in them as boys predicts that men as fathers will provide high levels of care for their children's physical-athletic development in adolescence.

Trying to Balance Work and Family

Most new fathers struggle to find a way to have it all, to provide for their growing family and be a nurturing, involved father at the same time. Finding the right balance between these two seemingly mutually exclusive options is something you'll be working on for the rest of your life.

Today's fathers say that they find being a father a lot more satisfying than their job. All over the country, fathers say they're being asked to sacrifice too much family time to the workplace. They say they want more work schedule flexibility so they can spend more time with their families, and they're turning down job promotions and transfers that would cut into that time.

But sometimes the pressure of being the breadwinner is too much. Six months after their children's birth, about 95 percent of new fathers are back working full-time. (Phil and Carolyn Cowan found that, during the same period, only 19 percent of women are employed full-time, and another 36 percent are working part-time.) Oh, and it gets worse from there. Rather than work a more relaxed full-time schedule, you'll probably work more hours after the birth of a child—122 hours a year more if it's a boy, 56 hours a year if it's a girl, according to a recent study by University of Washington economists Shelly Lundberg and Elaina Rose. (Not surprisingly, younger fathers, who are just getting their careers off the ground, generally have a tougher time balancing their work and home lives than older fathers, who tend to be more established and less worried about clawing their way to the top.)

The contradiction between what we say and what we do may not be as big as it seems. A lot of guys keep working full-time but find extra family time by cutting back on recreation, time spent with their friends, and even pesky things like sleep. Some even get kind of sneaky. A recent study by the Families and Work Institute stated that "some men had told friends at work they were going to a bar when in fact they were going home to care for their children."

No matter how you try to keep your work life separate from your family life, there's going to be plenty of spillover between the two, and that's not necessarily a bad thing. In his four-decade-long study of fathers, John Snarey found that, "contrary to the stereotype of rigid work-family trade-off, a positive, reciprocal interaction may exist between childrearing and bread-winning."

Other researchers have come to similar conclusions. "Before they became fathers, men did not appear to be conscious that home and work life often require different personal qualities," writes Phil Cowan. After becoming fathers, however, many men "described new abilities to juggle conflicting demands, make decisions, and communicate quickly and clearly both at home and at work . . . some described themselves as more aware of their personal relationships on the job, and more able to use some of their managerial skills in the solution of family problems."

FEELING A LITTLE GUILTY

A lot of men I've interviewed say that there's nothing like a long day at the office to make them realize just how much they miss their baby. And when they get home, they often feel guilty at having been away so much that they try to cram as much father/baby contact as possible into the few hours before putting the baby to bed. Unfortunately, there's no way to make up for lost time. But what you can do is maximize the time you do have. When you have an opportunity to be with your child, be there 100 percent. Forget the phone, forget the newspaper or the TV, forget washing the dishes, and forget eating if you can. You can do all those things after the baby goes to sleep.

GOING PUBLIC WITH FATHERHOOD

For most new fathers, the last few months of their first year as parents are a time of relative calm. They've dealt with the big emotional, professional, and personal hurdles of fatherhood and are now comfortably juggling their roles as husband, father, provider, and son. In short, they're finally feeling "like a family," and are entering what Bruce Linton calls the "community phase" of fatherhood. Other researchers have confirmed Linton's theory. "Parenting brings new levels of insight and social commitment," write the Newmans, "that contribute in positive ways to the overall evolution of the culture."

Many seasoned new fathers feel ready to socialize—along with their partners and children—with other families, and they use their fatherhood as a way to participate more actively in the public domain. They typically take on a more active role in their churches or synagogues, and they experience a heightened sense of public responsibility. Issues such as the quality of schools, city planning and zoning, the environment, and public safety become much more pressing than before. These feelings will get stronger as your child gets older, as we'll see in subsequent chapter.

Why Be Involved at This Stage at All?

Simple. Because the more involved you are in raising your children, the better father you'll be. Being an involved father is good for everyone: your kids, your partner, and even yourself. Here are some of the specific benefits to being actively involved with your infant.

BENEFITS TO YOUR BABY

- **She'll be smarter.** Numerous studies have shown that the more involved dads are with their infants, the better the infants perform on all kinds of tests of intelligence. Things like rocking, talking, cooing, touching, and encouraging independence make a big difference. And so do the father's skills as a playmate. "Fathers who were good at peek-a-boo, ball toss, and bouncing bouts had more cognitively advanced children than those who couldn't keep their children interested in their games," writes Ross Parke.

- **She'll have better friendships and fewer social problems later in life.** One fascinating new study found that babies who are deprived of quality time with their fathers in the first year of life often develop problems forming stable relationships later. Bathing and putting the baby to bed are especially important bonding activities. Other research shows that when dads are absent during infancy, their kids have worse relationships with their peers at 4–8 years old. Not having a dad around deprives them of the chance to learn the kinds of behavior that other kids value.
- **She'll be less anxious.** The more contact five-month-old infants have with their fathers (being bathed, fed, dressed, diapered), the more comfortable they feel around strangers, the less they suffer from stranger anxiety, and the better they handled stressful situations.
- **She'll be more independent.** Fathers tend to allow infants to explore, while mothers are more cautious and less encouraging of exploration. This is especially true of boys, who are encouraged even more than girls.
- **She'll be better coordinated.** Researcher Frank Pedersen and his colleagues found that the more actively involved a six-month-old baby has been with her father, the higher the baby's scores on mental and motor development tests.

BENEFITS TO YOUR PARTNER

- **She'll be a better mother.** The more involved you are and the more emotionally supportive, the more competent a caregiver your partner will be, and the better her relationship with the children.

BENEFITS TO YOU

- **It'll broaden your emotional horizons.** Having a child gives you a chance to feel and express all sorts of emotions that you may never have felt before. In turn, having opportunities to express your emotions to your children may allow you to become more expressive and gentle in your relationships with others, says Ross Parke.
- **It puts things into perspective.** Your ambitions and decisions and choices look very different when you consider them from the point of view of how they might affect your children or your family. Being able to step back and consider things more objectively makes you more sympathetic to others' points of view, too.
- **It's good for your health.** "Problems in a man's relationship with his child have a significant impact on his physical health, while his problems at his job did not," according to researcher Rosiland Barnett and journalism professor

The Importance of a Happy Marriage

Men's satisfaction with their relationships is a major factor in determining how involved they will be with their children. The more satisfying your relationship, the more involved and happy you'll be in your fathering role. But the more unhappy and volatile your relationship, the less involved you'll be, and the lower the quality of that involvement.

In addition, psychologist Martha Cox and her colleagues have found that the quality of a father's parenting is better when his marriage is better and that a supportive marriage can go a long way toward overcoming his lack of preparation for parenthood.

In case you thought you could keep the quality of your marriage a secret from your baby, forget it. Eleven-month-olds, for example, are less likely to look to their fathers for help in novel situations (such as seeing an unfamiliar person) when their fathers are in distressed marriages. Later on in life, children whose fathers are unhappy or overstressed "act out" more and suffer more from depression than children whose parents are in less stressful marriages, says psychologist John Gottman. And kids who watch their parents fight are frequently more aggressive, feel more guilty, and tend to be more withdrawing.

Overall, the quality of the marriage, whether reported by the husband or wife, is "the most consistently powerful predictor of paternal involvement and satisfaction," writes Shirley Feldman and her colleagues.

Caryl Rivers. "The men who had the fewest worries about their relationships with their children also had the fewest health problems. Those who had the most troubled relationships with their children had the most health problems."

• **You'll have a more successful career and a better life.** "Men who take an active role at home are—by the time their children are grown—better managers, community leaders, and mentors," according to researcher John Snarey.

• **It helps your self-esteem.** Men who take a more active role in running their households and rearing their children "tend to feel better about themselves and about their family relationships than men who are less involved in family work," according to the Cowans.

Staying Involved in the First Year

Over the course of the first few months of life, your infant will gradually gain control of her muscles, evolving from a little creature who can hardly lift her head to someone who can actually get her body to perform on demand. She'll also go from completely passively observing everything around her to actively interacting with the people and things that make up her world. There'll be so many physical, mental, and emotional changes, and they'll be happening so fast, that you won't want to close your eyes for a second. And while you're watching your baby develop, keep an eye on yourself as well: by the end of this year you'll be a completely different father than you were when you first brought your baby home.

What your baby needs from you is security and love. And the best way to give it to her is to spend a lot of time together getting to know each other and getting used to each other. It doesn't really matter what you're doing (although the activities described below are much better than watching television), or whether you're inside or outside. If you do go outside, strollers are nice, but if your back can handle it, a front pack is even nicer because it gives you and the baby more body-to-body contact with each other. Here are some great ways you can get to know your baby, stay involved with her, and help her grow during her first six months. I'll talk about the second half of the first year below.

- **Hold her.** Newborns love to be carried around, held in your arms, held in a pack, and so on.
- **Talk to her.** She won't be able to understand a word you're saying. In fact, she'll barely even know you exist. But talk to her anyway—explain everything you're doing as you're doing it, tell her what's happening in the news, and so forth—it'll help her get to know the rhythm of the language.
- **Change her diapers.** It doesn't sound like much fun, but it's a great time to interact with the baby one-on-one, to rub her soft belly, tickle her knees, kiss her tiny fingers. For at least the first month or so, she needs to be changed every two hours—baby's supersensitive skin shouldn't stew in human waste—so there are plenty of opportunities.
- **Stimulate her senses.** Let her smell everything in your kitchen (even the moldy stuff in the back of the refrigerator) and taste a few drops of things other than milk. Make sure she has a wide variety of things to look at—photos, mirrors, toys, people; expose her to lots of textures—smooth, soft, rough, bumpy; and be sure she has lots of different things to listen to—bells, whistles, your whole CD collection, and most importantly, plenty of conver-

sation. Whether you leave the radio on or carefully select a program, make sure there's plenty of variety in style, key, and tempo.

- **Play with her, but gently.** At this stage you can't do a lot of physical play with your baby beyond a little rolling around. Be sure to support her head at all times and never, ever shake her. This can make her little brain rattle around inside her skull and cause bruises or permanent injuries. And never throw her up in the air. Yes, your father may have done it to you, but he shouldn't have. It looks like fun but can be extremely dangerous.

- **Read.** At this age, you can read just about anything to your baby, from *The Iliad* to the installation guide to your dishwasher. The goal isn't to educate, it's to get her used to the sound of the language and to make a connection to a peaceful activity. So set up a regular reading time and place. "When children have been read to, they enter school with larger vocabularies, longer attention spans, greater understanding of books and print, and consequently have the fewest difficulties in learning to read," writes Jim Trelease, author of *The New Read Aloud Handbook.* Still not convinced? Try this: 60 percent of prison inmates are illiterate, 85 percent of juvenile offenders have reading problems, and 44 percent of adult Americans do not read a single book in the course of a year. Clearly, reading is an important habit to develop, and it's never too early to start. It'll be a while till you get much reaction from the baby. At about three months, she may start holding your finger while you read to her. At four months, she'll sit still and listen attentively while you read and may even reach out to scratch the pages of the book. At around five months, she'll probably start to respond to your pointing. At six months, she'll respond to what you're reading by bouncing up and down or chuckling before you get to a familiar part of the story. Look for books with simple, uncluttered drawings as well as poetry and nursery rhymes.

- **Get to know baby's temperament.** About forty years ago, Stella Chess and Alexander Thomas, theorized that children are born with a set of nine fundamental behavioral and emotional traits they called "temperamental qualities." These qualities, which experts now believe remain fairly consistent throughout life, combine differently for each child and determine, to a great extent, a child's personality and whether she will be "easy" or "challenging."
  - ◇ **Approach/withdrawal:** Your child's usual *initial* reaction to a new experience such as meeting a new person or tasting a new food. Approaching babies separate easily from parents and are excited by new people, experiences, and foods. Withdrawing babies are shy, have a tough time separating from parents, and take time to get used to new things.

◇ **Adaptability:** Similar to approach/withdrawal, but deals with your child's longer-term reactions to changes in routines or expectations, new places, or new ideas. Fast-adapting babies fall asleep easily no matter where they are, and are okay with changes in their routine or caregiver. Slow-adapting babies may have trouble sleeping in new places, and don't like to be picked up by strangers.

◇ **Intensity:** The amount of energy a child commonly uses to express emotions—both positive and negative. Low-intensity babies are laid-back and even-tempered. High-intensity babies react strongly (positively or negatively) and do everything (shrieking with delight or crying) incredibly loudly.

◇ **Mood:** Your child's general mood—happy or fussy—during a day. Positive-mood babies laugh and smile all the time and seem happy to see you. Negative-mood babies are fussy a lot, even for no reason.

◇ **Activity level:** The amount of energy your child puts into everything she does. Low-activity babies sit calmly in the car seat, don't move much while sleeping, and prefer low-energy games. High-activity babies move around constantly, and are almost impossible to dress, bathe, or feed.

◇ **Regularity:** The day-to-day predictability of your baby's hunger, sleeping, and filling diapers. Predictable babies get hungry, get tired, and fill their diapers at about the same time every day. Unpredictable babies are, well, unpredictable.

◇ **Sensitivity:** Your baby's sensitivity to pain, noise, temperature change, lights, odors, flavors, textures, and emotions. Low-sensory-aware (oblivious) babies love loud events like basketball games and concerts, and aren't terribly bothered by wet or dirty diapers. High-sensory-aware babies are easily overstimulated, startle and get upset at loud noise, and need to have diapers changed immediately.

◇ **Distractibility:** How easy is it to change the focus of your baby's attention. Low-distractibility babies are hard to soothe but don't seem to notice interruptions. High-distractibility babies have shorter attention spans but are easily soothed when they're upset.

◇ **Persistence:** Similar to distractibility, but goes beyond the initial reaction and concerns the length of time your baby will spend trying to overcome obstacles or distractions. Persistent babies are able to amuse themselves, like to practice new skills, and watch other kids to learn. Low-persistence babies have trouble keeping themselves busy, lose interest quickly, and take a little longer to learn to roll over, crawl, or walk.

Colic

Starting at about two weeks of age, some 20 percent of babies develop colic—crying spells that, unlike "ordinary" crying, can last for hours at a time—sometimes even all day or all night. The duration and intensity of crying spells peaks at around six weeks and usually disappears entirely within three months.

Since there's no real agreement on what causes colic or on what to do about it, your pediatrician probably won't be able to offer a quick cure. Some parents, however, have been able to relieve (partially or completely) their colicky infants with an over-the-counter gas remedy for adults. Talk to your doctor about whether he or she thinks taking this medication would benefit your child. Here are a few other approaches to dealing with colic (or crying babies in general).

- If you're bottle-feeding the baby, try taking her off cow's milk. Some pediatricians feel that colic may be linked to a milk intolerance and suggest switching to a non-cow's milk formula.
- Hold the baby firmly facing you, with her head over your shoulder and your shoulder pressing on her stomach.
- Put a hot water bottle on your knees, place the baby face down across it to warm her tummy, and stroke her back.
- Give your baby a gentle massage.
- Try swaddling. Being enveloped in a blanket may make the baby feel more comfortable.
- Reread the section on anger on pages 79–80.

If your baby is easy, great. If not, try to keep in mind that challenging children are challenging because of their innate makeup. Her temperament existed at birth. It's not her fault, it's not your fault, and it's not your partner's fault. It's just the way things are. Don't blame yourself, your partner, or your baby. There's probably nothing wrong with any of you.

In the second half of the first year, your baby will learn to crawl, sit up, and maybe even take a step or two (probably holding on to something). Here's how to stay involved at this stage:

- **Keep playing.** Although our society doesn't value play nearly as highly as some other parent-child pastimes such as feeding and diaper changing, it is nevertheless critical to your baby's development. Babies who are played with a lot, especially by their fathers, do better physically, socially, and mentally. For small-motor (coordination) development, play lots of games that involve picking up objects, organizing them, stacking, nesting, pouring, tearing, crinkling, and crushing. Puzzles are especially good starting at around a year, but get only the kind that have separate holes for each piece (each piece should also have a peg for easy lifting). For bigger-muscle development, try pushing balls back and forth, playing hide-and-seek, and chasing each other around the house on your knees. And for building hand-eye coordination, try spilling a bunch of Cheerios on your baby's high-chair tray and letting her pick them up. Whether she eats them or puts them back in the bowl is up to her. Don't spend a lot of money on fancy toys. Babies this age are more likely to be interested in labels and packing material than the toy itself. Hiding-and-finding games, such as looking for a favorite toy that you've hidden under a napkin, reinforce the important notion that things exist even when you can't see them. Stay away from anything made of foam (it's too easy to chew off pieces) or that might shed, anything small enough to swallow, or anything that has detachable parts, could possibly pinch the baby, runs on electricity, or has strings, ribbons, or elastic.

- **Keep reading.** At around seven months, your baby's grabbing and tearing are now slightly more purposeful, and you may notice an occasional attempt to turn pages. By ten months, she may follow characters from one page to the next. At a year, she'll be able to turn one page of her book at a time and answer questions like, "What does the duckie say?" The best reading position for your baby is to sit her on your lap with her back to your chest, holding your arms around her and reading from over her shoulder.

- **Keep playing music.** As before, the more—and the more variety—the better. But now try to choose recordings that have frequent changes in rhythm, tempo, and dynamics (loudness/softness). At nine months, your baby's attention span is still pretty short, and these contrasts will hold her interest longer and more easily. Try to avoid songs with words. Because your baby is rapidly developing her language skills, she may pay more attention to the words than to the music. Sing, whenever and wherever you can. And don't worry about being in tune—your baby doesn't care. As above, use nonsense syllables—dum-dee-dum kinds of things—instead of real words. Listen to music *you* like. Your baby will be paying close attention to the way you react to the music and will know if you've selected some "good-for-you" piece that you hate.

- **Keep talking.** There's plenty of evidence that talking to your baby can have some very positive long-term effects. So as you go through the day, identify everything you can, and tell the baby what you're doing, where you're going, what the weather's like, who won last night's baseball games, and so on.

Avoid Gender Stereotyping

You know the thing about how girls are sugar and spice and everything nice, while boys are snips and snails and puppy-dog tails, right? Well, as with most stereotypes, there is at the core a kernel of truth there: girls and boys *are* different, and they *do* seem to behave differently—even in early infancy. Girls tend to respond to sights and sounds earlier and more intensively than boys, and they also learn to talk earlier. Boys tend to cry more and are somewhat more physical and aggressive.

Well, that was easy. But here's a provocative question for you: Are the differences we see in boys' and girls' behavior real, or are we just imagining them?

Researchers John and Sandra Condry showed a group of over 200 adults a videotape of a nine-month-old baby playing. Half were told they were watching a boy, half that they were watching a girl. Although everyone was viewing the exact same tape, the descriptions the two groups gave of the baby's behavior were startlingly different. The group that was watching a "boy" "saw" more pleasure and less fear in the baby's behavior than the group that was watching a "girl." And when the baby displayed negative emotions, the boy group "saw" anger; the girl group "saw" fear.

So do these imagined differences affect the way adults interact with children? The Condrys think so. "It seems reasonable to assume," they write, "that a child who is thought to be afraid is held and cuddled more than a child who is thought to be angry." Other researchers have confirmed that adults do, indeed, behave differently with (perceived) boys than with (perceived) girls. Hannah Frisch conducted essentially the same experiment as the Condrys, except that in hers, the adults actually played one-on-one with two different children. One time the adults were told they were playing with a boy, one time with a girl. "The general picture which emerges," writes Frisch, "is one in which adults are playing in masculine ways with children whom they think are boys and in feminine ways with children whom they think are girls."

Researcher Beverly Fagot found that by treating boys and girls differently, adults may inadvertently reinforce sex stereotypes. For example, parents tend to react more positively to their daughters' attempts to communicate and more negatively to similar attempts by their sons, thus "confirming" that girls are more verbal than boys. Parents also react more positively when their sons engage in physical play and more negatively when their daughters do, thus "confirming" that boys are more physical than girls. So do boys play with trucks and girls with dolls because they want to, or because that's what their parents want them to? Think about that next time you're looking for a gift for your baby.

The whole point here is to show you how easy it is to fall into sex-stereotype traps. Sure, you'll still probably treat boys and girls a little differently; that's normal. But hopefully, now that you're a bit more aware of the dynamics, you'll be able to avoid the larger problems and give your kids a richer childhood experience.

If you have a boy, encourage him to communicate as much as he can. Don't discourage him from crying or from playing with dolls, and teach him that asking for help isn't a bad (unmanly) thing. If you have a daughter, encourage her to play physically and teach her that assertiveness and independence aren't unfeminine.

But whether you have a boy or a girl, make sure you aren't forcing your child into a type of behavior that doesn't fit his or her character or temperament. Trying to make your child conform to some kind of sexual stereotype isn't a good idea. But neither is trying to force a child away from the kind of behavior he or she is most comfortable with. The bottom line is that some boys, if you give them a Barbie to play with, will tear her head off and use her legs as a sword, or they'll chew their toast into the shape of a gun. And some girls are going to want to wear lace everywhere they go, and they'll wrap a toy truck up in a blanket and rock it like a baby.

"I gotta go play with my doll now, so that I'll be a really great dad someday."

- **Establish regular routines right now.** Getting your child used to eating, reading, going out, and sleeping at pretty much the same time every day will help build your child's sense of confidence and security.
- **Spend some time holding, hugging, and cuddling your baby, and be sure to tell her often that you love her.** Even if you think she doesn't understand what you're saying, your smiles and your voice tell her a lot more than you think.
- **Take breaks.** Don't feel that you have to entertain your child all the time. Sure it's fun, but letting her have some time to play by herself is almost as important to her development as playing with you. And don't worry: letting her play alone—as long as you're close enough to hear what she's doing and to respond quickly if she needs you—doesn't mean you're being neglectful. Quite the opposite, in fact. By giving her the space to make up games or to practice the things she does with you, you're helping her learn how to satisfy some needs by herself. You'll also be helping her build her self-confidence by giving her the opportunity to decide for herself what she'll be playing with.
- **Childproofing.** Once your baby realizes that she's able to move around by herself, her mission in life will be to locate—and race you to—the most dangerous, life-threatening things in your home. So if you haven't already begun the never-ending process of childproofing your house, get started now. Begin by getting down on your hands and knees and looking at the world from your baby's perspective. Taking care of those pesky electrical cords, covering up outlets, and putting locks on low drawers and cabinets is only the beginning. Crawl from room to room and you'll be amazed at the number of heavy objects that can be pulled down by little hands and the endless variety of things there are to smack one's head against if you're only 2 feet 2 inches and not so steady on your feet.
- **Take paternity leave.** Are you eligible for a temporary leave under the Family and Medical Leave Act? If you work full time and your company has 50 or more employees, you probably are. Even if you don't qualify that way, you may still be eligible under a state-mandated plan or by taking a personal leave of absence. Family Leave is a wonderful opportunity to get your involved fatherhood off on the right foot. But if you don't ask your employer and insist on taking advantage of your legal rights, no one else is gong to do it for you. Many employers are becoming more flexible when it comes to dads taking time off to be with their kids, but as a rule, they aren't the most supportive lot. There are some risks involved in taking Family Leave, but they're far outweighed by the benefits. Every man I've ever interviewed about Family Leave said he'd do it again.

3

The Evolving Father

TEACHING AND LEARNING FROM YOUR PRESCHOOLER

What image comes to mind when you hear the word *toddler?* Probably that of a small child, not nearly as helpless as an infant, walking, falling, walking again. A child brimming with confidence and eager to learn.

Much the same could be said about the fathers of toddlers and preschoolers. You've learned a huge amount in the year since your child was born, and you're getting a pretty good grip on this parenting thing. But as confident as you are, something still happens every day to remind you that there's still plenty more to learn.

The primary focus of your child's preschool years is going to be on developing and perfecting skills—physical as well as linguistic. You're changing too, of course, in ways you never would have if you hadn't become a father. During your child's preschool years, the most significant interactions you'll have with him are going to be physical, through play. At the same time this is the stage in both your lives when your relationships with each other will shape and solidify. It's also a time when you'll be figuring out exactly what your priorities are, what kind of dad you want to be, and how on earth you're going to accomplish what you want to in life.

What's Going On with the Kids

1-YEAR-OLD: PHYSICALLY

- Your bouncing baby is still expanding, but not nearly as fast as in his first year. Less growing means less eating.
- At the start of the first half of the year he can walk by himself—hands out and teetering—and he'll insist on doing so. He can run by eighteen months but mostly stops by falling down. After eighteen months he'll get the stopping thing under control, but corners will still present some difficulty.
- He can hold two objects in his hands at the same time, and if you draw him a straight line, he can copy it.
- He uses legs all the time, running and jumping and kicking. By his second birthday he may even be able to pedal a small tricycle.
- Favorite activities include emptying and filling (emphasis on the emptying)—especially things you don't want emptied, such as your refrigerator and dresser.
- He's fascinated by action-reaction and adores turning the lights on and off, opening doors and slamming them, and flushing the toilet repeatedly.
- He plays all sorts of physical games: chase me/catch me, rolling balls back and forth, and wrestling are big favorites.
- He stoops to pick things up, and most of the time doesn't fall. He can go up stairs by himself, holding on to the railing, but usually comes down backward.
- Fine motor coordination is improving. By now he can sort shapes with a shape sorter, builds a fine six-block tower, and is pretty good at undressing. Dressing is an entirely different story.
- He makes a formidable mud pie, spends hours opening and closing screw-top containers, and stacks, piles, tears, and pours anything that isn't tethered down.
- He's pretty good at handling forks and spoons, but he's no Emily Post. He holds his fork in one hand, picks up a piece of food, and pushes it onto the tines with the other.

1-YEAR-OLD: MENTALLY

- At the beginning of his second year your baby has an active vocabulary of 6–10 words—mostly body parts, a few animals, a few familiar people, and showstoppers like *yes* and *no*.
- His passive vocabulary (what he understands) is much bigger, though. When asked, he can point to his eyes, nose, and other body parts, and may even respond to simple directions, such as "Bring me my pipe and slippers."

- He will try to repeat everything you say, using a kind of shorthand. For example, if you say, "No, you can't pour your milk on the floor," he'll probably reply, "Pour milk floor."
- He's starting to grasp the symbolic use of words: If he knows the word *pool,* he may use it when he sees a duck pond, a puddle on the street, or even the ocean. He also might refer to every cat, horse, goat, pig, llama, or other hairy, four-legged animal as a "dog."
- By eighteen months he'll be trying to put phrases together ("gimme book" or "up me"). Near his second birthday he'll begin using language where he once used emotions: this is nice, especially when he says "change my diaper" instead of just shrieking.
- Nursery rhymes are very well received, and if you pause for a few seconds, he'll fill in the last word of a couplet ("Hickory, dickory, dock/ The mouse ran up the ___"). Unfortunately, this also means that if you're reading a familiar book and make a mistake, he won't let you get away with it.
- As his imagination develops, so will his capacity for pretending. He may crawl around the house pretending to be a dog, or may "eat" the drawings of food in your cookbooks.
- He'll start trashing your home by picking up, rotating, dropping, tasting, stacking (and knocking over), and throwing. Be patient—all he's trying to do, with everything he can get his hands on, is give himself a crash course in shape, texture, taste, density, balance, and aerodynamics.
- It finally dawns on him that things exist even when he can't see them, and he will search for objects he thinks might be hidden.
- A word of advice: toddlers love routines. Establishing rituals now, such as bath-story-bedtime and park-lunch-nap, will help you minimize some of the problems you're likely to encounter later on.

1-YEAR-OLD: EMOTIONALLY/SOCIALLY

- His never-ending search for independence starts—tentatively—now. He'll stroll a few yards away, casually looking back over his shoulder to make sure you aren't going anywhere. But independence is scary, so every few seconds he'll scamper back and cling to you for all he's worth. He'll repeat the process of going away and coming back at least through college.
- As he gets more secure with the idea that you'll always be there for him, fear of separation and shyness around strangers should decrease.
- Establishing independence involves a lot of limit testing, such as refusing to do just about anything you want him to—including eating and napping.

- He still plays alongside, rather than *with,* other toddlers. In fact, the only people he really wants to socialize with are you and your partner. He watches kids a lot and tries to imitate them.
- He may show his interest in other kids by physically exploring them, sometimes hitting, pushing, shoving, and hair-pulling. But he's not really being mean: he's still learning about the difference between animate and inanimate objects and is fascinated by cause and effect.
- He doesn't know how to share, so don't spend a lot of time trying to force him. He just hasn't yet picked up the ability to think about others' feelings or wants.
- He understands verbal humor now, particularly when it deals with incongruities. After refusing your lunchtime offer of a banana, a bowl of cereal, and a cheese sandwich, he may laugh hysterically if you suggest a spoonful of dirt. (After all, *even babies* know that people don't eat dirt.)
- He's developing a wider range of emotions: he's now quite affectionate with friends, family, stuffed animals, and pictures in books—he loves to "baby" dolls (and even parents), covering them with blankets and putting them to "bed." His whole body lights up when he's praised, and his feelings are genuinely hurt when he's criticized.

2-YEAR-OLD: PHYSICALLY

- Your toddler's appetite tapers off, and he starts getting picky, preferring the "white food group"—like rice and plain pasta.
- Enjoy his baby fat while you can, because it's melting fast. His little potbelly is mostly gone, and so are those wonderful little fat cushions on the bottoms of his feet.
- Gone too is his disproportionately giant head, as his body lengthens. And suddenly, there are all these teeth in his mouth.
- He doesn't need his hands for balance anymore, and he's losing that endearing Frankensteinian lumber. He runs without falling down, walks up and down stairs by himself, jumps off a low step, and rocks or marches in time to music.
- He's also adept at squatting and stooping and can even bend over to pick something up without crashing down.
- His attention span is still a bit iffy, so he seems to think with his feet—wandering aimlessly, stopping to engage in some activity or other, then moving on to the next. He can kick a ball and sometimes even controls where it goes.
- Now that his hand-eye coordination is improving, his fork-handling abilities

are much better, and so are his construction skills. He moves from simple block towers to long walls, houses, forts, and horse corrals.

* Pushing is nice. So is pulling, filling, and dumping everything he can get his hands on. He can turn the pages of a book, but almost never only one at a time. Give him a crayon, and he'll scribble emphatically, but without an agenda. By his third birthday, though, he'll try to imitate your writing and will be able to draw a fabulous "X."

* Early this year he still won't be able to differentiate between one side of his body and the other—when he points to something, he sticks out the fingers of both hands. But about six months from now he'll be able to control each side independently.

* Think your house is childproofed? You might want to revisit some of those doorknobs, cabinets, and window locks. You can bet that he has.

2-YEAR-OLD: MENTALLY

* Your child talks, and talks, and talks. Until now, he learned about his world *physically*: he had to touch, feel, or taste things before he could truly understand them. But now, *language*—questions, answers, explanations—begins to take over as the toddler's primary means of acquiring information.

* He uses 20–100 words and is learning 2–3 new ones every day. *Why* and *no* tend to be his absolute favorites. He can do some pretty good animal imitations.

* Listening is another story. Most of his words announce things that he's doing or seeing, and he doesn't respond much when you talk to him.

* He'll start this year with a passive vocabulary of 200–500 words, but by his third birthday he'll be able to understand the majority of the conversational language he'll use for the rest of his life, which means you'd better start spelling things out if you want to keep secrets from him.

* One of the more interesting steps in language-related development, according to child psychologist Selma Fraiberg, is that "language makes it possible for a child to incorporate his parents' verbal prohibitions, to make them part of himself." This isn't always 100 percent successful, though. You may find him sitting on the floor, eating sugar out of the box, and saying, "No, baby not eat sugar," between mouthfuls.

* He wants it, and he wants it now, and he wants to do everything himself, which means he gets insanely frustrated every time his desires outstrip his physical capabilities, which is most of the time. If you offer to help, you'll make him mad. If you don't offer to help, you'll make him mad too.

- Expect some spectacular tantrums as the "terrible twos" kick in. Most arise out of the frustration of having too few words to express what he wants.
- Routines, patterns, and symmetry are a must for the latter half of this year. Half an apple (or a cookie with a bite out of it) is completely unacceptable. And if you forget to fasten your seat belt before starting the car, you're likely to get a stern talking to.
- He learns the vocabulary of time between two and three. At this point he regularly uses *soon*, *in a minute*, and the always endearing *this day* (instead of *today*).
- He can now count to three and may even be able to recite numbers up to ten, but he doesn't really know what they mean.

2-YEAR-OLD: EMOTIONALLY/SOCIALLY

- The first few months of this year are happy and delightful. But starting at about two, your child becomes rebellious, defiant, negative, and exasperating. He doesn't know what he wants, but knows that he *doesn't* want to do whatever it is that you want him to. Get used to this now, because you'll be seeing it again when he's thirteen.
- He expresses his emotions physically more than verbally. If happy, he may jump up and down with glee; if angry, he may hit someone or throw something. Tantrums and mood swings happen daily as he struggles to gain some kind of control over his thoughts and actions. Giving him a limited number of choices (red sweater or blue one?) can help reduce tantrums by giving him more control over his world.
- Being contrary and difficult is a tough job for a kid, and he's likely to be tired a lot. Unfortunately, tiredness makes tantrums worse.
- He still plays alongside rather than with other kids. But, hard as it is to tell, he's slowly becoming more interested in them. You'll see this for yourself when he starts making a strange noise or using a word he never had before—the same noise or word used a few days before by the two-year-old at the park who your child seemed to be ignoring completely.
- He'll start off the year very possessive of his toys—offering them to others and then snatching them back. But by his fourth birthday, he'll show the first signs of cooperation—helping a playmate build or dig something instead of just trashing it.
- He's incredibly proud of the things he can do, and constantly seeks your approval. He'll beg you a hundred times a day, "Look at me!!!" as he climbs up stairs, fills a bucket with sand, draws a straight line, or rides his trike.

- His imagination is wild, and he can pretend to do anything with any kind of prop. Boys may turn dining room chairs into racing cars. Girls may spend a lot of time digging through—and experimenting with—your wife's cosmetics.
- He still finds the incongruous incredibly funny: try to put your foot into his shoes or wear his pants on your head, and you're likely to reduce your toddler to hysterical laughter.

3-YEAR-OLD: PHYSICALLY

- He's taller and thinner and has a full set of baby teeth.
- He spends most of his waking hours exploring the world and honing his motor skills. This means spending half the morning going up and down the same flight of stairs and the other half screwing the lid on and off his favorite jar.
- His average night's sleep is 10–12 hours. He usually wakes up dry, but accidents are still de rigueur. A few girls may show some interests in potty-training, but most boys won't.
- His dressing skills are improving. The shoes, he can put on himself. Snaps and zippers still frustrate him. And buttoning? Forget it!
- He can catch large balls if they happen to land on his outstretched arms.
- He walks and runs like a champ—usually without having to hold his arms out for balance. In fact, he's so good that he can even take corners at full speed. Once he does slow down, you might catch him practicing walking on tiptoe.
- And how 'bout those fine motor skills? Somebody's feeding himself with a spoon, and most of the food is getting inside him. He holds a crayon sort of like we do and traces some (very basic) shapes, most of which bear an uncanny resemblance to Mr. Potatohead.

3-YEAR-OLD: MENTALLY

- Your child will not stop talking. By now he has an active vocabulary of over 600 words and likes to arrange them in 3-to-5-word sentences.
- He's still not much of a conversationalist and prefers announcements and demands to give and take.
- He loves stories and rhymes, over and over and over and over. Not to worry: If you need a break, he's perfectly able to "read" you the book in his own words, using the pictures as a guide.
- He understands sequences much better than before: We went to the park, then we came home, then we watched a video.

- He's becoming aware of gender differences and stereotypes and understands that certain activities are "boy" things and others are "girl" things.
- He associates people with places, which means he may not recognize his favorite pediatrician if you bump into him in line at the grocery store.
- He's got *now, soon,* and *in a minute* down pretty well, but he's a little fuzzy on more abstract time. Words such as *tomorrow* and *today* are still a little unclear.
- He counts "One, two, a lot."
- Buy puzzles. He loves the relationship between whole objects and the parts that make them up.
- His imagination is soaring, and he loves dressing up. Cross-dressing is still pretty common at this age.

3-YEAR-OLD: EMOTIONALLY/SOCIALLY

- Whew, the terrible twos are pretty much over. Your toddler now says yes more than no. His improved coordination and growing control over his own actions mean he's less frustrated and a lot nicer to be with.
- Sometimes timid, sometimes adventurous, he may still have some trouble making up his mind—demanding to be taken to the car and then refusing to get in.
- He may also spend some time testing your limits, pushing you just to see what kind of reaction he can produce. Luckily, he's got a fairly short attention span and you can easily distract him, which makes it easier to avert a crisis. This is also a good time to remember the very important words: Choose your battles. Before reacting, take a second to figure out whether it's really worthwhile to stand your ground on some little thing like whether he's wearing matching socks or not.
- He's becoming a little less self-centered, changing from "I want" demands to "let's do" requests.
- He craves your approval and often does what you ask him to the first or second time instead of the seventeenth or twenty-fifth. When he does ignore you or misbehave, he may express some guilt or embarrassment later.
- Interestingly, your toddler may express a preference for the opposite-sex parent. This stage usually doesn't last very long.
- He still plays near rather than with other kids and isn't great at sharing. But by his fourth birthday he may actually do it without being prompted.
- He's becoming very aware of differences in race and gender, and the kids he does play with are more likely than not to be same-sex.

- His active fantasy life still includes dress-up and role-playing. It may also include some imaginary friends. These characters serve a very important purpose, helping him try out different behaviors and emotions and giving him someone to blame if things don't go right.

4-YEAR-OLD: PHYSICALLY

- No, you aren't imagining it: your four-year-old is even more active than he was at three. He will run and jump and hop on one foot and crawl and climb and skip and balance and do somersaults, and he will want you to do this with him.
- Roller skating is a distinct possibility, as is pedaling and steering his tricycle (or even a two-wheeler with training wheels) at breakneck speed. Thankfully he's a little more cautious on the stairs, putting both feet on each step.
- Using the above-mentioned activities, he will begin navigating impromptu obstacle courses. Make sure he has plenty of time and space to blow off steam.
- Meanwhile, on the small motor front, he loves painting with big, broad strokes and is getting quite handy with spoons, forks, and knives.
- He can get himself dressed and tie his shoes (if not in bows, then in knots) without much help, but he may not want to either.

4-YEAR-OLD: MENTALLY

- He's up to about 1,500 words now and will boost that to 2,500 by the end of this year. He still uses most of those words to tell you what's going on, but he begins to participate in—and even initiate—small conversations with other kids. If you ask him about his day, he may tell you, but chances are he'll make it up and exaggerate all sorts of details.
- He tailors his speech to his audience. He'll tell you, "I fell down outside and cut my toe." But he'll tell the baby, "Me hurt foot."
- He's so proud of his language abilities that he starts playing language games, making up silly names for objects he doesn't know. He'll be driven to hysterical laughter by the name-game song (Bill Bill bo bill, banana-fana-fo-fil, mee my mo mill, Bill).
- He identifies a few numbers and most letters—especially the ones that make up his name, which he may even be able to print. He also recognizes a few simple words that he sees regularly, such as *stop*.
- His grammar improves. He picks up some irregular plurals (one mouse, two mice, not mouses). But he still has trouble with some irregular past tenses,

saying things like "I goed to the zoo and seed a rhino," instead of "I went," and "I saw." When he makes this kind of mistake, don't correct him; simply repeat the sentence correctly.

- He's very curious and asks lots of questions, particularly about birth and death.
- He loves making big things out of little ones and is especially fond of connect-the-dots games.
- He still loves dressing up, but cross-dressing decreases as boys and girls tend to prefer "gender-appropriate" clothes.

4-YEAR-OLD: EMOTIONALLY/SOCIALLY

- His ability to feel and express emotions is increasing faster than his ability to manage them. He's often oversensitive, breaking into tears or becoming enraged for something insignificant or laughing for twenty minutes about something that wasn't that funny.
- He now plays *with* other kids. Actual friendships are developing, almost all of which are with same-sex kids. He has a new best friend every day.
- Along with friends comes peer pressure. Your child absolutely *must* have all those cool things his playmates have, and they can't live without what he's got.
- He's still not great at sharing, partly because he doesn't really get that other people have feelings that may be as important as his. Locking a friend up in a closet so he won't be able to leave is a pretty typical four-year-old way of keeping a play date going.
- He understands simple rules for games and usually follows them. But he'll often change the rules to suit himself.
- Until now, most imaginative play had to do with house and pretending to be mommy or daddy. Now, your child will more likely pretend to be an astronaut or a doctor a police officer or a butcher.
- He's still pretty self-centered, bragging about his accomplishments and getting jealous if you pay attention to anyone else.
- In an attempt to remain the center of attention, he tries to shock people by swearing, using his own made-up profanity, such as "doo-doo head."
- Your preschooler now prefers the same-sex parent and tries to be like him or her in every way. But no matter what gender you are, he loves to hear stories about your childhood—especially the times when you got into big trouble.
- He's more interested in sex now and may ask you about the mechanics. Long explanations are not necessary at this stage. Boys and girls both may extend their curiosity about sex into the pants of their friends. That's normal. Still, it may be time for a talk on privacy.

5-YEAR-OLD: PHYSICALLY

◆ He's down to 10–11 hours of sleep a night, but not because he's any less active than before. In addition to everything he was doing last year, he can catch balls on a bounce, throw overhand, jump rope, and stand on his head. He can even come down a flight of stairs, alternating his feet (as opposed to last season's two-feet-per-step approach).

◆ He's now able to take on more complex physical activities such as swimming or skiing.

◆ He may still like riding his trike, but if he hasn't already ridden a two-wheeler with training wheels, he's going to want to soon. But that phase will be short—by the end of the year he'll be ready to get rid of the training wheels.

◆ As his baby teeth fall out, you'll find yourself paying good money in the name of someone called the Tooth Fairy. And since the permanent teeth won't be along for a bit, you'll have plenty of time to enjoy the gaping holes in his smile.

◆ New, improved fine motor skills include: zipping, buttoning, and shoe tying.

◆ Everything is easier than last year. He can cut patterns with scissors and even draw fairly intricate pictures. So what if his people have eyes on the tops of their heads? At least they have necks.

5-YEAR-OLD: MENTALLY

◆ Your five-year-old is a real thinker. He loves to argue, reason, and prove his points. *Because* is the big word now.

◆ He still loves to be read to, but he's a lot more interested in trying to read for himself. He understands that books go from left to right and top to bottom. He especially likes jokes, nonsense rhymes, and silly stories.

◆ He draws letters and shapes and loves to write, especially his own name and short sentences like "I (heart) daddy."

◆ He begins to understand that actions have consequences. This won't keep him from misbehaving, of course, but at least it's on some back burner for later.

◆ He can memorize his address and phone number—and should, for safety reasons.

◆ He can count up to ten and may even have memorized a few more numbers past that. He loves to count and sort and organize everything he can—the number of squares on the sidewalk between your house and the park, the number of dogs you pass on the way there, how many green cars you drove by, how many kids have long hair in his preschool class, how many days till his birthday, and on and on.

5-YEAR-OLD: EMOTIONALLY/SOCIALLY

* Friends are getting to be very important. They continue to be almost exclusively same-sex. Preschoolers love to get together and construct elaborate fantasy play. But they spend more time talking about the rules and who's going to be whom than actually doing anything.
* He's pretty good at sharing and taking turns but may occasionally exclude some kids from the play group.
* He's much more interested in others in general. He now has conversations with people and may even ask a question now and then.
* His sense of empathy is growing. He notices when others are upset and may try to soothe them.
* Your preschooler has developed a fondness for rules—they offer some security in a world that he seems to have less and less control over. He likes to invent games and the rules that go with them and has no problem changing the rules if things aren't going his way. He can't always remember the rules he's supposed to follow, though: wash your hands after going to the bathroom, use a fork instead of your hands.
* He still has some trouble telling fantasy from reality and may be developing a fear of the unknown, which could include loud noises, the dark, strangers, and even some things he didn't used to be afraid of, like the mailman or the neighbor's dog.
* He likes to test his strength and show off how strong and capable he is. But he's not ready for competition, even with other kids—his ego is still pretty fragile, and he can't stand not to win.
* He's becoming more aware of the world around him and will notice differences between his family and other families—this one has two daddies, that one doesn't have any.
* He's also becoming more self-aware. He instinctively knows that he needs a little down time every once in a while, and he will go to his room or another quiet place where he can be alone.

Meanwhile, What's Going On with You?

RECALIBRATING YOUR LIFE

Before I had kids, I worked as a commodities trader, a labor negotiator, and a trade consultant—the kind of jobs you get with an MBA, which I have buried someplace in my attic. But before my first child was even born, I'd already reached the conclusion that being in business and being an involved dad—at least the way I wanted to do it—weren't entirely compatible. I'd published a few articles, and in a moment of feverish optimism, I quit my job to write full-time, which gave me the time with my daughter that I wanted.

I'm certainly not the only father to make dramatic kid-related career moves. Actor Mandy Patinkin gave up the work he loved to spend more time with his family. "I will not lose my family to this job," he said. Actor Ewan McGregor cut his schedule way back because of his daughter. And former secretary of labor Robert Reich gave up "the best job I've ever had and probably ever will" to spend more time with his family.

Okay, I realize that fatherhood isn't going have as dramatic an impact on everyone's career as it did on mine (and Patinkin's and McGregor's and Reich's).

"First of all, Harrington, let me tell you how much we all admire your determination not to choose between work and family."

In fact, making that kind of career transition isn't practical, or even desirable, for most dads. For some, the changes are more subtle. Here's how a U. S. Postal worker, for example, reacted when he was told he'd have to work nights:"I told them I could not work nights because I had a ten-year-old son, and I am a single parent. . . . Being with my son two days a week is not a good way to be a parent."

Not everyone responds to fatherhood by making changes at work. But I have yet to talk to a man who didn't change his life in at least *some* ways after becoming a father, ways he never would have considered if he hadn't had kids. Here are a few of the changes dads have made:

◆ **Moving to a larger (and usually more expensive) house.** When you've got a child, suddenly having a backyard or a playroom or an extra bedroom or two becomes very important.

◆ **Moving to a different neighborhood, city, or even state so the kids can have access to better schools.** Sometimes this is a change the whole family is okay with. But often this kind of change involves moving farther away from friends, family, movies, theater, museums, and other things that the parents enjoy.

◆ **Becoming the sole breadwinner.** A lot of women decide not to go back to work for a few years after having their babies. While it's great for the kids to have a parent around so much of the time, it puts a lot of financial pressure on Dad, including paying for that bigger house and its bigger mortgage.

◆ **Insurance and finances.** Parents have to worry about paying for college, and they're probably a little more conservative in their investments in general. It costs about $180,000 to raise a child through age eighteen (more if your child lives with you until he's thirty). Music lessons and private-school tuition bump that up even further. In addition, most financial advisers will agree that the more children you have, the more life insurance you should carry.

◆ **Nonhouse purchasing decisions.** Besides the new house, a lot of dads buy a lot of other things they never would have considered: a station wagon or minivan, backyard swing sets, Nintendo play stations, and on and on. When it comes to technology, kids often need much more powerful computers for school and play than we do for whatever we're using them for.

CONNECTING WITH YOUR CHILD

Before and during pregnancy, when women think about being a parent, the child they envision is usually a newborn. Men, including expectant and prospective dads, tend to imagine themselves with three- to five-year-old children. This was certainly true for me. In almost every dream or fantasy involving being a dad that I had before my kids were born, I was holding hands with a child, leaving

"Dad, would you please go back to doing the parenting, so that
I can do some of the childing for a couple of minutes?"

footprints on the beach, or playing catch—all things you can't do with an infant. We want to teach, and explain, and show. And even after the kids are born, it's hard for a lot of guys to get completely into the rhythm of being a dad with a tiny child who can't catch a ball or hold up his end of a conversation.

But in the preschool years, things change. Your child can laugh, and play, and listen to your stories, and may even be able to catch. Sure, he could do some of this before, but it's a lot more fun now that you can truly interact with your child, truly connect. The early childhood years are a time, says Selma Fraiberg, "when a baby and his parents make their first enduring human partnerships, when love, trust, joy and self-evaluation emerge through the nurturing love of human partners."

RECONSTRUCTING DAD

There's an old saying in the Talmud that a man has three names: the one his parents gave him at birth, the one that others call him, and the one he calls himself. A person's identity, according to the rabbis, is a rather amorphous thing. What the rabbis don't talk about is that all three of those names are subject to change over time—especially the one you give yourself. So who are you these days? The same person you were a few years ago? Probably not. And one of the biggest reasons you're not is that being a father has changed you.

Over a period of nearly two years, University of California–Berkeley researchers Phil and Carolyn Cowan asked a large number of men to draw a circle and divide it up into sections that reflected how important each aspect of their life felt—*not* the amount of time in the role. Over the study period, childless men showed a significant increase in the "partner/lover" aspect. But young fathers were squeezing "partner/lover" into a smaller space to accommodate the significant increase in the "parent" piece of the pie.

As the parenting pie grows, other things happen too. Here are a number of ways that the men in my survey (and several other studies as well) said fatherhood changed them:

- **Confidence and pride.** Having a close relationship with your child helps build his confidence and self-esteem. It also helps build yours. Being able to stop your child's tears, making him laugh, or knowing how much he idolizes you can make you feel incredibly competent, and the pride you feel when you see all the great things he can do becomes confirmation that you're doing pretty well at this whole fathering thing. For a while, at least, your child is going to share all your tastes—in music, literature, movies, art, career, politics, and food (as long as it's not too spicy). A lot of these things will change as your child grows up. But I can hardly describe the feeling of pride I get when my kids start discussing Hitchcock movies with my adult friends, belt out a few Janis Joplin lyrics, or pop in a CD of Elgar's cello concerto while they're doing their homework. But beware. Confidence and pride are often made of pretty thin veneer: any misbehavior—especially public—can suddenly make you feel you feel as though you've failed as a father.

- **Patience—and a better sense of humor.** Things are going to go wrong, whether you like it or not, and you have two choices: take everything seriously and try to change the world, or roll with it and laugh. Learning to laugh at yourself can rub off in other areas and might make you more understanding of the mistakes other people make.

- **Flexible thinking.** At this point it's almost impossible to tell the difference between your child's needs, your needs, and your partner's needs. In a perfect world they'd mutually reinforce one another. But on this planet, these needs "are to varying degrees in opposition, imposing frustrations and sorrows and forcing mutual adaptation," says the Group for the Advancement of Psychiatry

(GAP). As you get more experienced as a parent, your ability to prepare for the future and come up with contingency plans will grow.

You'll also learn the incredibly valuable skill of being able to see a variety of different points of view at the same time. For example, most new couples say that having children brought them closer together. At the same time, though, they say that labor around the house has been divided along traditional lines.

- **Return to childhood.** Having kids gives you a great opportunity to reread all those great books from when you were a kid and disappear back into the world of King Arthur and the Hobbit. It also gives you a rare chance to say words like "poop" and "pee" in public again.
- **Creativity.** A lot of parents suddenly get inspired to create. A. A. Milne (who wrote the *Winnie the Pooh* books) and J. K. Rowling (of *Harry Potter* fame) are just two who wrote for their kids. If you're giving your kids music or art lessons, you might develop a talent you never thought you had or rediscover the urge to perform at school talent shows.
- **Reordering priorities.** Having kids contributes to a heightened awareness of other's perspectives, says researcher Rob Palkovitz. A lot of guys admit that they were somewhat selfish and self-centered before having kids. This isn't necessarily a negative thing; it's simply an acknowledgment that having people depend on you and putting their needs before your own isn't something that comes naturally to most people before they become parents. What's especially interesting is that, according to Palkovitz, getting married didn't trigger this same realization.
- **Changing values.** Becoming a father will make you take a long, hard look at your fundamental beliefs and values. Things you may have thought were harmless when you were younger, such as not caring about money or material possessions, promiscuous sex, and even smoking a little dope, look completely different now that you've got a family to support. You'll start seeing the world in different terms. You may have thought about issues like pollution, terrorism, energy policy, Latin American debt, homelessness, AIDS, poverty, and even cloth vs. disposable diapers before, but now, instead of being abstract things that happen to other people, they're possible threats to your child and your family. We'll talk more about this in the next chapter. Having children will also help you clarify a lot of your beliefs. Teaching your child to say that the guy you didn't vote for in the last election is a jerk is one thing. But try explaining to your child—in terms he can understand—what war is, what the death penalty is, why some people are rich while others live on the

Costs and benefits of fatherhood

I realize that I may be making being an involved dad out to be something that's wonderful and fantastic and incredible every single minute. Well, it's not. The truth is that being a dad, just like anything else, has its ups and downs. It can be the greatest thing you'll ever do, and it can be the most frustrating. It creates opportunities for growth and fun, but interferes with others. The following table summarizes many of the benefits and costs associated with being an involved dad. It's based on Rob Palkovitz's and on my research.

BENEFITS

*   **Extending the family line.** Passing on your name, your line. Your children are your legacy.
*   **Satisfaction of watching children grow and develop.** You know that your teaching has made a difference in their lives, and you take joy in their accomplishments.
*   **Sense of pride.** You feel that what you're doing is right, that you've achieved something meaningful by making an investment in your children's development. This feeling comes whether or not you get compliments from others on how great a dad you are or on how great your kids are.
*   **Love received.** In a sense this is your compensation for being an involved dad. You get to be needed, loved, admired, and appreciated, and it feels great.
*   **Personal growth.** Maturity, self-discipline, role modeling, more emotional expressiveness. See this entire chapter for more.
*   **Perceptual shift/expanded self.** You're less goal-oriented, less driven, more interested in the family. Doing things for kids can be a tremendously satisfying experience.
*   **Fun.** Your kids give you all sorts of excuses to express joy, to experience life as a child again, to play and do things you'd never do without a child (go to a park or the zoo, collect baseball cards).
*   **Continued learning.** You can learn and develop skills and interests you never had before just to keep up with your kids. You can also relearn some of the subjects you'd forgotten long ago or learn some of the ones you never got around to in the first place.

- **Fathering gives life meaning.** Having kids may give purpose and direction to an otherwise ordinary life.
- **Enhanced marriage.** Some men feel that having kids makes their marriage better, giving Mom and Dad a shared focus in life and in their children's accomplishments. See below for more.

COSTS

- **Time.** For some men time is a metaphor for freedom or the opportunity to focus on themselves. Having kids requires giving up freedom to do what you want while you're with them. You may have to give up activities that brought you pleasure. (Although the opposite can be true: I rekindled an interest in martial arts when my youngest started taking karate.) You also may spend a lot of time thinking about them when you're not with them.
- **Sacrifice.** You may have to defer satisfying your own goals and dreams, or put off career advancement or continued education, in order to be the good provider. This tends to be much more common among men who become fathers young.
- **Finances.** Again, a more common worry among younger dads. It costs a lot to raise a child these days. (See page 112.)
- **Marital closeness.** You'll probably spend less private time with your partner. There'll be less time for physical and/or emotional intimacy, or even to talk over important issues.
- **Energy.** There's the sleep loss of early fatherhood, then the physical exhaustion of chasing a baby around, then more sleep loss when you start worrying about a sick child, or drugs and alcohol and sex and friends, or grades.
- **Potential.** All that time and energy you put into being a father is time and energy you could have devoted to writing a book, directing a movie, painting a masterpiece, inventing a cure for cancer....
- **Kids grow up and don't need you as much.** A lot of the meaning in your life will come from your relationship with your kids. If that relationship changes or gets strained, as it is likely to do as your child grows up and seeks independence, you may mourn the loss of meaning.
- **You get spread out.** All the demands on your time and energy leave you feeling like there isn't enough of you left.

street. You might find yourself changing your mind about a few things now that they might affect your family.

In 1998, NPR radio host Terry Gross did an interview that illustrates how fatherhood can cause values to change. Her guest, T. J. Leyden, worked for the Simon Wiesenthal Center at the Museum of Tolerance, fighting racism and anti-Semitism. But what made the interview riveting was that Leyden used to be a neo-Nazi and a white supremacist and had spent a lot of time recruiting teens into committing racist violence. What caused his dramatic turnaround? When his second son was four years old, Leyden heard him repeat some of the racist, anti-Semitic things Leyden had been spewing, and he was shocked. It was then that he decided to change.

Interestingly, older fathers report doing less of this kind of soul-searching than younger fathers. The older guys come into fatherhood feeling more mature and having had more of a chance to hone their philosophy of life.

REGAINING CONTROL

During your child's first year, you had to get used to the idea that your baby was pretty much running the show. It was the baby, not you or your partner, who decided when to eat, when to sleep, when he wanted to be changed, and

"You're not real experienced at this father business, are you?"

Power Struggles

Here are perhaps the three most important words you will ever hear as a parent: *Choose your battles.* Basically, this means that you should think carefully about whether it really matters whether your child wears one blue sock and one orange one instead of a matched pair. As your child gets older, he becomes more independent. And the more independent he becomes, the more he tends to resist the limits you set. It's all part of growing up: your child needs to know how serious the rules are and how you'll react when they're violated.

I used to spend huge amounts of time arguing with my middle daughter, trying to get her to put her shoes on before she got in the car. I'd threaten, cajole, plead, and bribe, and eventually, I'd wear her down, and she'd put them on. It was exhausting, but I considered it a victory. But the moment she was strapped in her car seat and I was behind the wheel, she'd yank off her shoes as quickly as she could and smirk at me in the rearview mirror. Eventually I gave up, and we're both a lot happier. And for about six months, my oldest daughter absolutely refused to sleep in her own bed. When I told her she couldn't sleep in our bed, she started sleeping on the floor, on the stairs, in the kitchen—anywhere but where we wanted her to. My wife and I argued with her for a while, but eventually decided that since she was getting a good night's sleep, we'd leave her alone. A few days after we stopped fighting with her, she retreated to her own bed.

More recently, a friend who lives in Chicago told me that his son suddenly began refusing to get into the family car unless he was stark naked. My friend and his wife made themselves—and their son—miserable for a few days before shrugging their shoulders and giving up. The three of them enjoyed several peaceful months—until that famous Chicago winter came, and their son rather sheepishly asked for some clothes.

Children, writes Ellen Galinsky, "have extremely accurate sensors and can tell when a parent is unsure of a limit and then will muster all of their force to dislodge it." Setting firm, consistent limits for your child is very important. But believe me, if you go to the mat to enforce compliance with every request you make, you'll spend a lot of unnecessary time butting heads with your child. And you won't have the energy to fight about the rules that really matter, like: Don't eat detergent, and Keep Mommy's bobby pins out of the electrical outlets.

119

when he wanted to play. Everyone else around him simply adjusted to his desires. As we discussed in the previous chapter, not being in control is hard. After all, we're bigger and smarter and older, and we should be in charge, damn it. But it doesn't work that way.

Fortunately, as your child gets older, things will change. There's an old saying that we spend the first two years of our children's lives teaching them to walk and talk, and we spend the next two years trying to get them to sit down and shut up. All that walking and talking requires a shift in the balance of power from your child to you. You're going to have to set basic boundaries for health and safety. And you'll gradually establish other rules, say for how to speak to and behave with other people, how to treat animals, when to go to bed, and so on. You'll also select your child's school and take your first steps toward overbooking him: soccer, piano, chess club, polo lessons. . . .

Don't expect much cooperation from your child, for two reasons. First, while you're trying to be the boss, your child is continuing his never-ending quest for independence, which involves rejecting you and your rules. Second, mentally, your child still thinks he's the center of the universe. Child psychologist Selma Fraiberg beautifully describes his attitude: "The magician is seated in his high chair and looks upon the world with favor. He is at the height of his powers. If he closes his eyes, he causes the world to disappear. If he opens his eyes, he causes the world to come back. . . . If desire arises within him, he utters the magic syllables that causes the desired object to appear. His wishes, his thoughts, his gestures, his noises command the Universe."

There are still plenty of times when you won't be in control at all, or at least not as much as you'd like to be. If your child is disabled or chronically ill, for example, his needs will still dictate your schedule. And, ill or not, when he throws himself down next to the bananas in the grocery store and has a huge tantrum, you'll remember the incredible frustrations of not being in control.

SEPARATION ANXIETY: YOURS

I don't think I'll ever forget the time I drove my older daughter a few blocks away from my house and abandoned her. Well, I didn't really abandon her, I just took her to preschool. But it was my first time, and somehow, I felt I'd done something wrong.

When our first child was born, my wife and I arranged our schedules so we could spend as much time with her as possible. And for the first two and a half years of her life, at least one of us was with her almost all the time. But as I sat in my car—having just dropped her off for her first day of preschool—I began to wonder what kind of parent I was, leaving her all alone with people I hardly knew. Would they read to her? Could anyone possibly teach her as well as my wife and I had? Who would encourage her? And who would love her? I was nearly overcome with a need to run back to the school, grab her, and take her home where she belonged.

After a few minutes of this sort of thinking, it became painfully clear that my wife and I had spent months preparing the wrong person for our daughter's first day of school. I fought the urge to go back to the school, and instead drove home and sat down in front of my computer. I tried to remind myself that—up until then, at least—I had actually been looking forward to having my daughter in school, knowing I'd have a lot more time to write. But as I stared dumbly at the screen saver, I kept thinking that maybe my priorities were in the wrong order. After all, what's more important, my getting to write a few articles, or making sure my children get the best possible education? Eventually, though, I had to admit that school was clearly the best place for my daughter—especially a school taught by teachers all our friends agree are gifted.

What it really comes down to, I guess, is that I knew I was going to miss my daughter while she was at school. I'd miss the wonderful times we had—the rainy-day matinees and museums and sunny-day outings, the hours spent cuddling on the couch reading the same book ten times in a row, or sitting at the table drawing. And most of all, I'd miss the long talks we had and the feeling of overflowing joy and pride I got from watching her learn new things and seeing how bright and articulate she'd become.

But missing her wasn't all there was. I was jealous, too. It somehow just didn't seem fair that my daughter's teachers—people who hardly knew her—were going to be the beneficiaries of so much of her company. Oh, sure, the two of us would still have plenty of afternoons together in the park, and we'd still make pizza dough, and soak each other with the hose while watering the garden, and hide under the covers in my bed. But no matter how much time we'd spend together now, I knew it would never seem like enough because I'd always remember the time when I didn't have to share her with *anyone*.

She was still so small and helpless, but at the same time, already off on her own. It really seemed like the end of an era. I remembered then (and still do now) going into her room at night when she was a baby and marveling at her angelic, smiling face and her small, perfect body. It was always a struggle not to wake her up to play. Thinking about it now, I realize that I was even jealous of her dreams.

I guess I should have known what I was going to feel as I dropped her off on her first day of school. I remember going to pick her up at the park a few months before. I stood outside for a few minutes, watching her chat and play with her friends. She seemed so mature, so grown up, so independent. Until that moment, I'd felt that I knew her completely. I knew the characters she'd pretend to be, I knew what she liked and didn't like, and we told each other everything. But watching her interact with other people—sharing secrets I'd never hear—I realized that the process of separating from our parents doesn't begin when we move out of their house at seventeen or join the marines, like I did. It really begins at three, in a park, digging tunnels in the sand with a friend.

Throughout his entire life, your child has been struggling to strike a balance between being dependent on you and independent from you. But he's not the only one in the family who's dealing with separation issues. As a father, you're probably

Your Child's Separation Anxiety

Think about things from a young child's perspective for a second (in this case I'm talking about kids under about eighteen months). For most of your life he controlled everything that happened in the world—who and what came and went, how long they stayed, what they did while they were there. But lately his grip seems to be slipping. Things seem to be coming and going all by themselves. And the people he thought he could always count on to be there for him have developed a nasty habit of disappearing just when he needs them most. Even worse, people he *doesn't* know—and isn't sure he even wants to know—keep on trying to pick him up and take him away. The universe is clearly in chaos, and given the way things are going, he can't really be sure that the people he's most attached to will ever come back.

All this, according to Philip and Barbara Newman, is what separation anxiety is all about. And the best way your child can put himself back in the driver's seat is to cry. It's as if he says to himself, "Aha! If I cry, my parents won't leave."

In an unusual but far-from-uncommon twist, many preschoolers develop some sleep problems: they view going to sleep as yet another assault on their ability to control the world. It can also be very confusing and frightening to go to sleep in the dark and wake up in the light, or to have you wearing one thing when you tucked him in and something else when you get him dressed in the morning. To a kid, staying awake can seem like a surefire way to make sure everything (and everyone) stays right where it's supposed to.

Not all kids get separation anxiety. Those who have had regular contact with lots of friendly, loving people will probably have an easier time adapting to brief struggling with an adult version of separation anxiety: a conflict between wanting to be needed by your child and wanting to push him toward independence.

The great irony here (to me, anyway) is that the attachment that we struggle so hard to achieve with our children is inextricably related to separating from them. In fact, "the task of becoming attached includes beginning to understand separateness," says Ellen Galinsky. It really seems that the stronger the attachment to the child, the more likely you are to be affected by the separation.

There are, of course, two common ways to deal with adult separation anxiety: push your child to be more independent, or encourage him be more dependent on you. Adopting either approach by itself will guarantee disaster for your child, for you, and for the whole family. As with just about anything else to do with parenting, the trick is to find the balance between the available extremes.

---

separations than those who have spent all their time with one or two people. They'll be more comfortable with strangers and more confident that their parents and other loved ones will return quickly.

As hard as separation anxiety is for your child, it's really a positive (albeit frequently frustrating) sign, marking the beginning of his struggle between independence and dependence. It's a scary time, and you can see his ambivalence dozens of times every day as he alternates between clinging and pushing you away.

At this stage, says British child-care expert Penelope Leach, "his own emotions are his worst enemy"—just when it seems that your baby should be needing you less, he actually needs you more. You're the grown-up, so it's up to you to help your baby make some sense of his conflicting emotions, as well as to nurture his independence while supporting his dependence. But beware: it's extremely easy to get trapped in a dependence/independence vicious circle. Here's how:

IF YOU...	HE FEELS...	WHICH, MAKES HIM....
Interfere with his independence and his developing ego	frustration, anger, and hate	anxious and afraid.
Interfere with his need to be dependent on you and his desire to cling	anxiety and fear	frustrated, angry, and hateful.

The first step is to become aware of what might be motivating you to take certain steps.

If you're pushing your child to be more independent, it may be because he's quieter, less curious, or more clingy than you'd like him to be. You might be worried that if he doesn't start learning to take care of himself, he'll grow up to be a wimp. Or you might resent your child for controlling you, for robbing you of your independence and making too many demands on your time and affection. This last feeling is especially common among fathers whose kids are temperamentally "difficult." And if you're a stay-at-home dad or if you're especially involved, you may be afraid that besides having lost your career, you've lost your prestige and your masculinity. The downside of pushing too much independence too soon is that you might end up being less affectionate with your child—especially if you have a boy. As a result, your child could end up feeling unloved and uncared for, as though you're trying to get rid of him.

Although pushing early independence tends to be thought of as a "dad thing," mothers are far from immune from trying to make their kids more self-reliant. At the same time, even though not wanting to let kids go is usually thought of as more of a "mom thing," there are plenty of dads who do it too. If you're encouraging your child to be more dependent, it may be because you're sad he's growing up so quickly. He's already outgrown some really adorable stages, and it's tempting to wish he'd stay this age forever. Or you might be feeling rejected when you want to sit quietly and snuggle with him, but he squirms off your lap and runs away. These feelings can trigger a lot of really negative behavior on your part. You might, for example, not give your child enough room to explore, or hover over him too much, never allowing him to make the mistakes he needs to make to learn from. You might limit his contacts with other people, feeling that any free time he has should be spent with you. You might spoil him by not setting adequate limits or disciplining him for fear of driving him away.

He may not show it, but your child needs you more than ever. He needs your support and love to let him know that growing up (which he's going to do whether you like it or not) is okay. Taking pride in his independence and all the "big boy" things he can do is an important part of building his self-esteem and independence. And finally, do you really not want your child to grow up? Do you really want to be changing his diapers for the next fifty years? I don't think so.

DEALING WITH THE DISAPPOINTMENT OF DISABILITY

One of the major themes in this book is the constantly evolving need to deal with the disparity between the way you dreamed your child would be and the way he actually is. A lot of the differences between reality and expectation have to do with choices and interests—the child choosing to join a motorcycle gang instead of going to medical school like you wanted him to, or the child having no interest in sports or in living out your dream to win an Olympic medal in the luge.

In most cases, parents manage to get past these things, and learn to accept their children as they are. But what happens if your child can't live up to your expectations or hopes because he's disabled or chronically ill?

You're likely to feel a wide range of emotions, from shock, disbelief, and denial to depression, anger, ambivalence at having a child at all, resentment at having to spend so much time and money on treatment, and even wishing that your child had died. Many of these more negative feelings will immediately be followed by profound guilt at ever having had the thought in the first place. Whatever your feelings, having a disabled child may do serious damage to your self-esteem.

Mothers and fathers react to a child's disability differently. Mothers typically worry more about the emotional strain of caring for a retarded child, how they'll have to reorganize their life around the child, and whether that will make them neglect other members of the family, according to Jaipaul Roopnarine and Brent Miller.

Fathers tend to worry more about practical things: the cost of providing care, and whether the child will be able to function in school. Dads also tend to be more concerned with their disabled children's (especially boys') social status and employment prospects, says Michael Lamb. Fathers with disabled children feel inferior, according to Lamb. They get less pleasure out of their disabled children, and "they end up with fewer reminders of their own value." Overall, Israeli researchers Malka Margalit and her colleagues found that fathers of disabled children derived less satisfaction from family life, perceived fewer opportunities for independence and personal growth and intellectual and recreational activities, and had less confidence in themselves than fathers whose children were not disabled.

How (and how well) you and your partner cope with a handicapped or chronically sick child depends on a fascinating collection of factors.

- **When you become aware of the problem.** The earlier the problem comes to light, the easier it is for parents to begin to cope. It's harder for parents to acknowledge a problem with a child who seemed perfect for a while.
- **How obvious the handicap is.** Fathers, according to Michael Lamb, generally feel more scrutinized by society, which makes them particularly sensitive to any perceived "imperfections" their children might have.
- **Birth order.** Fathers tend to be more involved with firstborn children who are handicapped than with ones born later.

- **The type of disability.** A physical or mental handicap seems harder for parents to adjust to than chronic illness. This is especially true for parents who are highly educated and who had high intellectual hopes for their child.
- **The gender of the child.** Sadly, since a lot of parents (especially fathers) have higher expectations for their sons than their daughters, they may react more negatively to a boy's handicap than to a girl's. Boys who are mentally retarded, for example, have a more negative impact on the family than retarded girls, says Lamb.
- **The couple's relationship with each other.** Couples who are more content and who have more social support are more likely to have favorable reactions to disabled kids than those who aren't as stable, according to Roopnarine and Miller.

Coping with the Death of a Child

Losing a child is every parent's worst nightmare, an ordeal no one who hasn't experienced it can possibly imagine. It can bring up grief, anger, denial, and even feelings of guilt at not having been there enough or inadequacy at not having been able to prevent the death.

Researcher Kim Wendee Schildhaus studied how couples adapt to and cope with the loss of a child and keep their marriage alive. She found that, as in most areas of parenting, men and women cope with the loss of a child differently. Women had two basic needs: one was to focus on the surviving children, if any; the other was support systems. Men did what men usually do: they tried to ignore their feelings and dove headlong into their jobs. The rationale for that kind of approach, says William Schatz, author of *Healing a Father's Grief,* is that since you've failed in your other societally approved roles, you can at least succeed at being a breadwinner. Unfortunately, that isn't an effective way of coping with grief—either in the short or the long term. "Grief will change you," adds Amy Hillyard Jensen, author of *Healing Grief.* "But you have some control over whether the changes are for better or worse."

Men are brought up to be tough, strong, competent, knowledgeable, and in control of our emotions. Weakness—especially tears—is discouraged. Anger and frustration are okay, but sadness and pain are not. This kind of socialization is very effective in a lot of ways. But when we face an emotional upheaval like the loss of a child, too many of us have no idea how to react.

- **How the father's parents respond.** Acceptance of the disabled child by the father's parents has a big influence on how well the father himself accepts the child, according to Lamb.
- **Whether you join a support group or not.** Men who get involved with other fathers of handicapped kids feel less sadness, fatigue, pessimism, guilt, and stress, and have more satisfaction, greater feelings of success, fewer problems, and better decision making abilities than dads who don't join groups, according to researchers Patricia Vadasy, Rebecca Fewell, and their colleagues.

There's no question that having a handicapped child puts a lot of stress on the entire family. Conflict, tension, and even divorce are more common in families with a disabled child. That's why it's especially important that you and your

---

Instead of acknowledging our grief and dealing with it, we ignore it. Instead of getting help, we pull away from the people closest to us. The results can be dangerous. "If feelings are left buried, they cause prolonged turmoil, bitterness, family problems, and even ill health," writes Schatz.

Besides being devastating to the parents, losing a child can also destroy the marriage itself. But it doesn't have to. Schildhaus identified a number of factors shared by couples who adapt to their loss and stay together. They:

- Accept different ways of grieving and allow each other space in the relationship without making judgments. Men and women have to accept each other's individual style.
- Believe in and utilize family support network, asking for help when needed, accepting it when offered.
- Focus on other children.
- Focus on work, job, career.
- Agree that the death of the child was the most tragic loss imaginable and that the thought of losing the spouse too is unbearable.
- Develop new friendship networks that include other parents who've lost children.
- Get therapy.
- Keep the memory of the deceased child alive.
- Communicate with each other.

partner get as much support as possible and that you communicate with each other constantly. When one parent backs off, that leaves the other parent with twice the burden. If your friends are able to step in, that'll certainly help. But you absolutely must explore every other possible resource. Start by getting some couples therapy. Then check with your child's pediatrician, parent support groups, and your local school district. In addition, About.com has a good collection of resources (*specialchildren.about.com/*), and *Exceptional Parent* magazine (*www.eparent.com/*) provides information, support, and resources for parents and families of children with disabilities.

Your child's disability will undoubtedly have an impact on how you treat him. You may respond by being overprotective, or you may be more lenient and lax about setting limits and enforcing them. Try not to do this if you can. Naturally, you'll need to adapt to your child's individual disability, but use this as a rule: As with any child, if you treat him as though he's weak and fragile, he'll grow up thinking of himself in exactly those terms.

Keep in mind that having a disabled child is not an all-negative experience. Most families get great pleasure out of raising their handicapped child, and many even go out of their way to adopt them. In addition, several studies have shown that handicapped children can actually have a positive effect on families, says Lamb. And at least one researcher found that some fathers in particular reorder their priorities to put their family first, discover new values, and experience personal growth as they adapt to their children's disabilities.

RECOGNIZING YOUR LIMITATIONS

Before Clint Eastwood (as Dirty Harry) was challenging people, "Go ahead, punk, make my day," he was advising, "A man's got to know his limitations." Phil and Carolyn Cowan found that one of the factors that differentiate fathers from nonfathers is that dads do a better job discriminating between what they can and can't control. This skill—as absolutely basic as it sounds—can actually take years to develop. "We heard men working on it when they discussed their struggles with wanting it all—job advancement, involved relationships with their wives and children, time for themselves—while accepting the fact that no matter how hard they tried, some things had to be put aside for the time being," write the Cowans. "It is our impression that as a group, men who were not parents had fewer competing demands to balance, were less aware of their limitations, and more invested in maintaining at least the illusion of personal control."

BROADENING (OR AT LEAST CHANGING) YOUR SOCIAL NETWORKS

For the first year or so of being a parent, your child will play with whomever you introduce him to; his first friends are most likely going to be your friends' kids. But as he gets older and starts showing interest in other children and making friends of his own, this will change: you'll start socializing with the parents of *his* friends. This will probably widen your circle of friends and may even make some of your adult relationships last longer than they would (or should) have, simply because the kids like playing together.

Being an involved father is also going to introduce you to all sorts of people you wouldn't have met otherwise: pediatricians, soccer coaches, teachers, babysitters. And who knows, you might end up becoming friends and spending time with some of them. And because you're a dad, which means being part of a family, you may be spending time with your parents, in-laws, or other relatives.

Expect continued change as far as your old, prefatherhood friends go. (See pages 83–85 in the previous chapter for more on this.). It may seem harsh, but the fact is that you may lose some friends (and they'll lose you). But you'll gain many new ones in the process.

LIBRARY BOOKS, OKAY. BUT CAN FATHERS BE RENEWED?

Well, according to sociologists, the answer is yes. The term *renewed fathers* refers to men in their forties or older who have grown kids from a previous relationship, but get remarried to younger women who want kids of their own. There are a lot of differences between renewed fathers and their nonrenewed brothers. First, the renewed dads tend to be more financially secure and less interested in career advancement. They also have more interest in spending time—and more time to spend—with their young children. Overall, the older the father, the more relaxed, caring, flexible, and supportive he is, according to my colleague Ross Parke. Parke has found that men and women age differently. Women get more task- and goal-oriented as they get older, while men get more nurturing. "Witness the man who was a stern parent turn into an old softie around his grandkids."

On the downside, a renewed father doesn't usually spend as much time playing with his kids as a younger dad who hasn't turned himself in for the deposit yet. "But his intellectual level is still high enough to more than make up for the difference," says Parke.

Integrating your old and new families can be enormously complicated—for your kids, your new partner, and you. Most older children feel somewhat abandoned and jealous when a younger sibling comes along. But if they aren't living

with you full-time, these feelings may get kicked to an even higher level when you start a new family. They may feel that your loyalty and your love (and sometimes your money) will be spent on your new baby, the one who's with you all the time, and they may resent having to share those things with anyone. They may also see how much more involved you are with their new half-sibling and resent that you weren't that way with them. (This may or may not reflect reality, but your kids' feelings are just as real either way.)

Children of divorce almost always harbor a secret (or not-so-secret) hope that their parents will get back together. But your having a new family with a woman who's not their mother may force them to confront their dashed hopes. At the same time, your new family may disrupt your older children's loyalties. On the one hand, they'll continue (as they should) to feel deeply loyal to their mother. On the other hand, they'll feel a naturally growing allegiance to the baby and to their stepmother. But as those newer relationships deepen, the children may feel guilty that they're abandoning their mother—as if allowing themselves to be part of a new family means that they have to stop loving her. This can sometimes make them lash out at you, the baby, and/or your partner. In their minds, if it weren't for all the changes that have been forced on them, life would have been great—or at least not any worse than it was before.

In intact families, women whose husbands are involved fathers are generally happier and more fulfilled. But if you're a renewed dad, your new partner may have a very different experience. She may have been very supportive of your relationships with your older kids. In fact, seeing how you related to your kids might have been one of the things that attracted her to you in the first place. But now that she and you have a child, she may resent the time that you spend with your other kids, fearing that you won't be as attentive to your new family.

This is almost exactly what happened with me. My two older kids are with me half the time, and we have a very close relationship. That's a wonderful thing for the three of us, but it sometimes makes my new wife feel excluded, as though she has me only 50 percent of the time. And she naturally worries about whether I'm going to have time (and love) enough for her and the child we have together.

As tough as your renewed fatherhood status is for your children and your partner, it's no less difficult for you. The comfortable, linear progression of your development as a father is now on two tracks. Usually you get married, have kids, the kids grow up and get married, and they have kids of their own and make you a grandfather. But if you're a renewed dad, you're literally in two places at the same time. You're still on your original track with your older children, but you're also starting the process all over again with your new family.

Sometimes it's easy—and fun—to be on both tracks. Having been through it before will probably make the early stages of fatherhood less stressful and more relaxing. Other times, though, you'll feel as though your two tracks are on a collision course. As we discussed in chapter 1, your new partner may interpret your laid-back attitude as a lack of interest or excitement. But the more time you spend with your new family, the more abandoned and resentful your older kids may feel, jealous of the things they never got. You might feel guilty too, about not having been a better dad the first time around. And if you spend more time with your older children, your new family will feel excluded.

All in all, you're in a tough spot, and you'll have to figure out a way to juggle the often conflicting needs of your two families in a way that works for everyone—including yourself. Whatever you do, don't give in to pressure or temptation to sever ties with your older children. They need you, and you need them, even if you don't get to see each other as often as you'd like.

Your challenge is to create a new family unit, one that integrates your older children, your new child, and your partner. Notice that I'm *not* saying to make the older kids part of your new family or to make the new family part of the old one. Either of those approaches will make one group or the other feel second

Issues for Adoptive Fathers

Adopted children and their adoptive fathers develop in very much the same ways as biologically related fathers and kids.

Perhaps the biggest (adoption-related) issue for adopted parents at this stage is whether and how to tell their children about the adoption. The consensus seems to be to hold off for a while, at least until the child is six. Before then, most children aren't capable developmentally of understanding what adoption means, and they haven't got a clue about how conception and birth really work. (They may be able to tell you all about how babies come from mommies' tummies, but they don't really get the process.) Adoption expert Gordon Finley tells a great story about a family with a three-and-a-half-year-old adopted child that went to the airport to pick up a newly adopted infant. "For a long period after," he writes, "whenever the family passed an airport, the oldest would point to the airport and talk about how that is where babies come from."

As we discussed in the previous chapter, many adoptive parents experience feelings of inadequacy at not having been able to produce their own children. By the time their children reach the preschool years, though, most adoptive parents have put aside their feelings about infertility and shelved their fantasies of having a biological child. Instead, they're "coming to see themselves as they really are, the eminently entitled and very 'real' psychological parents of their adoptee," writes Finley.

But thinking about telling their child about the adoption can bring back all the negative feelings about adoption—the infertility, the self-doubt, the conflicts with the spouse. Throw in a little fear that the birth parents will change their mind and the adoptive parents will lose the child, and you can see why this could be a very stressful time.

best. Instead, both groups have to understand that they're part of something bigger, and that your loyalties are not divided but are spread out evenly.

Why Be an Involved Father at All?

Well, as we've talked about in previous chapters, being an involved father is good for everyone: your kids, your partner, and even yourself. Here are some of the specific benefits to being actively involved with your preschooler:

BENEFITS FOR YOUR CHILD

- **Better friendships.** Three-year-olds who have positive relationships with their fathers have better friendships when they're five. The more negative the father-child relationship, the worse the quality of the kids' friendships.
- **More cooperation and self-reliance.** Children whose fathers regularly looked after them during their infancy and preschool years are more self-disciplined and have better social skills than others whose fathers spend less time alone with them, according to Kay Margetts, a researcher at Melbourne University in Australia.
- **Smoother separation from Mom.** During the time that their children are eighteen months to three years old, fathers play one of the most critical roles they will ever play in the life of their child: helping the child safely and securely separate from the intense maternal dependency of infancy, says psychiatrist Kyle Pruett. Pruett believe that as healthy as it is for young children to be depending on their mothers, they'll never develop their own

"Oh, good. Here comes Daddy, to bring us to our senses."

confidence if they don't ever establish their physical and emotional autonomy.

- **Better problem-solving skills and less frustration.** The combination of a father's more interactive play style and his less immediate support in the face of frustration helps kids adapt to new situations, explore the world more vigorously, and become more competent problem solvers, says Pruett. They're also more secure and less fearful when faced with new or strange things. Kids who have involved fathers have a higher tolerance for stress and frustration, skills that will help them a lot when they finally get to school. "Kids are better able to wait their turn for the teacher's attention, more confident in their abilities to work on their own, more confident, more willing to try new things," writes Henry Biller.

- **Smarter.** Sons of nurturing fathers score higher on intellect tests than boys whose fathers are less involved, according to studies conducted by Norma Radin. Kids growing up without involved fathers have more trouble solving complex mathematical problems than kids whose dads are involved.

- **More compassion for others.** First-graders whose fathers took more responsibility for limit setting, discipline, and helping children with personal problems and schoolwork had significantly higher empathy scores than kids whose dads didn't do these things, according to researcher Susan Bernadette Shapiro.

- **It sets a good example.** By being involved, you're demonstrating that both men and women can nurture. It shows young boys that being an involved father is something to aspire to when they grow up, and it shows young girls that they should expect their future husband to be an involved father as well.

- **They'll have fewer problems as teens.** The biggest predictor of whether a girl will take up sports or be physically active is having a father who plays (at wrestling, softball, basketball, whatever) with her when she's young. Adolescent girls who are involved in sports are less likely to drop out of school, get pregnant, develop eating disorders, put up with abusive relationships, smoke, drink, or develop breast cancer as adults.

- **They'll be more empathetic adults.** Several long-term studies have found that how compassionate adults (men and women) are and how well they are able to experience others' feelings depends more than anything else on how involved their fathers were during the preschool years.

- **It delays puberty and reduces early sexual activity for girls.** Girls who have close, positive relationships with their fathers during their first five years, and whose fathers were active caregivers and had good relationships with their mothers, enter puberty later in life, according to Bruce Ellis, a researcher at the University of Canterbury in New Zealand. "We've learned that girls who grow up without fathers tend to become sexually active at earlier ages, that girls without fathers tend to look for male approval in intimate relationships before they're emotionally ready."

BENEFITS FOR YOUR PARTNER AND YOUR MARRIAGE

♦ **More commitment to the marital relationship.** Men think about marriage and family differently from women. For men, "family" tends to mean a mother, a father, and some kids. As a result, once a man becomes a father, he also becomes very committed to keeping his family together. That way of thinking explains, to some extent, why after divorce men remarry sooner and more often than women. Women, however, can imagine themselves parenting without a man around and still consider themselves part of a family. That goes a long way toward explaining why about 75 percent of divorces are initiated by women.

BENEFITS TO YOU

♦ **You'll be less depressed.** Constance Hardesty and her colleagues found that low levels of paternal involvement can lead to depression. In other words, higher levels of involvement may promote mental health in men.

♦ **You'll have a longer, healthier life.** Involved fathers suffer fewer accidental and premature deaths, less-than-average contact with the law, less substance abuse, fewer hospital admissions, and a greater sense of well-being overall, according to Joseph Pleck.

♦ **You'll be a more effective parent.** Researcher Mary De Luccie did a study of 177 firstborn boys and girls in an attempt to figure out what made dads get involved and feel satisfied. She found that it was a kind of loop: fathers who were warm and firm with their kids felt they were doing a good job and thought they had good relationships with their kids. That, in turn, made them want to get even more involved. It just keeps getting better and better.

♦ **You'll get laid more often.** Being an involved father is the ultimate aphrodisiac. According to Aaron Hass, the most frequent complaint from wives about husbands is that they aren't involved enough with the children. And—from her point of view, anyway—if you don't love the kids, you don't love her. "A man, therefore, who does not actively father will inevitably trigger his wife's resentment," says Hass. The solution? Be an active, involved father. "There is no more powerful aphrodisiac to a mother than to see her husband lovingly engaged with their children," says Hass. "When your wife sees your involvement with her children, she will want to see you happy. She will, therefore, want to satisfy your sexual desires. She will be more likely to suggest that just the two of you get away for a night or a weekend so that you can have more intimate time together. She will be more open to sexual experimentation. . . . She will be more sexually creative. She will take pains to make sure the children are tucked away early in the evening so that you can have uninterrupted time together. And, of course, when your wife is happier, her own libido is more likely to assert itself." Whew! If that doesn't make you want to quit your job and take care of your children full-time, nothing will.

Staying Involved during the Preschool Years

* **Volunteer in school.** "Fathers' participation in early childhood programs will significantly benefit their own sense of contribution to the development of the *whole child:* a child who recognizes that men as well as women can nurture both in the home and in the school environment," write David Giveans and Michael Robinson.
* **Safety first.** In the toddler years, make sure the house is childproof. Crawl around checking for loose wires, choking hazards, bookshelves that might fall or get pulled over, ungated stairways, and other tempting dangers your child will want to explore. As he gets older, do periodic checks to make sure that knives, fertilizers, paints, poisons, and so on are locked safely away. Always insist on proper safety gear for biking, roller blading, or any other sport.
* **Make the house kid-friendly.** Put books and toys on low shelves so your child can have some control over what he reads and plays with.
* **Monitor the media.** This does *not* mean turn it off. Watching television and movies with your child can be a great way to talk about issues of morality, right and wrong, politics, and more. And don't believe everything you hear about how video games, superheroes, comic books, and make-believe violence in the media lead to aggression. Media critic Gerard Jones did an exhaustive study and found that, contrary to what we've all come to accept as the truth, fantasy violence often gives kids important coping skills. "Instead of banning head-bonking TV shows and gory games like Doom, we should harness the tremendous power of fantasy to help our kids better

navigate the world around them," he writes. It's an interesting argument, one that's worth investigating further.

- **Turn off the computer.** A recent study of preschoolers (age four to six) found that kids who spend a lot of time in front of the computer are less likely to be accepted by their peers. According to Theodore E. Gardner and Jeffrey R. Measelle, who did the study, kids who have trouble making friends when they're young often have trouble fitting in for years to come. Gardner and Measelle also found that heavy computer users tend to be more depressed than lighter users.

- **Take some breaks.** Airline flight attendants always advise parents to put on their own oxygen masks before helping their kids put on theirs. The same logic applies here: you can't be an effective parent if you can't manage the stresses in your own life.

- **Discipline, but don't punish.** It's your child's job to test your limits. It's your job to create firm limits and enforce them. Children need consistent boundaries and discipline; that teaches them self-control and gives them comfort and confidence that you really care about them. Being inconsistent or too much of a pushover (how many times have you given your child sixteen

"Not now, Benjamin—Daddy's having a little quality time with himself."

"last warnings"?) may make your child fear independence. Know when to compromise—and when not to (health and safety issues top this list). Above all, make sure you understand your child. Trying to discipline him without understanding why he's doing what he's doing is a little like taking cough syrup for emphysema: the thing that's bugging you goes away for a while, but the underlying problem remains—and keeps getting worse with time. The most direct way to solve this is simply to ask your child what's going on and why he's acting the way he is—in many cases he'll tell you. If he won't tell you or doesn't have the vocabulary to do so, make an educated guess ("Are you writing on the walls because you want me to spend more time with you?").

- **Read up on child development.** This may be one of the most important things that you can ever do as a parent, which is why I'm always amazed at how few people do it. At the very least it'll help you understand why your child is doing what he's doing. And chances are, it'll reassure you that a lot of those completely insane things your child does are absolutely normal.
- **Get involved in the day-to-day decisions that affect your kids' lives.** This means making a special effort to share with your partner such responsibilities as meal planning, food and clothes shopping, cooking, taking the kiddies to the library and the pediatrician's office, getting to know their friends' parents, and planning play dates. Not doing these things can give the impression that you don't think they're important or that you're not interested in being an active parent. And by doing them, you make it more likely that your partner will feel comfortable and confident in sharing the nurturing role with you. But make sure to log some private quality time with the kids too. Sure, somebody has to schlep them all over town to their ballet lessons or soccer practice, but those shouldn't be the only times you get to see each other.
- **Play.** A lot of what preschoolers learn comes from physically interacting with the world. Running, chasing, bouncing up and down on the bed, bike and trike riding, spinning till you drop, kicking things, dancing, gymnastics, and even pillow fights and other vigorous activities are great for exercising those growing large muscles. For small motor skills, puzzles, painting, drawing, stringing beads, pouring, ball games, and measuring are big favorites. And don't forget about imagination games. Children who have well-developed pretending skills tend to be well liked by their peers and to be viewed as peer leaders. It also helps them take the point of view of others and improves their ability to reason about social situations.
- **Cook.** This can teach your child many valuable lessons about textures, measuring, and how things change shape when they're mixed, heated, or cooled.

DONNELLY

*"No, I can't come and play now, Bobby.
My dad's teaching me how to eat pizza."*

Jell-O is particularly well suited because it even requires cooking. Be patient: making food with a child can be a tremendous mess—but an even more tremendous amount of fun.

- **Don't devalue the things you like doing with the kids.** Men and women have different—but equally important—ways of interacting with their children. Men tend to stress the physical and high-energy more, women the social and emotional. But don't let anyone tell you that wrestling, bouncing on the bed, or other "guy things" are somehow not as important as the "girl things" your partner may do (or want you to do). Reread the section above on the benefits involved fathers bring to their children. Ultimately, though, both kinds of interactions are indispensable, and it's a waste of time to try to compare or rate them.

- **Hang out together.** Go on a picnic in the woods, take a trip to the zoo, go to a lake and feed the ducks, do art projects together, do science experiments, or get a basic book on constellations and see how many you and your child can identify.

- **Spend time getting to know your child.** Watch him carefully to figure out what he likes to do and what he doesn't. Get down on the floor and play with your child on his level, and play the games he wants to play.

- **Talk to your child—and listen to the answers.** Ask a lot of questions about what he is thinking and feeling. It's especially important to do this with

Spanking

A few years ago, *Child* magazine polled its readers and found that 37 percent of parents discipline their toddlers several times a day, and 27 percent discipline their child *in public* several times a week. It's not all that surprising, then, that 39 percent of mothers spank their kids "often or sometimes" and 20 percent slap their kids' hands often or sometimes.

The big question, of course, is, Does spanking do any good? If you want to attract the child's attention in a hurry, the answer is yes. But if you're interested in any long-term positive effect, the answer is a resounding no. In fact, there's plenty of evidence that the long-term effect of spanking children is actually quite negative. (It's worth noting here that of the people polled in the *Child* survey, only 4 percent felt that spanking was an effective way to get kids to be good.)

Basically, researchers confirm just what you might expect: spanking children does little more than teach them to resort to violence and aggression to solve their problems—not exactly the message most parents want to get across to their kids.

I still remember very clearly a scene that took place a few years ago at a bus stop not far from my house. A rather agitated woman was trying to keep her two kids—about five and seven years old—from fighting. "How many times," she said, smacking the older child, "do I have to [smack] tell you [smack] not to hit [smack] your brother [smack]?" Any guesses about where that little boy learned to hit his brother?

Author Doug Spangler suggests that fathers who spank their children are sending some very specific messages:

- ◆ It's okay to hit another person.
- ◆ It's okay to hit another person who is smaller than you.
- ◆ It's okay to hit someone you love.
- ◆ It's okay to hit someone when you feel angry and frustrated.
- ◆ Physical aggression is normal and acceptable under any circumstances.
- ◆ Daddy can't control himself or his temper.
- ◆ Fathers are to be feared.
- ◆ Children must always be quiet around their fathers.

Research also shows that children who get spanked are more likely to suffer from poor self-esteem and depression, and have a greater chance of accepting lower-paying jobs as adults. While this may not be a direct cause-and-effect relationship, there is clearly some correlation between being spanked and poor self-esteem.

boys. And spend some time talking about your day. Doing this lets him know you value his company and, by extension, him.

- **Read.** Every day. Keep things interesting by acting stories out, improvising, and talking about the illustrations. And set a good example by making sure your child sees that you and your partner spend some of your free time reading—even if it's just the newspaper. Set up a low bookshelf where he can keep his own books.

- **Expose your child to music.** Your favorites are a place to start, but the bigger the variety your child is exposed to, the better. If you think he can handle his own CD or tape player, make him his own DJ. Three to five is the perfect age to start them on the piano or the recorder. Both are simple and allow them to make reasonable-sounding music almost immediately. Even if you don't want to start them on lessons, they can toot around on a kazoo or imitate you when you tap out various rhythms on the front porch.

- **Help your child build a healthy gender identity.** In the previous chapter we talked about how easy it is to fall into the trap of treating boys and girls differently. Given that kids learn most of what they know from adults, it shouldn't come as much of a surprise that this kind of gender-based double standard works just as well the other way. In other words, kids treat men and women differently.

  "Children learn the different roles that males and females play with children before the age of 3," writes researcher Beverly Fagot. "And once this difference has been learned, the children will react to adults outside the home on the basis of this learned differentiation." Fagot found that in preschool classrooms, kids "elicited many kinds of play behavior from the male teachers; but when children needed materials or needed some caretaking, they approached female teachers."

  So what can you do? Basically, just be a good role model. If you are a full participant in your home and you love, nurture, and care for your children, they—boys and girls alike—will come to realize that men can be parents too. Second, make sure your children get the message that men and women and boys and girls are not locked into any particular roles or futures because of their gender. Your children should be free to dream of becoming whatever they want to. This means that besides telling our daughters that they can grow up to be doctors, we need to tell our sons that they can grow up to be nurses (an idea my oldest daughter still has a problem with, even though the father of one of her best friends is, indeed, a nurse anesthetist).

So if your daughter (like mine) demands Matchbox cars for her birthday, tears the heads off her Barbie dolls, and refuses to be in the same room with a tutu, let her. And if your son wants to play with dolls or wear your partner's nail polish or lipstick, let him. A friend who has a particularly gentle, sweet little boy once confided that he was worried about his son's lack of physical aggressiveness and was concerned that he might be gay. Forcing your child into a particular type of behavior—either to conform with or buck gender stereotypes—can scar him for life.

- **Get involved in toilet training.** Strange as it sounds, this is related to building a healthy gender identity. Boys lag behind girls in toilet training (by six months for bowel training, sixteen months for bladder training), but there is no significant biological reason for the delay. Some experts believe that the real reason girls are "trained" sooner is that women have traditionally done the training, and girls have an easier time imitating their mothers than do boys. In addition, boys may not *want* to imitate their mothers, and they may balk at sitting down when urinating (it's no fun to sit when you can stand and make bubbles), and may resist Mom's instructions on how to grasp his penis—after all, she doesn't even have one!

Besides being done with potty training earlier, girls also have a much shorter time between bowel and bladder training (eleven months) than boys (twenty-one months). This difference may be the result of girls' not being taught to differentiate between the two functions. (Girls can't see either their urination or defecation and wipe after both, while boys *can* see their urine—and are encouraged to aim it—and wipe only after moving their bowels.) Overall, men and women traditionally have very different ways of teaching toilet training:

THE TRADITIONAL MALE MODEL TRAINING	THE TRADITIONAL FEMALE MODEL
• Urinary training precedes bowel training.	• Bowel control precedes urinary control.
• Urinary control is a stand-up procedure with emphasis on skill, mastery, and fun.	• Sitting down for all elimination, wiping.
• Wiping only after bowel movements.	• Wiping after both kinds.

THE TRADITIONAL MALE MODEL TRAINING	THE TRADITIONAL FEMALE MODEL
• Active participation and modeling by the father and/or other males.	• Use of the mother herself on the toilet as a model for imitation.
• Encouragement to touch and control the penis so as to aim the urinary stream.	• Discouragement from touching self.
• Greater tolerance for absence of bathroom privacy.	• Greater need for bathroom privacy.
• Control, function, and naming of urine is sharply differentiated from control, function, and naming of feces (boys tend to talk about "making pee-pee" as opposed to "pooping").	• Minimal distinction between bladder and bowel training in vocabulary, timing, or technique (girls tend to talk about "going to the bathroom").

"The female mode is compatible with and enhancing to the formation of a female gender identity," writes Moisy Shopper, who's done an exhaustive study of toilet training (well, someone had to do it). "The child is encouraged to be like mother; by seeing mother's eliminative functioning, they have an intimacy with each other's bodies that fosters the girl's gender *and* sexual identity." Using the female mode to train boys "in no way enhances the boy's potential for further body differentiation or supports the sexual differences between him and his mother," writes Shopper. "In fact, in many ways it is antithetical to the boy's maturation."

Basically, the primary role in toilet training boys should be yours. This, of course, does not mean that your partner can't toilet-train your son (except for providing a model for how to urinate standing up, there's no reason she can't) or that you can't toilet-train your daughter. Plenty of women support their sons' budding masculinity and encourage them to urinate standing up, holding their own penises.

A small number of mothers, however, won't allow their sons any autonomy, Shopper found; they feel "that *they* must hold their sons' penises as they pee." This is a rotten idea because your son may begin to question whether his penis belongs to him or to his mother, and that's just how serious sexual problems develop later in life. When boys have a male model, they are much less conflicted about becoming toilet-trained, since training no longer carries the connotations of gaining his mother's love, submitting to her, and becoming like her.

◆ **Keep your relationship with your partner healthy.** At least half of all married couples experience at least some stress and dissatisfaction with their marriage. There's no question that having a child can add to that stress. But according to Anne-Marie Ambert, becoming parents may actually reduce the divorce rate. Carolyn and Philip Cowan, for example, did a study of parents and nonparents and found that five years after getting married, 50 percent of the nonparents had divorced, while only 20 percent of the parents had. (See page 135 for one possible explanation.)

Among the top sources of marital spats are money, division of labor issues, and differences in parenting styles. As counterintuitive as it sounds, having a good fight now and then could be good for both of you. In fact, you may be far better off letting off some steam in her direction (in a reasonable way) than in suppressing it. "In trying to avoid conflict, we may create even more," says psychologist Brad Sachs. "What we risk by venting our anger out loud is generally far less threatening than what we risk by suppressing it," he adds. "Internalized anger causes emotional and physical symptoms like depression, alienation, ulcers, fatigue, backaches, and high blood pressure. Also, we have to remember that if we don't express it directly, it will come out anyway, but sideways, in a way we can't control. The phone message that we forgot to deliver to our partner, the medicine we forgot to give to the baby, the check we forgot to deposit, can all be passive aggressions directed against our spouse when we're afraid of what we're feeling."

Even more counterintuitive, fighting in front of your kids—within reason—could be good for them too. Naturally, you should avoid having *huge* fights in front of your children. (Kids are scared and confused when their parents yell at each other, and researchers have found that the angrier the parents, the more distressed the children.) But this doesn't mean that whenever the kids are around, you and your partner always have to see eye to eye (or at least seem to). In fact, just the opposite is true: "Children of parents who have regular and resolved fights have higher levels of interpersonal poise and self-esteem than those whose parents have chronic unresolved fights or those whose parents appear not to fight at all," writes Sachs.

Children can also learn a lot from watching their parents disagree—provided they do it civilly. "Occasionally divided ranks will encourage and

Dating Your Partner

Besides fighting, couples fall apart for other reasons. One of the biggies is that they don't spend enough time together. They both get so focused on the kids and doing everything for them that they forget to focus on each other, on themselves as individuals, and on the relationship. The result is that they lose track of the interests, passions, hobbies, philosophies, and other things that made them who they are and that brought them together in the first place. Perhaps the best solution to this problem is to schedule some dates. Yep, just like the good old days before you had kids. The basic idea is the same: the two of you go out and spend a few hours together staring into each other's eyes and getting to know each other. A few of the ground rules have changed, though:

- ◆ Don't try to make up for lost time. Packing too many things into a single evening can put a lot of pressure on you both.
- ◆ Make it clear that there are no strings attached. Either of you may be suspicious that the "date" will be used as a way of getting the other in the sack.
- ◆ If lack of sex has been an issue for you, however, you may want to schedule a date to do nothing but that.
- ◆ Don't talk about your child. Let's be realistic: your child and his life are what you're trying to get away from; he's the one who's consumed so much of your time that the two of you have neglected each other.

stimulate a child's capacity to negotiate, bargain, and present his own case against the opinions of others," writes child-rearing columnist Lilian Katz.

So let your child see you and your partner squabble about easily resolvable things, and schedule weekly or, if necessary, daily meetings *away from the kids* to discuss the bigger issues.

Big or small, if you do ever have a disagreement in front of your child, pay close attention to how you make up afterward. "It is probably useful for young children to observe how adults re-negotiate their relationship following a squabble or moments of hostility," says Katz. "These observations can reassure the child that when distance and anger come between him and members of the family, the relationship is not over but can be resumed to be enjoyed again."

4

The Confident Father

EASING INTO THE SCHOOL YEARS

Even though your child has been trying to establish her independence since she was born, she's spent most of her time at home, with you and your partner. And you've had a lot of control over her life—where she went, who her friends were, what she learned. Until now.

From the time your child starts kindergarten at about age five, school will become the focus of her life. And over the next few years she'll go from being able to read her name to plowing through 200-page novels. The ongoing process of separating from you and joining the outside world is getting more obvious by the day. Your school-age child has her own social life—one that often doesn't include you—and she's perfectly capable (or at least she thinks she is) of scheduling her own engagements and other activities.

Sure, as her dad you'll still be involved in your child's social and educational life, and you'll still have a lot of influence on the kind of person she becomes. But as she lurches unsteadily into the new world of school, peers, and teachers, you've got a lot of adjusting to do. You'll get occasional flashes of the future when she'll be a teen, and you may suddenly reevaluate your work-family balance, doing whatever you can to spend more time with your child because you know that the days of her cuddling up on your lap for a story are numbered. At the same time, you'll probably spend a lot of time thinking about the world your child is entering and looking for ways to change it, to make it safer and healthier.

What's Going On with Your School-Age Child

6–7-YEAR OLD: PHYSICALLY

- Your six-year-old is still very much a child, and her mouth is filled mostly with baby teeth.
- Her right- or left-handedness is pretty well established, and her hand-eye coordination and dexterity are getting better all the time.
- She can tie her shoelaces by herself, print her name and a lot of other words, handle a pair of scissors without drawing blood, and most of her art actually looks like what it's supposed to be. Control over small muscles (fingers, for example) is lagging, and she prefers doing things that work out the more developed large muscles (legs and arms).
- She's not gaining weight as fast as before (probably 3–6 pounds per year). That, combined with lots of physical activity, has eliminated most of her baby fat and makes her look pretty gangly.
- Her balance is excellent now, and she's ready to learn to ride a bicycle. She can catch small balls and connect fairly regularly with a baseball bat.

6–7-YEAR OLD: MENTALLY

- Pouts galore as your six-to-seven-year-old becomes increasingly taken with the notion that people are unfair and favor everyone else—especially younger siblings.
- Taking responsibility isn't her strong point, and she's quick with excuses. Still, she's starting to show some guilt about misbehaving. It's hard for her to make up her mind, but she's stubborn once a decision has been made.
- She lives in a black-and-white world with very little gray. She finds security in rules and makes up complicated games with extensive, ever changing regulations.
- The notion of "men's work" and "women's work" is beginning to dawn on her, and she may have some trouble dealing with the idea of a male nurse or female firefighter.

- She's getting mighty curious about reproduction and birth, but (thankfully) that's about as far as her interest in sex goes.
- She can tell time on an analog clock yet persists in asking time-related questions (how long till we get home?).
- She can separate fantasy and reality but may not want to—especially when fantasy yields money, as in the case of tooth fairies or Santa Claus.
- She craves knowledge and loves learning, adventure, and new ideas. Her vocabulary is over 2,000 words, which means she's got plenty of words to use when talking back to you. Questions are constant. With her increased attention span, she spends a lot of time reading and writing, though she may still reverse b and d.
- She loves magic, card tricks, and competitive games but can't stand losing.

6-7-YEAR OLD: EMOTIONALLY/SOCIALLY

- Your six-to-seven-year-old is a highly emotional creature, given to angry outbursts, mood swings, and difficult behavior.
- She wants to be the biggest, strongest, and have the most. She adores being flattered and becomes infuriated if you don't notice—and praise—her often. She's discovered that tattling is a great way to attract your attention.
- Her emotional range is fairly limited, and she tends to express herself physically more than verbally (hitting and pushing rather than discussing problems).
- She constantly starts more projects than she finishes, but by her eighth birthday she will be much better.
- Though still fairly self-centered, she can now (sometimes) see things from others' point of view and has a greater (but not too great) respect for their needs.
- "Real" fears, such as not having friends, or that something horrible that happened somewhere else will happen to her, begin replacing garden-variety childhood fears of witches and goblins and being flushed down the toilet.
- Her first steps away from her insulated little world and into the big world of school and peers scares her and even undermines her confidence. Her fragile ego doesn't deal very well with failure or criticism from others.
- Her playmates are generally of the same sex. She plays better with one friend at a time and demands loyalty (if you play with her, you can't be friends with me).
- She wants to tell you all about her day and everything that happened to her. And she does.

8-10-YEAR OLD: PHYSICALLY

- Your baby's looking like an adult! By ten girls are getting softer around the edges, while boys are getting firmer.
- But she still acts like a child, with energy to burn, fidgeting, and in constant movement. She does everything fast, shifting quickly between activities.
- All this activity takes its toll on both of you. She crashes hard at the end of the day and is still tired in the morning. So are you.
- She's between growth spurts, and the slower growth makes it easier for her to control her body. Coordination and small-muscle control are excellent. She can use both hands at the same time, which should help her make great advances in playing musical instruments.
- She's proud of her physical strength, agility, and stamina and loves to show them off.
- She's getting a little more adventurous when it comes to eating, and she may occasionally try something that isn't white (rice, noodles).
- Most of her baby teeth have been replaced by permanent ones. So a quick trip to the orthodontist and some squirreling away of money for braces may be in order.
- Now that she's using the computer and doing a lot more reading for school, keep an eye out for eyestrain.

8-10-YEAR OLD: MENTALLY

- She still loves praise but is starting to grasp the painful notion that the entire world doesn't revolve around her. She still loves competitive games but can now tolerate losing once in a while.
- Her awareness of time is growing. She knows her bed and wake-up times and may write out detailed hour-by-hour schedules of her day. Sequence and order make sense to her now, which enables her to concoct very elaborate stories about why she was late for school. It also enables her to comprehend death.
- Money intrigues her, and the more she understands what it does, the more interested she becomes in getting some of her own.
- Girls are more sex-aware than boys. Boys love to tell dirty jokes. Both genders are a little shy when it comes to sexual themes.
- Her mind is growing, and she loves to use it. She loves memorizing and now reads to acquire information as opposed to entertain. She prefers active

learning (going to see the lions at the zoo) to listening to adults drone on and on. Beware the know-it-all attitude this new knowledge gives her.

- Mathematical concepts are making more sense. She now understands about odd and even, larger and smaller, and groups (Ford, Chevy, and Lexus are all cars). She'll make endless lists of everyone she knows, organized by hair color or height.

- She defines herself in terms of what she can do (I can tap-dance, I can torture my brother, I can lift my daddy off the floor).

- Her stubbornness blossoms into perseverance, and she begins working on skills repeatedly until she masters them.

- Occasionally she thinks of the future, though mostly in terms of doing the same things that Dad or Mom have done in their lives.

- She's developing a sense of right and wrong! She tells the truth more often, exaggerates less, and has a pretty good understanding of actions and consequences.

- She may show couch-potato tendencies, enjoying TV, videos, and video games so much that she'll often pass up a chance to play outside in favor of sitting passively in front of a screen.

8–10-YEAR OLD: EMOTIONALLY/SOCIALLY

- She's outgoing and cheerful most of the time but seesaws back and forth between emotional highs and lows. Pouting is replacing violence as a way of expressing anger.

- She can be impatient too. She often has some trouble delaying her own gratification and is jealous of the time her younger siblings spend with you.

- Her confidence is growing, particularly about what she's learning at school. Her teacher can do no wrong, which means that should you ever disagree with either of them, you'll suffer her wrath.

- As her desire to fit into the group increases, her confidence in herself decreases. She wants to control younger kids, but she's usually worshipful of the older ones. She still tattles and often exaggerates the wrongs people are doing to her.

- She's more empathetic toward others but more critical of herself at the same time.

- She still enjoys spending time with her family, but as friends take on a more central role in her life, she'll spend less and less time with you.

- Guess what? She craves recognition from her peers more than from you, and they frequently resolve their problems by judging each other.
- There's little if any play with kids of the opposite sex. Boys' friendships are fairly smooth. Girls have endless spats, breakups, makeups. She has a handful of friends and a worst enemy. The lineup changes daily.
- She craves heroes—usually a teacher, coach, one of the adults who drives the carpool, or even a really cool teenager from the neighborhood—whom she'll try to please all the time.
- She's self-conscious and worried that everyone is looking at her all the time. Perfectly ordinary things become embarrassing. You, for example.
- She worries about the unknown—death, divorce, abandonment, high school, not being popular, growing up.

11–12-YEAR OLD: PHYSICALLY

- Girls are slouching toward maturity and are two years ahead of boys in maturity. Most girls have started puberty, while most boys have not.
- Fidgeting tapers off as she approaches her thirteenth birthday—cause for celebration all around.
- She's still very active, though, is often ravenous, and needs a lot of sleep (10–11 hours a night). Watch out for unnecessary dieting or skipping meals, which may indicate a predisposition toward bulimia or anorexia.
- Reaction time improves, and she gets stronger. She loves to learn complex physical tasks.
- She understands why exercise is good for her and may even see the value in warming up.
- Beware of her bite! She has most or all of her permanent teeth (28), unless her orthodontist has pulled some. Regular dental checkups are important.
- Enter pimples. And now that her sweat glands are fully operational, you may want to invest in some deodorant.

11–12-YEAR OLD: MENTALLY

- As she careens into teenhood, she becomes less cooperative, often doesn't respond when asked to help out, and is quick to criticize anything less than perfection in anyone else (especially you). Get used to the phrase "Why should I?"—you'll be hearing it a lot.
- Her behavior may remind you of the terrible twos: she does the opposite of whatever she's asked, cries hysterically for no apparent reason, has tantrums,

uses the word *no* more than any other in her rather large vocabulary, and slams doors a lot. Thankfully, she may also want to cuddle up on your lap and have you read her a bedtime story.

- She's ever more curious about sex but wants to get the skinny in all the wrong places: friends, magazines, television.
- Her mathematical skills have taken her beyond fractions and decimals to algebra, geometry, statistics, and probability. Hopefully she's learning the basic computer, library, and research skills she'll use in high school.
- She actively participates in adult conversation when she wants to, listening to what people say, asking questions, and making well-thought-out arguments. She also thinks critically and uses reason and logic, and she'll jump all over any mistake you make.
- Her sense of right and wrong is pretty solid, but she still adores getting away with whatever she can.
- She compares your family to her friends' ("But Jimmy's father lets him"), and you'll almost always come up short.
- Now that her abstract thinking skills are developing, she makes plans, sometimes weeks in advance.

11–12-YEAR OLD: EMOTIONALLY/SOCIALLY

- She's a mood ring on legs, alternating between murky frustration, burning passion, and blinding fury (generally reserved for younger sibs, whom she sees as worthless creeps).
- She becomes less embarrassed by your mere existence as she gains confidence with her friends. She still likes to spend time with her family but complains that you don't ever have time for her.
- She knows she's changing, and peer pressure will affect both you and her. "Fitting in" is a big deal, and requires keeping up with the latest fashions, movies, music, and trends. Aimless hanging out increases, and individualized activities decrease.
- Friends are getting more important, which makes sense, because it's about the only area of your child's life that she has complete control over. Both genders usually have only a few close friendships, though. Secret clubs and passwords are used to deepen friendships by keeping others out. Boys and girls live in very different social worlds. Boys go to parties to eat and hang out, girls go secretly hoping something will happen.
- Girls' friendships are intense and marked by spats and fights and tearful

reunions. Boys quarrel with each other a little more than they did before but still less than girls.

◆ She's codifying her world, and the rules (for you, anyway) just got more stringent. She may swear like a sailor, but parents should never swear in front of kids.

◆ Your eleven-to-twelve-year-old actually wants to grow up! In fact, she may even hate being seen as a child. So what if her hygiene slips a little or if she skips an occasional bath or shower?

Meanwhile, What's Going On with You?

WHO AM I GOING TO BE THIS WEEK? THE EVOLUTION OF A CONFUSED FATHER

For the first five or so years of your child's life, you had two dominant ways of interacting with her: caregiving (feeding, changing, driving to the doctor, walking around trying to get her to stop crying) and playing (wrestling, rolling balls back and forth, hide and seek, reading stories).

But now that her needs are different, you'll have to recalibrate your parenting—again. One of the big shifts, according to researcher Robert Bradley, is that your role in her life will evolve "from caregiver and organizer of experiences to that of mediator and guide." As she gets older, your role in disciplining her will increase (not in a harsh way, but in the way the word was originally used: to train or instruct). "During these middle years the father can be a teacher, coach, confidant, and pal as well as an authority figure," write Bryan Robinson and Robert Barret.

Most dads instinctively understand all this and respond to their school-age kids' changing needs by making fundamental changes to their own personalities, and by altering the way they see themselves and the ways others see them. Here's how this plays out for a lot of dads:

◆ **Honing your skills as a role model.** You've always known that what you do influences your child. Just think about the way she imitates your mannerisms and of all those times you've heard her swear and then realized that she's repeating *your* words. But seeing your child pretend to smoke a cigarette or drink a beer or copy any of your bad habits is going to make you think a lot more seriously about the way you behave. Of course you never fudged on your taxes, but some dads who did think twice about that now. Rob

"Father would be much happier if you wouldn't."

Palkovitz found that a lot of dads gave up destructive or risky behavior, criminal activity, drug abuse, or bungee jumping. A lot of young dads also change their attitude about their health. Most men don't go to the doctor (for themselves, anyway) unless a woman in their life forces them. But kids often motivate us more than we or anyone else can. A lot of dads of school-age kids start going, or at least they're more receptive to the idea when their partner raises it. All of a sudden being around for their kids seems a lot more important. They may start exercising more regularly, eating better, and even cutting down on the amount of junk food that makes its way home from the grocery store—partly for themselves and partly to encourage their kids to get into the same good habits.

- ◆ **Slowing down and smelling the roses—for a millisecond.** A lot of men find the start of their kids' school career to be very stressful; they suddenly realize that they haven't spent as much time with the kids as they wanted to, and now the kids are practically leaving home. . . . In a way our kids give us a time limit. You may not feel that you've aged since becoming a dad, but seeing how quickly your child has grown makes you realize that she—and you—aren't going to be young forever. A lot of men I interviewed said that they tried to take it a little easier, sometimes cutting back at work or working a more flexible schedule, and even turning down promotions or transfers that would take them away from their families. I remember becoming a lot less obsessed with being on time, and insisting that everyone else was too.

- **Pondering ye olde values, ethics, morality, religion, and spirituality.** About 80 percent of the men in Rob Palkovitz's study and a similar majority of the dads I interviewed said that they'd made some kind of shift in their basic values or life priorities. Also, since teaching right from wrong is such a stereotypical dad thing, it's not surprising that a lot of dads spend some time thinking about it. Some dads took on a more active role in their children's religious education (most of us tend to leave those things up to our partners), which often meant increasing their own church or synagogue attendance and/or sending their kids to religious school. About half of Palkovitz's sample didn't make any changes at all. Religion was already central in their lives, or they'd had such bad experiences as kids or young adults that they were turned off for good. Younger fathers in particular were less likely to take any big steps either way. Their religious and spiritual views tend not to be as fully developed, and they're not as sure as more mature dads what they're embracing or rebelling against.

- **Experiencing more empathy.** As we discussed in previous chapters, becoming a father has opened up all sorts of emotional doors for you, allowing (or forcing) you to experience feelings you didn't even know you were capable of, everything from joy and pride and intense love to fury, disgust, and jealousy. There was one feeling, though, that may have been left off the list: empathy. Sure, you've always been able to imagine what your child is feeling, partly because you have some conscious or subconscious memories of what *you* felt like when you were a kid. During the early school years most children can't really express their emotions verbally as well as they'd like to, which makes it hard for parents to really know what's going on inside their kids' hearts and minds. But helping her try to express them by trying to give words to her feelings will teach her to express them better. Later in the school years she'll begin using words to express many of her innermost feelings, and to be truly empathetic, you need to really listen to her—not just to the words, but to the emotions behind them. Connecting with your child on that kind of level leads to a far deeper kind of empathy than you experienced before. Interestingly, as the Group for the Advancement of Psychiatry (GAP) writes, "to be able to feel what the child feels enlarges the parents' capacity for empathy in other interpersonal relationships." Doctors who are parents, for example, are better able to empathize with their patients, which is something a lot of parents instinctively feel. Think about when you take your child to the pediatrician. You probably never asked whether he has kids of his own, but don't you really want to know whether he does? This isn't to

155

say that childless people shouldn't be allowed to be pediatricians or that pediatricians with children are naturally better. That's not true at all. What is true, though, is that as we become more empathetic with our children, we naturally want people to be more empathetic with us.

• **Expanding your (previously narrow) horizons.** The personality overhaul that your school-age child has triggered in you is going to rub off in other areas of your life too. If your years of parenting have taught only one thing, it's the value of contingency planning, of having a backup plan just in case Plan A goes terribly wrong. That's a skill you may have already brought to your workplace. You might find yourself interested in mentoring younger coworkers, taking them under your wing. You're likely to be a more outspoken and confident advocate for your children, whether it's at a parent-teacher conference, or asking a waitress to take back an undercooked steak she brought to your child. Because you love your child more than anything in the world, you're going to learn to think more flexibly and creatively. You'll teach yourself to accept her rejection while swallowing your pride and supporting her at the same time. That newfound ability to adapt your thinking and responses to other people's irrational behavior might make you a little more tolerant when those around you act like complete idiots. And as your child picks up new abilities and skills and brings home new interests and passions, you may find yourself learning about things you never heard of or never cared about before. Who knows, you could find yourself studying the rules and strategies of soccer, learning to tie fourteen kinds of slipknots, becoming an expert rock climber, solving quadratic equations, or conjugating irregular Latin verbs.

EMBRACING THE PLAN GONE AMUCK

As we've discussed, your child's growing independence and how the two of you deal with it plays a major role in how you both develop—she from a child into an adult; you as you change and grow as a father. Besides that, though, there's another major issue that you've dealt with before and that you'll be dealing with for the rest of your life: the difference between the way you planned or imagined or hoped that your life would turn out and the way it actually is.

The years between about thirty-three and forty are what Daniel Levinson calls the "settling down phase." This is typically the time when fathers (and men in general) focus their energy on taking their place in society: on "making it," on advancing in the workplace, on family and friends, on success. The days of figuring out what you're going to do when you grow up are pretty much gone. You no longer have infinite choices. Any door you open or any choice you make requires closing other doors and missing other opportunities. The worst part about this phase is that each choice makes you grow up a little, and the more you grow up, the more you have to give up. This isn't all bad, of course. For every one door you close, you open a dozen windows—you may lose out on one opportunity, but you'll have all sorts of others you never knew existed.

Are you the kind of *über*-father you'd imagined you'd be ten years ago? Had you even planned on being a father at all? Are you able to spend as much time with your family as you want? Do you have the kind of relationship with your kids that you imagined? How does your relationship with your partner compare to the way you thought it would be? Are you living in your dream home in your dream neighborhood? Are you sending your kids to the kind of schools you'd planned on? Are you giving them the life and the things you wanted them to have? Are you keeping the promise you made to yourself when you were a teenager to never, ever raise your kids the way your parents raised you, or have you forgotten and slipped into doing exactly what they did? Do you have the education you wanted? Have you traveled everywhere you wanted to go? And where are you in your career? Are you as far along as you'd hoped? Are you even doing the kind of job you thought you'd be doing?

Your life today may be superlative, or it may. . . not. But no matter what it's like, chances are there are at least a few things about it that have turned out differently than you'd planned—not necessarily better or worse, just different.

The difference between fantasy and reality can cause a tremendous amount of conflict, and there are three basic ways to deal with it. First, you could get absolutely paralyzed and horribly depressed that your life hasn't turned out the way you'd hoped. Second, different or not, you might choose to be perfectly happy with life just the way it is. Third, you can adopt a kind of serenity-prayer attitude: enjoy the things that are going better than expected, accept the things you can't change, fix the things that aren't, and get clear on the difference between the three options. Life is far from over, and there's still plenty of time to fulfill at least some of those dreams.

TAKING PRIDE IN (AND DIALING DOWN YOUR DISAPPOINTMENT IN) YOUR CHILD'S ACCOMPLISHMENTS

This whole fantasy-vs.-reality thing also plays out in our relationships with our kids. One of the best things about being a parent is that it gives you a chance to go back and do all those things you loved doing as a kid, all the things you missed out on, and all the things you wish you'd done differently. It's like having a second childhood.

"Just remember, son, it doesn't matter whether you
win or lose—unless you want Daddy's love."

The problem, however, is that some parents have long forgotten whose childhood it really is. Too many parents "expect their child to be their ambassador out in the world," writes Ellen Galinsky, believing that "what the child does reflects upon them." This is especially true if we've fallen into the incredibly common trap of living our life (or at least part of it) through our child, of expecting our children to live our unfulfilled dreams and do as well—or better—than we ever did. You might, for example, want your child to do or like or excel in some of the same things you did when you were that age—could be sports, or music, or science, or public speaking, or anything else. Or you might want your child to do or like or excel in some of the same things you weren't so successful at when you were a kid.

"The child acts as a mirror for his parents," writes the Group for the Advancement of Psychiatry (GAP). "If his behavior expresses positive aspects of the parents—if he is loving, happy, intelligent, creative—his parents feel that these qualities are reflections of themselves. They feel satisfied with what they have done thus far and more able to go on successfully." At the same time, though, if your child doesn't do well, doesn't live up to your expectations, or gets into trouble, you'll feel that you've failed. Your little attempt at immortality, at having the world recognize your true greatness, isn't working out quite the way you wanted.

In his best-selling novel *Something Happened,* Joseph Heller does a beautiful job of capturing just how difficult it is for so many dads (and moms) to stop seeing our kids as extensions of us. "My little boy is having a difficult time of it in school this year in gym, in math, and in classes stressing public speaking, and just about everywhere else it seems," writes the narrator about his nine-year-old son. "He is, I'm afraid, starting to 'let me down.'"

"Parents may experience intense emotional reactions to their child's behavior," write Philip and Barbara Newman. "They can make you feel warm, joyful, and proud. They can make you feel furious, guilty, and disgusted. . . . It's one thing if someone else's child is rude or selfish. But if your own child is rude or selfish, intense feelings of anger, disgust, or embarrassment may be stimulated. You may feel pleased by the successes of a neighbor's child, but the success of your own child gives rise to the peculiar parental emotion called 'gloating.'"

Trying to relive your life through your kids is a rotten idea for everyone. As with everything else in your life, your child is going to turn out differently than you'd planned. Taking her failures too personally (including her failure to act like you want her to), setting your expectations too high, or pushing her to be someone

*"Please Daddy. I don't want to learn to use a computer.
I want to learn to play the violin."*

she's not (you, for example) puts way too much pressure on her. Wanting to make your child part of whomever you wish you could have been isn't a bad thing to do—it can expose her to all sorts of great opportunities you never got to experience. The key is not to get upset if your child doesn't want to be you. Your disappointment could lead you to reject her, and that same disappointment, which she'll see no matter how you try to cover it up, could completely undermine her self-esteem. In addition, it could make her feel guilty and inadequate because she can't make you happy, according to psychiatrist Stanley Greenspan. The fact is that kids need to be themselves. More important, they need to know that being themselves is okay, and they need to have the freedom and encouragement to develop into the adults they're supposed to develop into. Those are things that only you can give them.

(Interestingly, even the way your child looks can impact how you treat her. What if she looks just like a relative—living or dead? Well, if you like that relative, you're in great shape. But what if you hate the relative? Or what if you're divorced, and your child looks just like your ex?)

The bottom line is that the more realistic your expectations, the better off you'll be. So relax. No matter how well or badly your child does, her successes and failures are *not* a referendum on your parenting skills. You had your turn. Now move over and let someone else have a clear shot at being the kid.

CONFRONTING YOUR DEMONS—AND PUTTING THEM TO WORK FOR YOU

Like it or not, who you are as a dad right now has a lot to do with the kind of childhood you had. "To brew up an adult," writes Roger Gould, "it seems that some leftover childhood must be mixed in; a little unfinished business from the past periodically intrudes on our adult life, confusing our relationships and disturbing our sense of self."

But your own often-zany childhood experience does not have to have a negative impact on your fathering. In fact, for most men, it's just the opposite. Most fathers try hard to give their children the positive things they experienced during their own childhood, to spare their children the pain they themselves experienced, and to make sure their children never lack what they did.

Researcher John Snarey found that that men with positive memories of being fathered used their fathers as models. In other words, if a boy's father gave him a good education, was warm and nurturing, and supported his emotional and physical growth, he tended to do the same with his kids when he became a father himself. At the same time, when men had negative memories of their fathers (for example, their dads didn't provide a good education or a stable economic situation, or relied too much on physical punishment), they tended to use their father's shortcomings as motivation to do better.

Were you an only child? If you loved being one, you might want only one kid. If you hated it, you might want to have a large family. The same applies if you were one of nine kids. If you got lost in the shuffle, you might want a small family. If your brothers and sisters put together a championship baseball team, you might want to have nine or ten kids of your own. If you never graduated from high school, you might do everything you can to ensure that your children get the best education possible. If you grew up rich, you might want your kids to learn what it's like to have to earn their own money. And if you grew up poor, you might want to make sure they never have to go without the things that money can buy. Ultimately, having kids isn't exactly a second chance to live your own life. You can, though, boost the odds that the next generation has it better than you did.

MAKING THE WORLD A BETTER PLACE AFTER A LONG DAY...

Toward the end of your child's first year you probably went through what psychologist Bruce Linton calls the "community phase." You felt confident in your fathering abilities, you probably started to do more socializing with friends and family, and you may even have gone out on a few dates with your partner— all of which expanded your world beyond your immediate family. When your child reaches the school years, you'll go through another community phase, but this one involves a much bigger community: the world. And this one is going to change the way you think about that world.

Remember how you used to roll your eyes when you were little and your parents started blathering on about "When I was a kid, we didn't...," or "When I was your age, blah, blah, blah never existed...." Well, it's finally happened: *you're* the droning fossil now, looking back and comparing the world you grew up into the one you're trying to raise your child in. It seems so much bigger than it did then, with so many more opportunities. At the same life feels less secure, more dangerous, and more threatening. Think about all those things you never noticed when you were a kid, but have suddenly become important now that your child is taking her first tentative steps into the larger world: drugs, alcohol, crime, poverty, overpopulation, homelessness, and on and on. And while you're at it, throw in the dangers that didn't exist back then but that do now (AIDS, terrorism, global warming, and so on). All and all, the world may seem like a pretty scary place for a kid to be all by herself.

Speaking Up—Why We Don't and When We Should

Most of us know what we'd do (or at least what we *think* we'd do) if someone tried to hurt *our* children. But why—when someone else's kids are being abused—are we quiet? Is it that we just don't care? "Not at all," says psychology professor Mark Barnett. "Historically, children have been regarded as personal property. And we still tend to believe that parents have the right to deal with them however they see fit."

Another reason we don't speak up when we see someone treating a child inappropriately is that most of us try to blend into our surroundings, praying that someone else will take the lead. But when no one does, "we downplay our own reactions and convince ourselves that what we initially thought was abusive behavior really wasn't that bad after all," claims Dr. Ervin Staub. Staub refers to this extremely common phenomenon as "pluralistic ignorance."

But hesitating to "butt in" and taking one's cues from others are definitely not the only factors that keep our lips locked. Imagine this scenario: you're walking home alone at night when you see a large man come out the door of a house, carrying a screaming child. He quickly stuffs her into the back seat and is about to peel out when he sees you staring suspiciously at him. Are you face to face with a violent kidnapper, or just a frantic father taking a sick child to the hospital? If you play it safe and say nothing, you are probably experiencing one of the other feelings most likely to keep people from speaking up: fear of putting oneself in physical danger.

For better or for worse, passersby almost never have a *legal* obligation to do anything. (Doctors, dentists, teachers, social workers, and in some states photo processors, however, *are* required to report suspected abuse to the proper authority.) But there are clearly times when all of us have a *moral* obligation to do something. Suzanne Barnard, a spokesperson for the Children's Division of the American Humane Society, suggests the following guidelines:

- If an adult is causing a child serious or life-threatening injury (hitting hard enough to leave a mark, or actually drawing blood), do something.
- If a child has been abandoned, or negligently left in a dangerous situation (locked in a car in hot weather with the windows closed), do something.
- If the child's actions make it reasonably clear that he or she is scared, or that the person doing the suspected abuse is a stranger to her, do something.

For some of us, of course, confronting others is no problem. "I'd rather risk embarrassing myself to save a child," a friend of mine once told me, "than have to live with myself knowing that I could have done something but didn't." Of course, "confronting" doesn't have to mean "attacking." "If you can approach the parent in a non-judgmental way, there are things you can say that can help defuse the situation," says Barnard.

The National Committee for the Prevention of Child Abuse (NCPCA) endorses the following approach:

- Divert the *adult's* attention away from the child by sympathizing or by offering some praise for the child—"My child did the same thing just yesterday" or "She has the most beautiful eyes."
- Divert the *child's* attention by talking to her, or pointing out something of interest.
- Say positive things—negative remarks or looks are likely to increase the parent's anger and could make matters worse.

But for many of us, approaching a stranger—even to do something as simple as ask directions—is simply too embarrassing or daunting. So if you can't, don't feel guilty—you're not a wimp. You still can make an anonymous report to the appropriate authorities, who will check it out for you.

If you're in a store, contact the manager immediately and have him call the police (or call yourself if the manager refuses). If you're outside, try to get the adult's license plate number and then call 911. If you're concerned about a neighbor, call your county child protective service and give them the address.

But what about when the situation is not so clear-cut, or when you're seeing something that looks more like a flash of temper than a case of prolonged abuse? After all, as parents, we've all come close to "losing it" on a particularly bad day. And what about that kid you know who's always covered with bruises?

Before calling the police, take a good, long look at the situation and make sure your suspicions are reasonable. As you well know, children are always having accidents, and a few bruises and cuts are usually not an indicator of abuse.

If you need help evaluating what you've seen, or if you want to know how to make a report in your area, call the Child Help USA National Child Abuse Hotline:

1-800-4-A-CHILD or

1-800-2-A-CHILD (TDD) for the hearing impaired

www.childhelpusa.org

That thought can be a real wake-up alarm, a call to change things, to do whatever it takes to improve our communities and our world. This is a time when dads "become more aware of, more vocal in, and more vigilant regarding community issues," writes Rob Palkovitz. "Men become more community centered when they have children growing up in a community, not only for the interest of their own children, but for the good of the children in the community."

Other researchers have reached similar conclusions. "Those men who live with their biological or adopted children are significantly more likely to belong to service clubs and school-related organizations," says David J. Eggebeen, a research associate at Penn State. "Children are the mechanism that lead men who are fathers to become a cub scout leader, scout master, community league basketball coach, little league coach and school board member."

Roughly speaking, there are two types of community involvement. Formal involvement, according to Palkovitz, includes things like building ball fields and playgrounds, putting up speed bumps, joining neighborhood watch groups, coaching, scouting, and getting involved in the PTA. I talked to dads who volunteered at homeless shelters, cleaned up litter from local freeways, became Big Brothers, took petitions door to door, and even ran for city council. It was as if there was a sudden shift from "Someone ought to do something about that!" to "I'm going to do something about that, damn it!"

Not everyone reacts this way, of course. Palkovitz found that even dads who don't participate formally get involved informally: "Informal community involvement was represented by more awareness and outgoingness within neighborhoods, encouraging kids to come in off the streets into gyms, and so forth." Other informal activities might be talking to parents and the police about unsafe or questionable behavior or conditions and trying to keep drug dealers out of the neighborhood.

My Child Dumped Me; or, Coping with Your Separation Anxiety

By the time your child is six, she's probably already had some experiences with preschool or day care, and she's spent some pretty good chunks of time away from the house. But there's something about starting the first grade—that's "real" school, after all—that's different.

A lot of dads I've spoken with have said that while the start of their children's school years was a happy occasion, it was also a little devastating. On the one hand, we're proud that the kids are getting bigger and smarter and better

"Soon you will be entering a phase, son, in which you will no longer pay attention to anything I have to say. Please let me know when that changeover occurs."

looking and stronger, but at the same time we have this general feeling that they're slipping away. The issue isn't the number of hours away from home. It's that we're slowly becoming aware that our kids don't need us as much as they used to, and we're losing our ability to influence them. Until recently you were your child's primary source of information about the world. Sure, teachers, peers, and the media had something to say, but your child came to you for the final word, and you had a lot of control over what she learned or didn't learn.

That's all changing now, big-time. Over the next few years what your child's friends and teachers say will carry more and more weight in her mind. She'll also be influenced by her own reading. During the next few years your child will gradually shift from reading as entertainment (which kids do through the second or third grade) to reading to learn, which starts happening in about the fourth grade. Between the friends, the teachers, and the books, your child will be exposed to all sorts of new ideas and thoughts and philosophies that you have very little control over.

Okay, it's going to take a little doing to get used to relinquishing control over your child's education, but you can handle it. What's going to be a lot tougher is to come to terms with her budding independence. It wasn't all that long ago that she wanted to hold your hand all the time and have you watch every somersault and hang up all those "You're the best daddy in the world" notes that she made for you all by herself.

But now, as she develops deeper relationships outside the home, her relationship with you and your partner will change. There'll be no more—or at least a lot less—snuggling in bed as a family to read stories or watch videos together; she may get embarrassed about being hugged or kissed by you, especially in public; she may not want to talk to you about her day; she always has someplace else she'd rather be and may hardly want to spend any time with you at all. Getting recognition and acceptance from you won't be nearly as important as it used to be. Instead, life will be more about fitting in with the new crowd and being accepted by them. It's a normal part of life. She needs to prove to herself and others that she can make it in that big world out there. And in her mind, the only way to show her independence and fit in with her friends is to reject you. Doesn't make a lot of sense from the adult perspective, but those are the cold, hard facts.

Novelist Joseph Heller does a great job of capturing this dynamic. "My boy has stopped talking to me, and I don't think I can stand it. He doesn't seem to like me. He no longer confides in me. 'Are you angry with me?' I inquire of my boy. 'No I'm not angry.' 'You don't talk to me much anymore.' 'I talk.' He shrugs."

But as normal as it is for her to push you away, it's just as normal for you to feel confused. You'll be proud that your child is growing up, and you'll want to encourage her independence. At the same time, you'll want to keep her close to home, where you can protect her from the world. But watch out: you may have other, more selfish reasons for not wanting to let your daughter go. You'll mourn the loss of your close relationship, and you'll feel hurt by her rejection. Having a child dependent on you made you feel important and needed, and you don't ever want to forget how her hugs and kisses melted you.

It can be very tempting to take your child's rejection personally and "get even" by pulling back emotionally or even physically. Big mistake. Try to remember that you're the grown-up here, and it's up to you to behave like one. Your child may act as though she doesn't need you, but deep inside she does—and she knows it. So don't stop being affectionate (just respect her wishes and don't kiss her in public), and don't stop trying to communicate. Your new and improved role now is to set boundaries while keeping the door open, to steel yourself

*"O. K., here I am in the fourth grade, but is that really
what I want to be doing with my life?"*

against the sting of rejection but remind your child that you love her and that you'll always be there for her. You need to show that support unobtrusively, without feeling hurt, disappointed, or angry, according to the Group for the Advancement of Psychiatry (GAP). You also have to discipline yourself not to expect much back from you child. It won't be easy, but you'd better try: "Parents who need reassurance of the child's faithfulness are the unhappiest people in the world," writes the GAP.

Sometimes parents—mothers and fathers—respond to their child's rejection by seeking attention elsewhere, possibly by having an affair. Most parents, of course, don't do this. But among those who do, it's common that their children are "difficult:" intense feelings of rejection can come up when a child is more strongly attached to one parent more than the other. The parent who feels left out may look for a more sympathetic shoulder to lean on. Or sleep with.

Dads and Boys, Dads and Girls

Most fathers claim they treat their sons and daughters the same way. But in reality, that's just not the case. The truth is that fathers (and mothers too) treat boys and girls very differently. We've talked about this a little in previous chapters, but some of it bears repeating here. For example, parents tend to encourage boys' independence more than girls', and they're more protective of girls than boys. (As a friend who has sons once said, "It's easier raising a boy because you only have one penis to worry about.") Academically, parents—again, mothers as well as fathers—are more likely to push their sons than their daughters. Dads in particular are usually more physically playful with their sons than their daughters. There are, of course, plenty of exceptions, but generally speaking, this is the way it is.

This means that your relationship with your daughter is going to be very different from the one you have with your son. One interesting thing that happens to the father-son relationship during the school years is the development of competition. Sounds silly, I know. A grown man compete with a fourth-grader? A fourth-grader compete with his dad? But the truth is that this is exactly what happens.

From the father's sometimes way-too-mortal perspective, the son is a threat, living proof of the father's mortality, the one who will soon take the father's place in the world of men. The boy is healthy, has his whole life ahead of him, and the father, though far from being on the way out, is probably noticing a few aches and pains that didn't used to be there. The result is, as we talked about at the beginning of this chapter, that a lot of dads start exercising more, eating better, and generally taking better care of themselves, in an attempt to keep up with their kids, especially their sons—and it only gets more intense as the sons (and the dads) get older.

Some of a son's competitiveness with his father is oedipal (fantastic news if you're a Freud fan), which is just a fancy way of saying that deep down inside he loves his mother, wants to keep her for himself, and feels that he has to overcome his father to win her love. The human mind is a very warped thing, isn't it? Another part of the son's competition has to do with how the males in our society (and in most others as well) generally interact with each other: constantly sizing one another up, seeing where they fit in, and trying to be better, stronger, richer, better looking, more powerful than everyone else. There's plenty of dispute as to whether that competitive drive is the result of socialization or genetic wiring. My vote says it's mostly hardwiring.

Part of the father's role is to guide his son through this oedipal phase by helping him separate from his mother and from the world of women. No, this isn't some kind of misogynistic rant. Boys need to model themselves after men in order to develop a healthy gender identity; women simply can't provide that kind of direction. It's a lot harder for boys to learn what it means to be masculine than for girls to learn what it is to be feminine. Most teachers are female, and so are most baby-sitters and day-care workers, which means that girls have constant access to female role models, and boys don't have anyone to look to. In addition, "the messages from adults are not consistent," says gender-role expert Carole Beal. "Mothers and teachers would like boys to behave one way—masculine, yes, but also neat, well-mannered, and considerate—while fathers and male peers encourage other types of behavior, including rough physical play and indepen- dence." The result is a lot of boys who are confused about what it means to be a man. Fortunately, you can do something about that. "Fathers' warm, close, guid- ing support encourages their sons' acceptance of them as their primary models," says John Snarey. "Fathers' broad support of their sons' physical-athletic, intellec- tual, and social-emotional development promotes this transition and the contin- uation of their boys' sense of basic trust and autonomy."

As odd as it sounds, fathers also play a very important role in helping their daughters develop a healthy gender identity. A girl's primary identification will be (and should be) with her mother. At the same time, a healthy physical-athletic dad-daughter relationship will help her "avoid an extremely traditional sex-role identification," according to Snarey. In addition, a girl looks to her father—the very first man in her life—to demonstrate how she can expect to be treated as she grows. Challenging her, supporting her, having high expectations, and making her feel loved, respected, and important are critical, especially as she approaches puberty. "The girl who receives the least amount of male attention at home is the one to seek it most aggressively outside the home—namely at school," writes Nicky Marone in *How to Father a Successful Daughter.* "Any girl who has doubts about her worth can find encouragement by capitalizing on her helplessness, flaunting her youthful sex appeal, and abandoning (in many cases permanently) achievement-oriented behavior." Not to put pressure on you or anything...

A Special Note to Adoptive Dads

As we've discussed elsewhere in this book, adoptive fathers develop and change in basically the same ways as biological fathers do. For the most part, adoptive children and biological children develop in the same ways too. But there are some interesting and important differences.

Researchers, for example, have come to completely opposite conclusions about adoptive kids' mental health. Some says adoptive and biological children are about the same. Others say that adoptive children have more behavioral and psychological problems as well as difficulties adapting to new situations. What most agree on, though, is that children who were adopted after age one or so, or who bounced from home to home before finally settling down with one family, are at greater risk for emotional and psychological problems.

Some of these problems are exaggerated by the normal developmental stage the child is in. Preschoolers, for example, can't really grasp what adoption means. They understand the word, but they can't truly grasp the idea of having had any other family than the one they're living with now. But in the school years, they can. And during these years, when being accepted and fitting in are getting more and more important, the idea of having been given away—no matter how well you explain it—can feel like rejection to some kids. They may take it personally, thinking that they were put up for adoption because they were bad or because they're flawed in some way.

Despite all this, a lot of adoption experts feel that the school years are the perfect time to tell your child about her adoption. Besides her ability to understand that concept, there are three other good reasons. First, by the time she's six or seven, she'll probably be feeling secure enough in your family not to be shattered at the thought that she was adopted, according to Dr. Steven Nickman. Second, there's a pretty good chance that your child is going to have a unit in school on

Why Be an Involved Father at All?

Well, as we've talked about in previous chapters, being an involved father is good for everyone: your kids, your partner, and even yourself. Here are some of the specific benefits to being actively involved with your school-age child.

biology or genetics, and the issue of hereditary traits and blood relatives will probably come up. Third, waiting until your child is a teenager could hurt her. "Disclosure at that time can be devastating to children's self-esteem and to their faith in their parents," writes Dr. Nickman.

Some kids who find out they're adopted are incredibly curious and ply their parents with thousands of questions. If so, try to answer them—but don't give them any more information than they're asking for. It's tempting to respond to a question like "Where did I come from?" with a whole long explanation about sperm and eggs and birth mothers and adoption law, when all that is necessary is "Norfolk, Virginia." Others kids seem completely uninterested. Still others might actually be dying to ask but may worry that their questions will offend you. No matter how your child responds, it's critical to speak openly and honestly and let her know that you'll be available to answer questions any time she has them. If she's more on the silent end, revisit the issue from time to time. Don't push, but asking whether she has any questions every once in a while can really help.

Also, think about this: in keeping with the general black-and-white world she lives in, a six-to-seven-year-old may still believe that she was either adopted or born, one or the other, as if being adopted didn't have birth as a prerequisite. For that reason, the National Adoption Information Clearinghouse (*http://www.calib.com/naic/*) suggests that when you tell your child about her adoption, you help her understand that she was *born* first, and that "all children, adopted or not—are conceived and born in the same way. The birth came first, then the adoption."

If it's okay with your child, introduce her to some other adoptees, including some adults. She might find it helpful to see that being adopted doesn't have to have any impact on how successful you can be in life. But make sure you leave the option of whom to tell about the adoption up to her. She'll appreciate that you trust her to manage that information.

BENEFITS FOR YOUR CHILD

- **Better concentration and problem solving.** "Frequent opportunity to observe and imitate an adequate father contributes to the development of the boys' overall instrumental and problem–solving ability," writes Professor Henry Biller. The results for girls weren't quite as strong.
- **It just might make her smarter.** Dozens of studies demonstrate that children whose fathers are nurturant (warm, helpful, encouraging) and

Coping with the Loss of Your Own Father

For most men, the years between eighteen and thirty-two are among the best of their life. They're in peak physical and mental form, and they're building their own lives and careers and exploring all that life has to offer. But 20 percent of these men get a shock that's hard to recover from: the death of their father. Losing one's father is almost always a shock, but at this age it's particularly devastating for several reasons. First, so many men are still dependent on their father for guidance, finances, even emotional support, and they haven't had a chance to fully move away from the father's influence to establish themselves, says Neil Chethik, author of *Fatherloss*. Second, because the loss of the father is usually unexpected, most of the sons have unfinished business—the "I love yous" that were never said (by either side), unexpressed resentments, and so on.

We've talked a little about the father-son relationship in this chapter, and we'll go into it in more detail in later chapters. One of the major themes of that relationship is competition—the father's desire to remain strong and virile and the son's desire to equal or better his father's accomplishments. According to Chethik, the death of a father during the son's early adulthood can disrupt the process of the son becoming his father's equal. The result can last a lifetime. In the first month after their loss, 21 percent of the sons in Chethik's study who lost their father between eighteen and thirty-two used alcohol or nonprescription drugs to help cope—more than three times the rate for men who were over thirty-two when their father died. In the longer term, it's not surprising that so many men who are young when they lose their father suffer from depression, withdraw socially, and have constant self-esteem problems, the result of never having been able to get to "prove" themselves by "beating" Dad, or never having been accepted by Dad for the things they did.)

involved (spending at least two hours a day with their kids) get higher grades and score better on vocabulary and intelligence tests than children whose fathers scolded them or reprimanded them. Researcher Norma Radin found that the father's presence raised kids' math scores. How? "One possible explanation," she wrote, "is that fathers tend to engage in more physical activities with their children and this appears to enhance the children's comprehension of spatial relations which is related to mathematical ability." Overall, "the more time the child spends with a nurturant father the greater are the benefits to his problem–solving ability and intellectual functioning," according to Michael Lamb. These results are true for both boys and girls.

- **It may make them more popular, assertive, and resilient — especially girls.** Children (daughters in particular) who are exposed to high levels of paternal play and attention at this stage are more popular and assertive with their peers later in adolescence. They're more likely to make friends, and they keep those friendships longer. On the other hand, kids whose fathers are too intrusive and authoritarian tend to be the ones who get rejected by their peers. Studies by Ross Parke and others of extremely successful women have shown that they're more likely than less successful women to have had a high level of paternal support, stimulation, and high expectations from Dad. And other researchers have found that regardless of gender, kids who had warm and loving fathers when they were five years old had longer marriages, were better parents, and had closer friendships as adults.

- **They stay in school longer.** Compared to kids growing up in families without a father, kids with involved dads had half the risk of dropping out of high school. They also had higher test scores, higher GPAs, better school attendance, and higher college expectations.

- **It makes life easier for difficult kids.** Hard-to-handle kids and those with learning disabilities have higher feelings of self-esteem and well-being when their fathers are involved in their lives, compared to similar kids whose dads aren't as involved.

- **They have greater self-control and take more responsibility for their actions.** "By actively choosing to be involved, the father presents his child with an especially salient model of responsible behavior," writes Lamb. "Through emulating their involved father, children are more likely to demonstrate moral behavior."

- **It helps minimize the effects of divorce.** After their parents divorce or separate, about a third of children suffer a decrease in academic performance. Even after their parents divorce, kids who have a good ongoing relationship with their father do better in school and have fewer social, emotional, and physical problems than kids who don't see their fathers as much.

BENEFITS FOR YOUR PARTNER AND YOUR MARRIAGE

- Men who are actively involved fathers when their kids are young have more stable marriages and rate them as better and more satisfying than men who aren't as involved with their kids. As John Snarey put it, "Fathers who provided high levels of childhood social-emotional support during the childhood decade and high levels of intellectual-academic and social-emotional support during the adolescent decade were themselves, as men at midlife, more likely to be happily married."

BENEFITS FOR YOU

- ◆ Being involved—especially in the first ten years of fatherhood—makes men more generative later on, meaning that they're more concerned with making life better for the next generations.
- ◆ Contrary to what you might think, being actively involved in caring for their children doesn't seem to have a negative impact on men's careers. Actually, it seems to make men more upwardly mobile in their careers than dads who aren't as involved. This is especially true for fathers who promote and support their kids' social and emotional development.

Keep in mind that being there and being involved is a function of quality time and quantity time—both together. Kids whose dads are around but don't spend

"O. K., kid. Busy man here. Quality time. Here we go."

much time with them end up doing about as poorly as kids whose fathers aren't around at all. In fact, according to Henry Biller, "a son who had a father who was highly nurturant but seldom home may feel frustrated that his father was not available more often or may find it difficult to emulate such an elusive figure."

Staying Involved during the School Years

The best way to be involved at this stage is to take an interest in your child's life, be supportive, and make her part of your life. Be aware that she's using you as a role model, so set a good example. Here are some specific things you might do during these years:

- ◆ **Drive like a demon.** Get involved in the carpool, take the kids to their piano lessons, and soccer practice, take them shopping with you and to the bank and everywhere else you go.
- ◆ **Go back to school (your kids' school, that is).** Volunteer to talk to students about what you do, help a teacher in the classroom, go on a field trip. In most schools men are in short supply, so your being there will be an inspiration to other kids as well as yours, showing them—and the school administration— that men care. (Besides cooking spaghetti lunch fund-raisers four or five times a year at my kids' school, I also do a few presentations on how books are written.) And be sure to go to as many parent-teacher conferences, school plays, concerts, sporting events, and science fairs as you can. Again, it's a great way to show your kids and everyone else around that school and learning are important.
- ◆ **Talk, talk, talk, talk.** And then talk some more. Have some serious conversations about drugs, alcohol, sex, peer pressure, and all the other things you dread talking about. You may have had some of these talks before, and you'll probably be having some of them again, so get used to it.
- ◆ **Listen.** School-age kids have a lot they want to talk about—and they have a lot of interesting things to say, too. So set aside some time every day or at least every few days to turn off the cell phone and the television and the computer and focus 100 percent on your child. Resist the urge to give advice— just listen.
- ◆ **Play.** Kids this age need a lot of exercise, half an hour a day at a minimum. Some they'll get at school, some they'll have to get at home. Encourage her to get into team sports, but make sure not to push her into something she doesn't want to do. She may very well be a good enough athlete to compete

*"I know sex is no longer a taboo subject. I just don't feel
like discussing it all the time, thank you."*

in the next Olympic games, but is that what *she* wants, or is it what you
want? If you push too hard, her resentment may drive her away from sports
altogether. If she prefers to do her sports alone, roughhousing is still a
welcome activity for most kids this age, as are shooting baskets and jogging.

- **Give your child the opportunity to take on more responsibility.** This can
  mean getting a job watering the neighbor's garden, doing some meal planning (or even cooking), and scheduling the activities for a whole weekend.
- **Give your child lots of opportunities to develop her own skills and interests.**
  Encourage participation in art, music, and anything else (from raising roses
  to breeding iguanas) she's interested in exploring on her own. You might
  also try to develop a shared activity.
- **Take an interest in your child.** Get to know her friends by helping them
  schedule play dates and sleepovers and by offering to invite a friend or two
  along on one of your outings. Take an interest in her schoolwork by going

to PTA meetings, attending parent-teacher conferences, helping out with homework, and/or volunteering in your child's classroom. All these things help your child understand that you're interested in her all the time.

- **Teach your children well.** You've still got a few years before your child decides she knows everything better than you do. Until then, take advantage of her relatively open mind to take her to interesting places, show her interesting things, and teach her as much about the world as you can. Now's the perfect time to talk about money, how people earn it, taxes, interest, investing, charity, comparison shopping, and more.

- **Never stop reading.** Your child is doing a lot of reading on her own now, but that's no reason to stop reading to her. In the unlikely event that she doesn't want you to read to her, have her spend fifteen to twenty minutes per night reading to you. Ideally, though, both of you should read to each other. This is especially important for boys, who consistently score lower on reading and comprehension tests than girls. Girls in this country generally learn to read faster than boys. A lot of experts think that's because most preschool and elementary school teachers are female, which gives girls a same-sex role model. Henry Biller points out that in Japan, where about half of elementary school teachers are men, boy's and girls' reading scores are equal. In Germany, where the majority of school teachers are men, boys not only score higher than girls but are also less likely to suffer from severe reading problems. And don't forget to encourage writing skills too.

- **And don't forget yourself.** Keep reading about how your child is developing physically, mentally, emotionally, and socially. The charts at the beginning of this chapter are a good place to start. You'll be amazed at how reassuring and calming it can be to find out the difference between normal and not normal.

- **Get a grip.** Then loosen it. Your child's getting more and more independent, but you don't have to let go of her completely. You do need to step back a little, though, and think about what she really needs and what she wants, as opposed to what *you* want her to be. Remember, she's a separate person, not an extension of you, and it's time to start shifting your role from being involved in everything to being a mentor. It's a hard lesson to learn, but the sooner you get comfortable with the idea, the better off you—and she—will be.

5

The Challenged Father

SURVIVING AND THRIVING IN THE TEENAGE YEARS

One of the horrid little secrets about fatherhood is that sometimes it's . . . not fun. I know, I know, I shouldn't say things like that, but it's true. Throughout our children's lives, all parents have the occasional why-did-I-ever-have-kids? day. But during the teen years it's not uncommon for dads to watch helplessly as those days sometimes blimp into weeks and then months. Roger Gould found very much the same thing in his landmark studies back in the late 1970s. The teen years, he said, will likely be the least satisfying time of your life as a father. (They're not going to be that much fun for your teen either, but we'll talk about that later.) It's nothing to be embarrassed about, I assure you. The only people who don't go through this are the people who don't have kids.

Of course there's all the head-butting that dads and teens do. But at the same time, your child's teen years are a time of real growth and self-examination for *you*. It's during this stage that the aging process will really sink in. Before now you knew you were getting older because you kept having birthdays, and you stopped getting carded at grocery stores and bars, but you probably didn't feel much different from when you were twenty. But get ready, because this is gradually starting to change—you'll have a few more aches and pains that you didn't before, and it might take a little longer to recover from your weekend basketball game with your buddies. At the same time, you'll watch with envy as your teen steps into a world of unlimited possibilities and choices, and you'll become aware that your options are far more limited. Your teen's largely responsibility-free life is in sharp contrast to your life, which is filled with work, mortgage payments, carpools, and other obligations. He's entering his physical and sexual prime, and you're leaving yours. And as he looks toward the future, you can't help but reevaluate the past.

What's Going On with Your Teen

13 – 14 - YEAR - OLD: PHYSICALLY

- As far as sexual development goes, girls continue screeching ahead of boys (don't miss "A Dad's (Brief) Guide to Puberty" later in this chapter). Most girls are looking "womanly," but most boys this age still look, like, well, boys, especially when placed next to high-schoolers. No matter what they look like, though, both genders are starting to have sexual feelings, which they and you may find disconcerting.
- In the beginning, these feelings tend to be geared at the self, rather than others, which means that they'll "stumble" onto masturbation soon, if they haven't already.
- As peer pressure increases, along with the belief that everyone else is doing it ten times a day, the likelihood of your teen having sex increases stratospherically.
- Your teen's still getting taller and heavier, but thankfully, that whole four-inches-per-year thing is over. Noses, however, have their own growth spurt about now, which can be cause for great alarm. Ditto for acne.
- Overall health and hygiene may start to slip a little.

13 – 14 - YEAR - OLD: MENTALLY

- Your teen is starting to think more about the larger world and how he fits into it.
- Teens just entering high school will have to deal with the shock of going from the top of the middle school heap to the bottom of the high school one. There are unfamiliar settings, new people, new rules, and new expectations. Those with fashion-conscious teens could find this development costly.
- Overall, your teen may not seem to know whether he wants to grow up or not. He knows he's outgrowing kid stuff but may still like reading picture

books or playing with younger kids (except for younger siblings, who are the perennial cause of misery).

- He craves independence but isn't yet able to accept the responsibility that goes with it. As a result, bouts of poor judgment and impulsiveness are still quite common. He might suddenly announce a passion for a brand-new sport or music or art or even science.
- Likewise new religious and moral beliefs. Experimentation is common at this stage, so don't panic if you hear some talk of a God you've never heard of.
- The "get away from me" vs. "I need you" syndrome begins as your teen vacillates between the belief that he knows everything and can do anything, and his fears of inadequacy, helplessness, and failure.
- As he tries to separate himself from you, he may temporarily veer into a path of rudeness, arguments, and defiance—stopping along the way to break as many rules as possible.
- With the above syndromes in place, privacy will become the catchword of the day. And he needs it. Private time allows him to exert some modicum of control over his thoughts and environment without having to suffer through all those lectures on what you did when you were his age.
- And who knows, a day—or an hour—later, your teen may be respectful, cooperative, responsible, and will come looking for your advice, guidance, or even just a hug.

13–14-YEAR-OLD: EMOTIONALLY/SOCIALLY

- The flip side of your teen's need to separate from you is his need to be accepted by his peers. As he begins to rely on them for emotional support, they will have a great influence on his choice of clothing, hair color, music, activities, and on whether or not he starts smoking, drinking, or experimenting with drugs. (This threatens to bankrupt you too.)
- This struggle to find his moorings in the social scene and fit in with the "in" crowd is accompanied by much blushing and multiple bouts of crushing loneliness.
- At this state, the dating thing is still a little unclear. Friendships and group activities tend to be with members of the same sex and are usually driven by common interests such as sports.
- Still, kids have opposite-sex friends, and making out at parties is always a crowd pleaser. Most attempts to go further are usually pretty clumsy.
- On the emotional front, your teen is a lot better able to manage his emotions

than he was only a year ago, and he's now quite adept at articulating his emotions verbally—especially when expressing his judgments of you.

- None of this prevents him from acting like a much younger child once in a while, probably in an attempt to get more attention from you as the occasional terror of growing up sets in.

15–16-YEAR-OLD: PHYSICALLY

- Girls are still more physically mature than boys. And by now most teens have had sex, or at least gotten to third base (which today means oral sex, not heavy petting, as it used to when we were all chaste teens). Information on STDs, condoms, AIDS, and so on is essential.
- Raging hormones may have your teen flip-flopping between hysterical laughter, tears, oversensitivity, and complete insensitivity.
- The only constant is his self-consciousness about his body, whether what's going on is normal, and whether he's attractive enough. Even more time will be spent in front of mirrors than before. Girls may start dieting (which can lead to eating disorders), and boys start bulking up (which can lead to steroid abuse).
- Hygiene may improve along with the desire to impress new love interests.
- Teens need more sleep now than at any other time since they were infants, so oversleeping is common.

15–16-YEAR-OLD: MENTALLY

- As worries about the world beyond high school begin to take hold, your teen will take a greater interest in career and in education.
- All those moral and religious beliefs are firming up. Many teens get very involved in social causes, serving meals in soup kitchens, organizing AIDS walks, volunteering, and so on. Many teens get rigid and judgmental, lecturing you on the lousy religious and moral choices you've made at this point. Others continue to dabble.
- Thankfully, your teen will start taking more responsibility for his actions and may look for role models (sorry, not you). Rebelling against you and everything you stand for is a crucial pastime.
- Even though deep down inside he knows he needs a structure, he'll complain that your stupid rules are limiting his freedom. True independence— at least in his mind—can only be won through being "different" from the rest of the family. If that doesn't work, conflict will have to do.

- He wants a relationship with you on his own terms. That means that you are demoted from actually controlling his life to the menial position of on-call consultant, available to answer questions, but only when asked for.
- Struggling with the "Who am I?" question, he may spend countless hours staring off into space, thinking about himself, his hopes, and dreams. He'll start projects and drop them halfway through. He'll also "try on" different identities: changing the spelling of his name or asking to be called something else altogether; adopting phony mannerisms, handwriting, or a bizarre accent; sporting clothes or a new hairstyle just for the shock value; and wanting (or even getting) a tattoo or body piercing. Some sexual experimentation is common at this stage.
- A lot of teens will take a particular class because they heard it was easy, or someone they have a crush on is taking it, or the teacher is supposed to be cool. Since school guidance counselors are working triple time, it's your responsibility to make sure your child is taking the classes it'll take to get him where he wants to go in life.

15–16-YEAR-OLD: EMOTIONALLY/SOCIALLY

- The peer group becomes even more important than before. He'll confide in them more and more as his opinion of you and your credibility slips. At the same time, he starts breaking away from his peers or at least trying to carve out his own identity.
- Social circles broaden one day, then shrink the next, as your teen's focus shifts from simply being popular to creating and maintaining closer, lasting friendships.
- Friendships in the middle teen years deepen as kids develop more emotional depth. Your teen will have his first experiences with powerful positive and negative emotions (compassion, love, hate) directed at non-family members.
- Pairing off with members of the opposite sex now goes into high gear.
- He'll seek out more role models and mentors. Even though he's rejecting you, he knows that he still needs to have an adult around to give him some guidance.
- Your teen isn't good at taking criticism from anyone. But because of your privileged status, just about everything you say will be "stupid" or "annoying." He'll also interrupt you a lot, claiming he knows everything you say before you even finish the thought.

17–18-YEAR-OLD: PHYSICALLY

- Boys have finally caught up to girls physically, and sexual energy is rampant.
- Physically, most teens at this age are fairly comfortable with their bodies.
- Although they feel and look like fully developed adults, their brains are still growing. The frontal lobes, which regulate little things like self-control, emotional maturity, and emotion, are in a period of rapid expansion.
- Most teens have experimented with drugs and/or alcohol, and they're in real need of support and honest information—especially about the dangers of driving under the influence of drugs or alcohol.
- Overall health and hygiene become downright adult as teens prepare themselves to leave home and enter college or the work world.

17–18-YEAR-OLD: MENTALLY

- Congratulations, the high-conflict days of your relationship with your teen are almost water under the bridge.
- Amazingly enough, he's beginning to see you as a real, live person, and—even though he'd never admit it in public—he values your opinion.
- This does not mean he will listen to you, however. It is still imperative that he reject your world, if only to show you how responsible he is (especially if he needs the car keys).
- Be wary of overt displays of self-confidence—it may just be an act. Believe me, he's questioning the important choices he's made, like where to go to college. He's excited but scared about leaving home and worried whether he'll be able to make it without the safety net you've been providing for so long.
- The search for identity narrows from "Who am I?" to "Which is the real me—the way I am with my friends, the way I am with my family, or the way I feel inside?"
- He also has a much clearer picture of his assets and inadequacies and is beginning to feel bad if he hasn't lived up to his own or others' expectations.
- Moral views are pretty solid now, as are empathy for others and an ability to compromise and to work with others toward a common goal. He still may suffer from a wide-eyed idealism and announce plans to rid the world of racism, poverty, and other societal ills.
- Interests are more stable, and he'll now finish most projects that he starts.

17–18-YEAR-OLD: EMOTIONALLY/SOCIALLY

- By now your teen has had at least one significant romantic relationship, and at least one significant breakup.
- Your teen increasingly relies on role models and mentors—usually teachers, coaches, or other adults. The fact that you may have given the same advice weeks ago means nothing.
- His friends still play a major role in giving him the courage to stand up to you, the theory being that if things don't work out at home, the supporting friends will always be there to provide the emotional support he needs during tough times but can't ask you for.
- As a graduating senior, he's finally made it to the top of the social ladder. But dread ensues at the prospect of leaving good friends behind, the fear that new ones will be hard to make, and having to start over again at the bottom of a new social ladder in college.
- Driving becomes a big issue here. Not letting him drive is pretty much your only remaining method of wielding control.
- Slowing hormones mean more emotional stability—just in case you do take away the car keys.

Meanwhile, What's Going On with You?

TIME KEEPS ON SLIPPING, SLIPPING, SLIPPING...

However it happens for you, one day you're going to have to admit that you're not as young as you used to be. For some guys it's those first-thing-in-the-morning aches and pains. For others, it's having to get bifocals, or take cholesterol-lowering medication. For me it was having to get to my karate class thirty minutes early so I could warm up before the warming up, otherwise I'd spend the next three days stooped over, nursing a pulled muscle. As much as people talk about how aging is a natural part of life, it's not pleasant.

This does not mean that you should start shopping for wheelchairs. However, you will be making some adjustments. You'll spend a little more time playing chess and reading, and a little less on physical activity. And when you do something active, you'll take it a little easier. The no-pain, no-gain days and that play-through-the-pain attitude are heading south fast; it's just not worth it anymore.

What often makes aging even tougher is having to deal with kids who are getting more and more active all the time. Driving them around to their various sports leagues or even coaching a team might feel as though your age is being rubbed in your face.

Even the way you think about your age is changing. For the first thirty-five to forty years of our lives, we tend to think of our age as the number of years since birth. And while that's what our birthdays still mark, most guys over forty have started thinking of their age in terms of how many minutes till we die. That shift, that awareness of our own mortality, can trigger all sorts of things, one of which is a general feeling of "fish or cut bait." This is a time when a lot of men reexamine their lives, review opportunities lost and opportunities seized, and come up with an honest assessment of where things stand. It's a time for accepting reality or doing something to change it, which means that major upheavals— including major career changes and divorce—aren't uncommon. After all, we just don't have as much time left to fool around. (Some men respond to this by fooling around with other women.)

At work, most fathers of teens are fairly well established in their careers— those who aren't tend to get more serious. Many who are reevaluate their commitment to their jobs and their families and realize that no one on his deathbed wishes he'd spent more time at work. Some men also start coming to terms with the idea that those big plans of youth—the executive job, the summer home, the world travel, being president of the United States, playing a violin solo with the New York Philharmonic, the umbrella drinks on the beach—just aren't going to happen.

There are some advantages to getting a little older, though. This time, from the late thirties to the mid-forties, is what Daniel Levinson calls the "mid-life transition." And according to Levinson, who did a groundbreaking study on male development, this stage "is often the fullest and most creative season in the life cycle. [Men] are less tyrannized by ambitions, passions, and illusions of youth . . . more deeply attached to others and yet more separate, more centered in the self."

This is certainly true of your attitudes toward money. In the earlier days of fatherhood, say from the late twenties through the late thirties, most guys don't worry a great deal about money. But when the house is invaded by teenagers, things tend to change. Suddenly concerns like saving for college, retirement, home repairs, car payments, and all those other things that have been sitting on the back burner, are boiling over.

Not to mention that sex can actually get . . . better. Your sex drive may not be quite what it used to be, and you may not be having as much sex as you were a few years ago. But chances are you can last a lot longer than when you were

Of Young Dads and Old Dads

It may seem obvious that at the same time as we're developing as fathers, we're developing as men as well. What's a little less obvious, though, is that the two developmental paths aren't always parallel. This means that two fathers of fifteen-year-olds—one in his thirties, the other in his fifties or sixties—are probably going to parent very differently.

A man who was in his teens when his first child was born will be the father of a teenager when he's in his late twenties or early thirties. Men that age are typically not so far out of college, not yet solidly established in their careers, and are trying to carve out their place in the world. They may also still be doing some experimenting—trying lots of new things, taking risks, having a great time. But when a guy that age has a teenager—who is going through the very same risk-taking and limit-pushing stage—there can be problems.

As we talked about in chapter 3, older dads—guys who became parents for the first time when they were in their late thirties or older—are less physical with their kids but more intellectually stimulating. They also tend to be more interested in parenting, more involved in daily child care, and more likely to have a positive experience as fathers. What's especially interesting is that the children of older dads feel more appreciated than children of younger fathers, according to Ross Parke and Brian Neville.

younger, and most of the guys I've interviewed have told me that sex got better and the orgasms more intense.

IT'S TOUGH BEING (AND HAVING) A TEENAGER

The poet Ogden Nash wrote that "the trouble with a kitten is that eventually it becomes a cat." In a lot of ways you could say the same thing about children. They're cute and soft and cuddly when they're small, and when they get into trouble it's kind of endearing. When they get older, you still love them just as much, but they aren't quite as cuddly, and they've become so independent that you don't have much control over their lives anymore. And when they get into trouble, it's not nearly as cute.

Over the next few pages I'm going to discuss some of the tough situations your former kitten might get himself into. As you're reading these sections, keep a few things in mind:

"This is a nice restaurant. Turn your cap around."

- Testing limits and taking risks are part of your teen's job right now. It's part of his natural development.
- The teen years may be tough for you, but they aren't any easier for your child. It's a confusing and sometimes frightening time, and your child needs your love and support more than ever.
- Your child may literally be "not all there." You hear a lot about how 95 per-cent of a child's brain development happens by age five, and that's true. But according to Michael Bradley, author of *Yes, Your Teen Is Crazy,* "the most advanced parts of the brain don't complete their development until adoles-cence is pretty much done." The specific parts that are still growing are the ones that control impulsive behavior, judgment, and the ability to understand consequences. This goes a long way toward explaining why teens do some of the things they do.

DRUGS AND ALCOHOL

By their senior year of high school, almost half of teens have sampled at least one illegal drug—marijuana, cocaine, ecstasy, amphetamines, or something a lot stronger, such as heroin or PCP. Thankfully, most kids who experiment with drugs do so only once or twice and then stop without having caused serious harm to themselves or anyone else. Some will continue to use drugs infrequently, to get into the "in" crowd, or just because it's fun. A small minority, though, will develop more serious drug-related problems.

There's a lot of disagreement about the connection between smoking marijuana and using harder drugs. While it's not clear that smoking itself actually leads to anything else, there's little question that people who smoke marijuana are more likely than those who don't to be in an environment where other drugs are being used. And just being around harder drugs increases the chances that kids will give them a try. A recent study by researcher Judith Brooks and her colleagues found that teens who use marijuana tend to have lower educational and occupational expectations; are more likely to be suspended or expelled from school or get fired from a job; and are more likely to be on welfare and to be an unmarried parent.

Despite everything you hear about the "epidemic of drug abuse" and "the war on drugs," the fact is that alcohol poses a far, far greater danger. There may be as many as 3–4 million teenage alcoholics in this country. About half of all seventh-to-twelfth-graders drink, and about 20 percent do so at least once a week. Half of teen drivers have driven drunk, and about three-quarters have been a passenger in a car driven by someone who's been drinking.

Alcohol is linked to depression and psychiatric problems, and it's a factor in 50 percent of all violent crimes. Drinking also plays a significant role in three of the leading causes of teen death: car crashes, suicide, and murder. All told, ten to fifteen times more teens die from alcohol-related causes than from all illegal drugs combined.

If you discover—or even suspect—that your child is experimenting with drugs or alcohol, you'd better snap into action right away (see "Cries for Help," below). Yes, there's a big difference between *use* and *abuse*. But alcohol is a lot more available now, and the grass your child is smoking or the coke he's snorting are a lot more powerful than what you may have had access to when you were young. And the fact is that a onetime binge or drug experiment can kill. Symptoms you might want to keep a lookout for include:

- A dazed or unfocused look.
- Dilated pupils when there's plenty of light around.
- Obvious signs of being high—slurred speech, poor coordination, and so on.
- Clothes reeking of marijuana. This doesn't mean that he's actually been smoking, but it's a good clue that he's been someplace where others have.
- Breath smelling of alcohol or cigarettes.

- Burning a lot of incense or scented candles, spraying room fresheners in his room or car, constantly chewing gum or sucking on mints, wearing a lot of perfume.
- Big mood changes.
- Lying all the time, when he has been honest until now.
- Money or valuables missing.
- A change in friends.
- A fake ID.
- Words or expressions you've never heard before. Ever heard of grypton, Georgia home boy, Cadillac express, embalming fluid, or snowbirds? Well, they're all slang names for various drugs.

The Partnership for Drug Free America has a section on their Web site (*www.drugfreeamerica.org*) with a pretty comprehensive glossary of common drug terms.

DEPRESSION AND SUICIDE

One of the hallmarks of the teen years is feeling misunderstood—by you, their friends, their teachers, their siblings, the world. And it's perfectly natural for teens to experience short periods of depression—a few days, perhaps a week. Symptoms of depression might include:

- Spending lots of time alone.
- Dark, depressive poetry.
- Major change in social circle.
- Significant weight loss.
- Promiscuous sex with many partners.
- Major change in school performance.
- Behavior problems at school or at home.
- A vacant expression.
- Lack of interest in things that used to be a source of happiness.
- Apathetic attitude, never initiates activity.
- Seeming withdrawn.
- Frequent running away from home.
- Drug or alcohol use.★
- Giving away all his possessions.★
- Threats or conversation about suicide, or saying things like "you'll be sorry when I'm gone."★
- Sudden violent behavior.★
- Self-mutilation or torturing animals.★

Again, most of these symptoms (except for ones with the ★) are normal in small doses. But if they go on for more than a week, or if your teen does any of the things marked with ★, get some professional help, and get it fast. Adolescent suicides have tripled since 1970; it's now the third biggest cause of death among young people. More girls threaten suicide, but boys are four times more likely to actually follow through. Most of these kids are not "bad" kids, and they don't have big drug or discipline problems. They're just kids who need something they aren't getting.

Pay special attention if any of the following risk factors are present: a major event such as moving, divorce, birthdays, or graduation; a break with a girlfriend or boyfriend; having a friend or family member who committed suicide; or being gay (sexual identity is a factor in about 30 percent of all teen suicides).

Some experts say that part of the reason for teen suicide gets back to the brain-development thing we talked about in "It's Tough Being (and Having) a Teenager" (page 186). It may be that teens don't fully grasp the idea that death is final. They may see suicide like bankruptcy—as the way to get rid of some problems, but not the end of life.

WHY THEY DO WHAT THEY DO

Besides the brain-development issue, there are a lot of reasons why teens engage in risky or dangerous behavior, whether it's unsafe or promiscuous sex, doing drugs, drinking, or whatever. Here are a few:

- **Ignorance.** They simply don't have enough information on the risks involved in what they're getting into—pregnancy, AIDS, overdose, etc.
- **Rebellion.** Ignoring your No is the perfect way to piss you off, and rebel against what they see as arbitrary, unfair, authoritarian parenting on your part.
- **It's fun.** They may be trying something out for the rush, to escape boredom, to get away from their problems, or even "just for the hell of it."
- **To feel better.** A lot of teens are self-conscious, shy, or feel unsure or unhappy about various parts of themselves. A drink or two or a couple hits on a joint can reduce those inhibitions.
- **Peer pressure.** The desire to be accepted by friends is a powerful motivator. Peers can make drinking or doing drugs or having sex a requirement for admittance to the "in crowd." But peers aren't all bad. They can also discourage risky behavior by making it a reason to be excluded.
- **Because they have to.** This is a particularly common excuse for less risky behavior, such as cheating. Your teen may rationalize cheating by saying that if he didn't, he wouldn't pass a course and wouldn't be able to get into college,

or that if he didn't help a friend, she would end the friendship. It can even be a way of "getting back" at a teacher whose expectations and demands, your teen feels, are too high.

DATING, SEX, LOVE, AND, WELL, MORE SEX

If you've heard all the talk about the epidemic of teen pregnancy and reached the conclusion that most teens are having sex, you'd be wrong—but not by much. A recent study done by the Centers for Disease Control and Prevention found that from 1991 to 2001, the percentage of high school students who ever had sex dropped from 54.1 percent to 45.6 percent. Over the same period, condom use by sexually active kids increased from 46.2 percent to about 58 percent. These two factors are undoubtedly responsible for the decrease in teen pregnancy rates and in sexually transmitted diseases (STDs). That's the good news.

There's also some bad news. You don't have to be a math whiz to see that despite the decrease, almost half of adolescents have still had sex. And those who are, are starting younger than you or your partner did. Interestingly, most adolescents

"But, Dad, in your day sex was still in the future."

aren't doing it because they want to. They watch television and see kids their age having casual sex five times a day, they hear all their friends talking about it, and they feel pressured to do it too. In one study, almost a quarter of teen girls said their first sexual experience was "voluntary but not wanted," according to Kay Hymowitz, author of *Ready or Not*. And kids as young as thirteen or fourteen who *aren't* having sex worry that there's something wrong with them, even though about three-quarters of the ones who *had* sex at that age say they wish they'd waited.

Oh, and it gets worse from there. The 54.4 percent of teens who aren't having sex aren't necessarily virgins, depending on how you define "having sex." In one study of ninth-to-twelfth-grade students, psychiatrist Mark Schuster found that almost a third of "virgins" had engaged in masturbation with a partner of the opposite gender. Nine percent of girls and 10 percent of boys had performed oral sex with a partner of the opposite gender. One percent had had opposite-gender anal sex.

Whether they're having "real" sex or not, the results are the same: teens who start early are more likely to do drugs, smoke, drink, get worse grades, get pregnant, or contract an STD than their peers who keep their pants on for a while longer. If this all sounds pretty grim, it is. But there's actually plenty you can do to help.

- **Talk.** The National Campaign to Prevent Teen Pregnancy took a poll in 2000 asking what teens want from their parents. Here's what they said: "Begin the conversation about sex when we're young and maintain an open-door policy as we get older. Teach us by what you do, not just by what you say. Give us good, honest answers in a straightforward way. Support us in all of our endeavors, and most of all, play an active role in our lives. . . . Finally, no lectures, please. Remember, we really care what you think, even if we don't always act like it."

- **Listen.** A lot of teens are afraid of their sexual urges and desires and may worry that they're crazy for thinking about sex all the time or masturbating. Reassure them that the urges are normal, but that it's within their power to control them. Pay special attention to a child who tells you he or she is gay. All teens have a strong urge to fit in, but being gay is a sure way to stand out, which is not a good thing. The result is often depression, which is why gay teens are particularly susceptible to getting involved in self-destructive behavior like drinking, smoking, doing drugs, and even suicide. If your child does come out to you, stay calm. Your dreams of having grandchildren may have just vanished, but it's more important to help your child find himself.

- **Take a stand.** Some studies show that abstinence programs work; others show that they don't. There's also plenty of debate about whether sex ed classes have any effect on reducing sexual activity or increasing use of

Dealing with Teen Pregnancy

Every year more than a million babies are born to teenage mothers. If you were a teen when your child was born, there's a greater chance that she will become a teen parent too. But even if you weren't, there's still a chance that your child could get (or get someone else) pregnant.

If this happens, it's going to be hard to stay calm. You'll probably be angry at your child's carelessness and worried about his now-diminished chance of finishing high school and getting a good job. Throw in your own feelings that you've somehow failed as a parent, and you've got a recipe for parent-child conflict.

If you have a daughter, it's essential that you help her consider her alternatives as quickly as possible. Basically, there are three (two if you're philosophically opposed to abortion): end the pregnancy, have the baby and give it up for adoption, or have the baby and keep it. But tread lightly and let your daughter make the final decision on her own, hopefully with some input from the baby's father. "Girls who have been psychologically forced to have an abortion or give a baby up for adoption often become pregnant again soon after, 'replacing' the baby (and the decision) that was taken from them," write Laurence Steinberg and Ann Levine, authors of *You and Your Adolescent.*

If she decides to abort, she should get some information from your local chapter of Planned Parenthood or a similar organization. The earlier the procedure takes place, the less risky it will be to your daughter. If she chooses to have the baby, make sure she gets good prenatal care immediately. If she's considering the adoption route, check with her doctor or a local adoption agency as soon as possible.

Regardless of the options she's considering, encourage her to include the baby's father in the decision. He and your daughter may have broken up, and you may be furious at him for getting your daughter into this situation in the first place (even though she bears an equal share of the responsibility). But regardless of what anyone thinks, he has a legal right (and I'd argue, a moral one too) to be part of the process. He may want to contest the adoption or, if your daughter decides to keep the baby, he's responsible for eighteen years of child support.

If your son has gotten his girlfriend pregnant, encourage him to get involved in whatever decisions are being made, since they affect him too. This may be hard if his girlfriend or her parents refuse to have anything to do with him—a lot of boys want to be involved but get pushed out of the way by the girl or her parents. It

(continued on following page)

(continued from previous page)

also may be hard if he's angry at the girl for getting pregnant or for breaking up with him, or if he feels that she tricked him.

If your child, boy or girl, decides to go through with the pregnancy, understand that you'll probably be asked to take on some of the physical, emotional, or financial care of your grandchild, because your child will have a tough time providing any of those things. "Teen parents are still partially children themselves," writes Jerrold Shapiro. "They find it hard to be self-sacrificing or wise enough to provide something for their own children that they have yet to experience personally."

The best thing you can do to help your teenage child/parent is to make sure he or she stays in school. Girls who drop out usually don't come back. And adolescent boys who drop out are also less likely to eventually graduate from high school than their nonfather peers, according to University of North Carolina researcher Ted Futris. "Early childbearing can disrupt development and reduce prospects of realizing one's potential.... Consequently, adolescent fathers are more likely to get low paying jobs and eventually disconnect from their children both socially and financially." The same thing applies to girls as well.

contraceptives. What does work, though, is getting good, solid information from *you*. Kids whose parents disapprove of early sexual activity and of the easy availability of contraceptives are less likely to have sex early, according to Kay Hymowitz. Make sure your child knows that sex may be a lot of fun, but it's also a big responsibility. It can also cause permanent damage or even kill.

- **Emphasize education.** Fifty-seven percent of teens with a C average or lower have had sex, compared to only 26 percent of kids with a B+ average or better.
- **Teach them to say no.** Girls and boys both need to learn to refuse sex when they don't feel comfortable as well as to take no for an answer. Don't make the mistake of thinking that only girls can be coerced into having sex. Boys often feel pressured into it too—sometimes by their girlfriends, sometimes because they're afraid that if they don't, people will think they're gay, sometimes to earn status with friends.
- **Know the risk factors—and reduce them where possible.** If you smoke, drink, are too permissive, live in a very low-income or low-education neighborhood, are single, or were a teen parent yourself, your child has a greater chance of starting to have sex early. Same goes if your teen entered

"Daddy, this is Fletcher—unplugged."

puberty early, has low self-esteem, started dating young, does poorly in school, or works outside the home more than nineteen hours a week.

- **Monitor his dating activity.** The earlier he starts dating, the sooner he'll have sex. If you notice that your child is spending a huge amount of time on the phone, has a lot of opposite-sex friends, and has friends who date a lot, he won't be far behind. You can delay serious dating if you institute some rules and stick to them. These four are a good place to start.
    - ◇ Establish a curfew.
    - ◇ Group dating. No couples-only events.
    - ◇ Date only kids the same age.
    - ◇ Meet the dates. It gives you a chance to see what's going on, and more importantly, it shows you care.

But what if your teen is already sexually active? There's plenty to do besides just throwing up your hands. The first step is to emphasize safety and remind him often about using contraception. Only 35 percent of fifteen-to-seventeen-year-old girls relying on condoms use them consistently. And only 40 percent of those taking the pill take it every day, which they need to do for it to be effective. It's critical to understand that while the pill is extremely effective at preventing pregnancy, it's useless when it comes to stopping gonorrhea, syphilis, AIDS, and other STDs.

A second alternative is to suggest that your child become a "virgin" again—in the real sense of the word. It may be hard, but it's perfectly possible for a teen who's been sexually active to stop. He or she will probably need a lot of support and encouragement from you, though.

A FEW OTHER POTENTIAL TROUBLE AREAS

* **Eating disorders.** Ninety percent of people with eating disorders are girls. Anorexia and bulimia are the two most common. Anorexics literally starve themselves to death. They've severely underweight but complain that they're fat and weigh themselves compulsively. Anorexics tend to be good, well-behaved kids who have very low self-esteem. If you notice that your child has suddenly lost a lot of weight, has stopped having menstrual periods, has brittle hair or nails, or feels faint when standing up, take her to see your pediatrician. Bulimia is marked by binging and purging (self-induced vomiting). It's a little harder to spot, since it doesn't involve the dramatic weight loss of anorexia. But if you notice your child eating huge amounts of food and then spending a long time in the bathroom (running water to hide the sound of vomiting), or her dentist says the inner surfaces of her teeth are decaying (could be from stomach acids), see her doctor immediately.
* **Crime.** Criminal activity, especially violence, used to be thought of as a "boy thing." But no more. About a third of those arrested for property crimes and more than half of those arrested for loitering and curfew offenses are girls. And about 25–30 percent of kids arrested for violent crimes are girls. Violence is the second leading cause of death for teens. In major cities, though, it's number one.
* **Getting a job.** On one hand, having a job may seem like a great way for your teen to build independence, learn some skills, and get some valuable lessons about earning, spending, and saving money. On the other hand, though, there are some risks involved. The combination of access to money, older coworkers, and being out of your sight increase the risks that kids who work outside the home will get involved in smoking or drinking or have sex early.
* **Tattoos and piercings.** Try to talk your teen out of this. There's no guarantee that his taste in art will be the same in twenty years, and having a tattoo

removed can be expensive and even more painful than getting it done in the first place. Done wrong, piercings can cause infections or nerve damage. Even done right, belly button rings take most of a year to heal, and nose rings make everyone look like a bull.

YOUR TEEN AND YOUR MARRIAGE

The top two things couples fight about are finances and division of labor. For families of teens, though, there's a third factor: the teens themselves.

When there's a teen in the house, a couple's marital satisfaction tends to drop. The main reason is style differences between parents. Generally speaking, dads are more supportive of their teens' transition from child to adult. They tend to support and encourage independence and reasonable risk taking, while moms are more cautious (just like it was with your two-year-old). Dads are more concerned with grades and results. Mothers tend to be more concerned with how the kids *feel* and about the process of growing up.

These differences in approach may also lead to disagreements between the parents about things like privileges, rules, curfews, driving, responsibilities, chores, grades, consequences, going to college, and so on. So who's right? Whose approach do you go with? Well, you and your partner are going to have to work that one out. And the only way you'll be able to is to talk, talk, talk—and listen, listen, listen.

Try as much as you can to reduce the stress in your marriage. Your adolescents' overall health and well-being is closely tied to how well you and your partner get along. Couples whose marriages are satisfying are more responsible and more sensitive to their children's needs, while unhappy couples are more distant and less likely to be active, involved parents. Marital conflict also adds to teens' stress, say Reed Larson and Maryse Richards, and it "weakens the relationship with parents that are often their most helpful buffer *against* stress." Get some marriage counseling if you need it.

AND THEN THERE'S THE D WORD

Whether you filed for divorce or she did, you're going to be going through an emotional roller coaster the likes of which you've never seen before, and things are going to be tough for quite a while. "Fathers encountered marked stresses in practical problems of living, self-concept and emotional adjustment, and interpersonal relations following divorce," say researcher E. Mavis Heatherington and her colleagues Martha Cox and Roger Cox. "Low self-esteem, loneliness, depression, and feelings of hopelessness were characteristic."

Most of what you're experiencing now and will be going through for the next weeks and months and maybe even years will come under the general heading of "grief," which is really a complex set of emotions that evolve in a fairly predictable way over time, according to Elisabeth Kubler-Ross, an expert in grief, who in the late 1960s identified five distinct stages that people go through when they're told they have a terminal illness. In the decades since, many people—including me—have come to believe that Kubler-Ross's stages apply equally well to other kinds of grieving, including the breakup of a relationship.

Naturally, these stages aren't set in cement, and each man experiences them in his own way. Don't expect to go through these stages and be done. You might get bogged down in one stage or another for months or years, you might skip one altogether, or you might even return to one three or four times. It's really more of a lifelong process; you might go through the same issues many, many times. You might even feel that you've finished with one stage, but then something can happen that triggers the whole process again, although maybe a little less intensely. Let's take a look at these stages in a little more detail.

- **Shock and denial.** Most relationships don't end by mutual agreement. One of the partners has usually made the decision long before telling the other. This gives her (and with 70 percent of all divorces filed by women, it's safe to say "her") the chance to get a little used to the idea, to prepare for the upcoming changes, and maybe even to start a new relationship. Many men respond to being handed divorce papers by simply refusing to believe that the relationship is over.

- **Anger.** For most men, being angry is safer (and more socially condoned) than being sad or depressed. Being angry feels kind of energizing, filling your head with all sorts of ideas and giving you the motivation to try to do something about your situation. But all that may be something of a mirage. "Angry adults feel they are taking steps to stabilize their out-of-control experience, and this tends to make them stay angry," writes Shirley Thomas.

- **Bargaining.** A lot of guys run around trying to reconcile with their exes. Another approach some men (and women) use to maintain contact with their exes is what psychologist Richard Austin calls *negative intimacy*—hassling, fighting, arguing, harassing, spying, calling in the middle of the night, making threats, and so on—which keeps you and the ex involved, but in a very unproductive way.

- **Depression.** Anger may be the easiest emotion to express, but depression is by far the most common. It can ambush you, suddenly overwhelming you with feelings of hopelessness, helplessness, and sadness. On the positive side, depression may actually be a good sign: it means that you're beyond the denial phase, and you're seriously dealing with the reality of your situation.

- **Acceptance.** One day—this could be several years from now—you'll get comfortable with the idea that while you can't control what goes on around you, you *can* control how you react. In a sense, this realization is like a line separating your old life from your new one. It doesn't mean, of course, that your old one is over, just that you can focus more on the new one now that your anger, depression, and other emotions no longer dominate.

Okay, that's the grief process. But as you're working your way through those five stages you'll experience a lot of other emotions as well:

- **Relief.** If you initiated your breakup, you might be euphoric at having left a bad relationship. And if you didn't initiate it, you can still feel relieved anyway: "If you can step back for a moment and let go of the hurt, chaos, and shame created by the situation, you might just realize that your ex did you a favor by ending things," says psychoanalyst Mary Lamia.
- **Paralysis.** Feelings of being unable to function—physically or emotionally—are completely normal. So are worries about money, whether you'll ever be able to see your kids again, how you can help them cope with what's going on in their lives, whether you'll be able to take on the responsibilities of being a single parent, or that the world is falling apart.
- **Loneliness and isolation.** If you're like most men, your partner probably took care of managing your social calendar, but you're on your own now. As a result, you may be experiencing a rather drastic change in your social life. Couples tend to hang out with other couples, and you, as a single guy, may be very much left out. Plus, other friends may have taken sides and dumped you altogether. Being alone, however, can be a great thing, giving you a chance to think or spend time with yourself—maybe for the first time in years. Many men are grateful for the opportunity, but too many simply can't handle it. I developed a sudden, fanatical interest in square dancing. Thankfully, I'm over this now, but some men throw themselves just as fanatically into their jobs or their hobbies, while others spend their time pouting or drinking.
- **Abandonment and rejection.** When you lost your wife or girlfriend, you may have lost your best friend and closest confidante, leaving you with the feeling that you haven't got a friend or source of support in the world. Sometimes these feelings snowball, and you might imagine that your ex must have been right to reject you because you're a lousy husband, a lousy

Help Your Kids Cope with Your Divorce

One of the major concerns newly single fathers have is how to help their children deal with the dramatic changes going on in their lives. Here's a brief guide to what your children may be going through and how you can best help them cope.

"Adolescents tend to be egocentric," write Laurence Steinberg and Ann Levine. "They see divorce as something you are doing to them. Getting angry at the parent who is moving out is dangerous, because that parent might not want to see them anymore. Getting angry at the parent with whom they will be living is also dangerous, because that parent might abandon them, too." A lot of teens whose parents are breaking up disengage from the family and spend more time with friends. This is a mixed blessing. Many become more mature, develop deeper friendships, and explore extracurricular activities and other interests. But others, trying to be too independent too fast, run away from home, slip into drug or alcohol abuse, have sex too early, or behave in other self-destructive ways. Here's how to help them cope:

- **Watch out for depression.** If your child is emotionally withdrawn, has problems in school that last for more than a semester, loses interest in friends and other pleasurable activities, has prolonged mood swings, or completely changes his group of peers, get some professional help.
- **Pay attention.** Divorcing and divorced parents are less likely to monitor their teens and to set the limits they need—but this is a time when monitoring and limits are more important than ever. Boys are more likely to respond to the divorce by acting out or falling in with a bad crowd, girls by getting depressed. Kids of divorce, regardless of gender, often develop some health problems, partly from having fewer regular meals and eating more junk food.
- **Give your child a vote on scheduling.** Teenage girls sometimes prefer to live with their mothers, while boys prefer their fathers. Either way, if your kids want to spend more time with their mother, let them—but don't let

man, and a lousy father, and that it's only a matter of time until your children reject you too. She may have, but your kids never will.

- **Guilt.** Just about everyone has something to feel guilty about. If you were having an affair or left your ex for someone new, you're probably feeling at least a little guilty about the pain you caused her. And even if you didn't do anything wrong at all during your relationship, you may blame yourself in yourself be cut out altogether. And keep in mind that sometimes a child will insist on staying with the parent who appears most vulnerable, in an attempt to try to protect that parent.

◆ **Maintain as close a relationship with him as you can.** Because women get sole or primary custody about 80–90 percent of the time, children's relationships with their fathers suffer more than their relationships with their mothers. However, how well your child gets along with you is a major predictor of his long-term adjustment to the divorce. Try to schedule some one-on-one time with your child to talk or just to hang out.

◆ **Don't make him your emotional support.** He can't possibly grow up healthy if your emotional neediness makes him feel obligated to take care of you or guilty if he doesn't want to.

◆ **Get along with your ex.** The three most significant factors in postdivorce adjustment for children are the degree of parental conflict, the degree of legal conflict, and the mother's hostility toward the father. And never, never, never badmouth your ex in front of your child. Children understand that they're half Mom and half Dad, and they take any criticism of one as a criticism of that part of themselves.

◆ **No more big changes.** Kids who adjust best are the ones with the fewest disruptions to their school, homework, meals, extracurricular activities, chores, and bedtime routines. A divorce is enough of a shock to your child. Moving to a new house, switching schools, and having to find new friends can be too much.

◆ **Control your emotions.** Your child will model his coping behavior on yours. If you fall apart, get depressed and withdrawn, or run around blaming everyone else and acting like a victim, so will he. But if you can keep it together—at least in front of him—he will too. That said, do *not* stifle your feelings and plaster a fake smile on your face. It's fine to be sad or angry— just don't wallow in your grief.

some way for hurting your children, especially if you were the one who initiated the end of the relationship.

◆ **Frustration with other people.** If you're lucky, you'll always have someone around who can comfort you. But you'll be astounded at how unintentionally insensitive some people will be. Friends and family were constantly asking me whether I'd heard anything from my ex or telling me that they'd just

If You're an Adoptive Father

"The central issue of adolescence is identity formation," says adoption expert Gordon Finley. And one of the central issues of identity formation is the question, Where did I come from, and where am I going? Some adoption researchers suspect that the search for identity is harder on adopted teens than on nonadopted ones. After all, biologically related kids may be trying to find out who they are and where they're going too, but deep down inside they at least know where they came from. Adopted children, on the other hand, don't have that biological foundation to fall back on—especially in cases of international or interracial adoption.

Many adopted teens develop a particularly strong capacity for empathy, which may drive them to find answers to unanswerable questions such as, How could my birth parents have given me up?

Either way, one thing's for sure: your adopted teen is going to be spending some time thinking about his birth parents. "The adolescent adoptee's fantasies about his or her birthparents may have a more powerful impact on him or her during adolescence than at any other stage of the adoptive family life cycle," writes Finley. As a result, it's not uncommon for adopted teens to passionately throw themselves into a search for their biological parents. They may threaten to run away and maybe even do it.

All this focus on your child's birth parents may be hard on you, and could make you feel unwanted or unappreciated. His accusations that you don't know him and never cared about him anyway will hurt you, and his budding sexuality may bring up unpleasant memories of your own (or your partner's) fertility issues. But try to be as understanding as you can. Part of your adolescent's search for identity involves putting some distance between you. Sometimes that distance is physical, sometimes just emotional.

So facilitate your child's search for his birth parents and try to find some other adopted teens for your child to talk to. Getting support from people with similar concerns can often be a big help—you might also want to try it yourself. Most important, never let your child forget that you love and support him. It's important that both of you understand that permanent parent-child relationships can be "based on their shared life experiences rather than blood ties," says Finley. "Family emotional and psychological connections can remain permanent in the absence of blood ties."

seen her, apparently not bothering to consider that I really didn't want to think—let alone talk—about her at all, and that doing so was incredibly painful. I was also stunned at how many intelligent people tried to fix me up with other women just weeks (or in a few cases, days) after they found out I was getting divorced. I think they honestly believed that I should just "be strong" and "move on."

BECOMING AN ELDER STATESMAN

At age thirty-five, according to Daniel Levinson, most men still feel connected to people in their twenties and consider them peers—and the people in their twenties may still consider thirty-five-year-olds to be peers too. But for a man on the other side of forty, things change: all of a sudden he's the boss, the senior guy, and even the oldest twenty-somethings are in a different generation. A guy in his forties can't be the up-and-comer anymore—he's supposed to have up and come already. At forty, Confucius wrote, "the father is no longer suffering from perplexities." At fifty "he knows the biddings of heaven." The ancient rabbis were pretty much in agreement: at forty, they wrote, "the father is understanding." At fifty it is "the time for giving counsel."

It's no wonder, then, that the teen years are typically a time when fathers commonly take on a mentoring role. They know themselves pretty well by now, they're confident with who they are, what they know, where they're going in life (or at least where they've been), and it feels good to be able to help out the next generation. But as Levinson says, mentoring isn't just a one-way street. It's a way for a man to "maintain his connection with the forces of youthful energy in the world and in himself. He needs the recipient of mentoring as much as the recipient needs him."

Being a good mentor, does, however, require a certain sort of selflessness. A mentor who isn't confident in himself might end up taking advantage of the relationship. I had a professor in graduate school, for example, who assigned students detailed research projects every semester and then sold the results to his consulting clients. There's also the possibility of feeling jealous of a mentee who surpasses his mentor. This last point is particularly poignant if the person you're mentoring is your own child (see "What, Me? Jealous?" below).

Besides being a mentor, you may find yourself getting more involved in your community. In previous chapters we talked about how fathers, more than non-fathers, tend to do things to make the world a better place, whether it's joining the neighborhood watch, coaching a soccer team, running for Congress, or even picking up trash in a nearby park. As you age, that overall attitude won't change. But toward the end of your kid's teen years you'll probably notice a subtle difference: you're becoming an elder statesman here too. Instead of just joining a civic group, you'll probably be on the board of directors. Instead of coaching a team, you might be involved in organizing the whole citywide league. And instead of getting out there and marching or building houses for Habitat for Humanity, you may write them a check.

WHAT, ME JEALOUS?

Well, if you think about it, it makes good sense. Your teen is *soooo* young. He's at the early stages of his independence, just starting to form other relationships, experiencing first loves, first kisses, graduating from high school and going on to college, and is in peak sexual, physical, and mental condition. The same goes for

"Dad, can I borrow the carpet tonight?"

girls, of course. If your son is going out with girls at a younger age than you were, you might be proud of his budding masculinity and/or envious of it. Any or all of these things may make you think about and reconsider some of the choices you made when you were young. And the clarity that only twenty-five years of hindsight can offer may make you wish you could have done things differently, fixed mistakes, picked another major, gone out with a different girl, not wasted so much of your youth, or whatever. But you can't. You made your choices and are looking back on them. Your child has his whole life ahead of him.

Toward the end of the teen years your child will probably start getting ready to move out of your house. As we've talked about earlier, this will bring up all sorts of issues, in particular fear of not being able to protect him from the world and sadness at the change in your relationship with each other. But don't be surprised if you suddenly find yourself jealous—or even resentful—of your child's freedom to pick up and go wherever he wants to. Meanwhile, you're working harder than ever so you can provide for your family. It doesn't seem fair. You may not really want to go anywhere, but it sure would be nice to have the option available. . . .

YOU AND YOUR FAST-TRACK CAREER, BUT AT WHAT COST?

Fathers have always had an uneasy relationship with their work. We need our jobs to pay the mortgage and keep shoes on everyone's feet, but they also make it hard to spend as much time with the family as we'd like to. Problems at home interfere with concentration and productivity at work, and problems at work become an easy excuse for fathers "to cut themselves off from the life of the family and focus on their own needs," write Reed Larson and Maryse Richards.

In our society all of us—men and women—have been socialized to view a man's worth in terms of his income. That, naturally, makes work the centerpiece of men's existence, the place where we define ourselves, the place where we compete against each other for power, prestige, women, recognition, money. When we're young, it also has a more sinister impact. "Many men see work success as the route to immunity from death," writes Roger Gould. "It's as though we had a pact with the world, if we continued to be good boys and worked hard, if we sacrificed and succeeded, the fear that we would be annihilated, which terrorized us as little boys, was never to return again. . . . It's a tempting vision, because it connects with the way many of us want to see the world. If one success doesn't do it, then the next level of success certainly will. We never know when to stop, for success and total peace might be just beyond the next bend in the road."

But by the time our kids are teenagers, we wake up to the harsh reality that work isn't going to keep us alive. In fact, it might kill us. And if it doesn't do that, it could very well kill our relationships with our children. Spending a huge amount of time at work trying to achieve success (whatever that means to you) can really cut into the little time you have to spend with your kids. "In essence, men sell their souls for a feeling of triumph with so little lasting power that they constantly have to sell more of themselves to buy more of it," says Gould. "When the craziness is finally exposed, they feel cheated."

Behind Slammed Doors: What Your Teen Is Really Thinking

No matter how tall or strong or adultlike your teen seems on the outside, on the inside he's still a kid, which means he thinks about the world and everything in it very differently than we do. Independence, for example, is all about control, at least from your child's perspective. And it doesn't taste nearly as sweet if it's given— it has to be taken, on the teen's terms. To make matters worse (or better, depending which end you're on), taking independence isn't enough unless it hurts you. This hurt may be either real or fantasy. Either way, though it exists for your child.

"In our pious, tortured logic, we believe that because they have let us know what they want for us, they must be controlling us," writes Roger Gould, offering a rare glimpse into what teenagers think about their parents. "But we can control them by causing them pain, by defying their wants and expectations. We gain power at their expense, then we hate them for being weak and vulnerable.... We push them into ridiculous authoritarian positions, then scoff at their folly. Though rationally we see their pain, we can't stop ourselves. All we see emotionally is a world of power plays, hostility, deception, and self-deception." Pretty scary stuff, isn't it? Fortunately, it doesn't last forever.

While it does last, though, try to be patient. Your teen's behavior and words may seem like attempts to push you away, but they're really not. Hiding underneath all the "I hate you's" and the "you never let me do anything's" and the anger and the sullen refusals to help out around the house is a child who's trying to sort out his identity, figure out who he is, and where he fits in the world. He's a child who desperately wants to be a grown up but who knows deep down

SEPARATION ANXIETY STUFF AGAIN?

As in every other stage of your child's development, his major job as a teen is to separate from you. And as in every other stage, his struggle toward independence can cause a lot of conflict between the two of you.

A lot of the problem is that you know, deep down inside, that it's not going to be that many years until your child moves out of the house. How old were you when you left home? seventeen, eighteen, nineteen? Of course your child may be back in a few years, but that isn't going to make letting go much easier. According to Gould, one of the biggest fears parents have while their kids are teenagers is that they won't be able to protect them. The world can be a pretty scary place, and they're about to take off on their own. It's also hard to come to

inside that he's not. On the one hand, he still looks up to you, respects you, wants to please you, and craves your guidance and approval. On the other hand, he resents you; your very existence is a daily reminder that he's still dependent. As a result, he'll test you constantly, making a power play, pushing and cajoling, and trying to get you to give in any way he can.

Most of the time your teen's testing behavior will be fairly innocuous—not pleasant, but ultimately harmless. We'll talk about dangerous and truly out-of-control behavior on pages 210-11. The trick to handling the day-to-day annoying behavior is to be as tolerant as possible. Try to see it as a symptom of the struggle to carve out an individual identity. And train yourself not to be suckered into responding to your teen's baiting and taunting. The minute you try to explain to him that you really don't hate him or that you do in fact let him do plenty of things, he's got you on the ropes and there's no way you can win. Resist the urge to come out swinging, preaching, responding to his anger with anger of your own, demanding that he comply. If you do, he'll take things up a notch or two, finding bigger and more extreme ways of enraging you and doing exactly the opposite of what you want—even if you're 100 percent right.

Overall, the more tolerant you are, and the more you explain and discuss and solicit his input, the less likely he'll be to mouth off. So as long as chores, school-work, and basic behavioral standards are being maintained, give him some leeway to express himself his own way. Sometimes you'll feel like chucking him out the nearest window, and if you're worried that you might, walk out of the room. But be sure to come back. A lot of time the hidden message behind your teen's fighting words is the need for a hug. But he'll never admit it.

terms with the fact that your child doesn't need you as much as he used to. That can bring up all sorts of mixed feelings, everything from pleasure and pride to resentment and anger.

At the same time, you're trying to make sense of your life, trying to get everything in order and settled, trying to be a loving dad. You want people to notice what you're doing and what you've done. Not only that, you want recognition and affirmation that you've made the right choices in your life, says Dorothy Martin, an expert in fathers and teens. But along comes your teenager, who's trying to carve out his own identity. He's feeling insecure and moody and is focused on himself. If you were hoping that your child would see that you have needs too, give it up. "The deep egocentrism of the early adolescent shields the child from recognition of the father's needs and his developmental passage," writes Martin. "The adolescent push toward independent identity is expressed in the defiant rejection of a caring father." Interestingly, boys and girls sometimes have different ways of separation. Boys are more likely just to storm away and not talk. Girls are more likely to start fights and arguments—which serves the purpose of both separating and maintaining a connection.

Your teen may not be the only person in your house trying to establish a new identity. In a lot of "traditional" marriages (where Dad is the breadwinner and Mom has stayed home with the kids), the woman takes advantage of her teen's independence to explore some freedom of her own. She may return to work or change her life in other ways that may have an impact on your marriage. See the sections on communicating with your partner toward the end of this chapter.

RECALIBRATING FATHERHOOD

Ever since your child was born, a huge part of your identity has been tied up in being a father. You may not have realized it, but it's true. A lot of men in Rob Palkovitz's study "were so invested in their roles as fathers that they could not articulate or even imagine what their lives would be like without children. . . . Thinking from a perspective outside of fathering was a novel or foreign concept." I hope you're used to that way of thinking, because it's never going to change. No matter how old your children get, you're always going to be a father.

What is going to change, though, is what it means to be a father. When your child was younger, you were the nurturer, teacher, playmate, disciplinarian, and lawmaker. But that's not enough anymore. (Actually, it may be too much.) At this point, you need to be the guide and mentor, the consultant who's brought in for meetings once in a while but who spends the rest of the time on call. Your skills as nurturer, teacher, playmate, disciplinarian, and lawmaker will still come in handy, but in a different way: on your child's terms rather than on your own.

Naturally, as the definition of fatherhood evolves, so does your relationship with your child. You're no longer the invincible superdaddy, the guy who's stronger, smarter, richer, and better-looking than all the other daddies. Now you're the old man, the one your child has to rebel against to become independent.

It's sometimes very hard to acknowledge that your relationship has changed, but you really have to. Not only that, you have to actively facilitate those changes, and accept that your baby is becoming an adult. Clinging to the way things used to be, trying to keep your child from growing up, or being overprotective can create terrible problems for both of you.

Another thing that can cause problems is humor. "Men resolve their dual agenda for their home life—recovering from the stress of their jobs and spending time with their families—by being a recreational leader, or sometimes a jokester," write Reed Larsen and Maryse Richards. "Yet while humor is ice-breaking and fun, it can also have costs. If fathers make everything into a joke, their adolescents may start to suspect them of not taking their feelings seriously." Humor can be a great way to teach, but teasing and being sarcastic is not, they say.

Interestingly, fathers and their children often have very a different take on their relationship and on the time they spend together, with fathers generally perceiving a closer relationship than the teen. "Adolescent and father may be together, in the same activity, but their experience is different," write Larsen and Richards. Teaching your child and taking pride in his accomplishments may still make you feel warm all over, and getting asked for advice may make you feel loved and needed. But your child is likely to see your attempts to teach as pedantic, and your pride as intrusive. "Dad may be trying to create enjoyment, but his son's or daughter's pleasure lags behind his. This is, of course, partly because for adolescents, friends are where the fun is."

THE BATTLE TO STAY YOUNG

As part of your tacit competition with your son, you may find yourself doing all sorts of things to recapture your youth or fight off your age. A lot of dads in their late thirties to early fifties and older start dressing more hip, get contemporary haircuts, lift weights, jog, take martial arts classes. They often develop an interest in whatever music or movies or television shows or video games their sons are into. And of course there's the stereotypical red Midlife Crisismobile that shows everyone you've still got what it takes to be a man.

"What's this they say, Billy, about a new, more virulent strain of teenager?"

A Date with Delinquency

Parenting an adolescent isn't a particularly easy thing to do even under the rosiest of circumstances. Having a healthy, well-adjusted, top-performing, polite, well-groomed, socially conscious teen would certainly make the process more enjoyable for everyone, but what if, despite all the wonderful things you've done for him, he turns out the very opposite?

They don't prepare us for that. Simply put, it can be devastating. When a child has severe behavior problems, is rebellious, or gets into major trouble in school, parents' initial reaction is to blame themselves, to ask themselves what they did wrong. Things get worse, from the parents' point of view, if their child lands in jail or acts out in a particularly public way that embarrasses them. To make matters worse, most of the professionals these parents come in contact with—doctors, teachers, psychiatrists, lawyers—blame them too, says Anne-Marie Ambert, a psychologist and expert in child development. Parents of delinquent teens suffer in a variety of ways, she says. They might start drinking too much, find it hard to concentrate at work, feel increased stress or shame, imagine that others are blaming them, and find all sorts of excuses to stay away from their teen. They begin to see themselves as parental failures, and they feel socially isolated.

Even worse, they feel that they can no longer trust a child who has lied to and betrayed them. Ambert found that these feelings of mistrust can set off a vicious circle: the parents react by becoming more controlling and monitoring their child's friends. That, naturally, makes the child accuse the parents of not trusting him (which is true) and rebel even more. He blames his parents for everything, and takes no responsibility. At the same time, parents who are in denial about their own contribution to the problem can be quick to blame the outside world (school or friends) or attribute their teen's behavior to a specific cause, such as Attention Deficit Disorder (ADD).

If you're in denial, wake up. If you're blaming yourself, stop. Continuing on either of those paths will do absolutely nothing to change your teen's behavior and could land you in a position of loving your teen very much but not really liking him. This could eventually destroy your relationship with him.

If he's doing anything that could be harmful to himself or others (running away, behaving violently or threatening to, abusing drugs or alcohol, having sex with a lot of different people), get him to a child psychologist or psychiatrist right away. He needs the kind of help you're probably not able to provide.

For less dangerous behavior (things like cutting school, being disrespectful, staying out past curfew, failing classes) you're going to have to get tough. This means letting your teen know very clearly what your minimum behavior standards are and what kind of behavior is unacceptable. Do this in writing and be as specific as possible. Teens are brilliant in finding loopholes in rules. Next, come up with a list of consequences. Taking away phone privileges, car keys, free time, and social privileges are great attention getters. But be sure to include some positive consequences as well. Doing things right, for example, might earn your teen a curfew extension for a few hours or something else that indicates that you trust him. Violating one of the rules, though, might result in not being able to go to that concert he'd already bought tickets to.

Keep in mind that this whole being-tough thing is going to be hard on you too. Most of us aren't used to catching our kids being good. If they do what they're supposed to, we hardly notice because we expect good behavior. Kids often find that incredibly frustrating, so rewarding good behavior once in a while will greatly increase the odds that it'll continue. Conversely, when it comes time to enforce the rules, you have to learn to stand your ground, not giving in to whining, cajoling, threats, tears, screams, or manipulation. If you let your teen steamroller you one time, it's guaranteed that he'll try it again.

Dads of daughters do a lot of the same things, but with the added agenda of looking cool for her friends. Most guys will never do anything about it, but even the thought that a teenage girl might find him attractive is enough to make your whole day.

Getting in shape and expanding your pop-culture horizons is great. It gives you some valuable insight into what your kids are interested in. But don't take it

Gender and Conflict

DADS AND SONS

Relationships between a father and his teenage son can get very complicated. On the one hand, boys typically feel closer to their fathers than girls do (more on that below). There's more man-to-man talking and more camaraderie. On the other hand, dads tend to have higher expectations for their sons and are tougher on their sons than they are on their daughters. And a father is more likely to put pressure on a son than a daughter to live the life he wishes he had or to avoid the mistakes he feels he made. Fathers want to retain their authority in the family, but conceding power to Dad makes the son feel weak and ineffective.

Three major themes influence father-son relationships, says psychologist and fatherhood expert Jerrold Shapiro. First, the son is the rejector of what the father has accomplished. Second, the son will replace the father in the world of men. And third, the son's emergence as an independent man is a powerful symbolic reminder of the father's mortality. Author Mark Goldblatt summed it up in a pretty interesting way: "Sons are their fathers' only natural predators," he wrote. "If we do not surpass the lives of our fathers, we kill them with disappointment. If we do surpass them, we kill them with envy." These issues of mutual jealousy and competitiveness loom large and can drive father and son apart. (See pages 204–5.)

DADS AND DAUGHTERS

Father-daughter relationships can be equally complicated, but for other reasons. To start with, fathers generally feel more alienated from their teen daughters than from their teen sons. Some of the problem may be the male way of expressing approval. Fathers (and most other men) tend to focus on external factors: accomplishment and performance. Their daughters (and most other females), however, too far. No matter what you do, how much you try, or what kind of clothes you wear, you're not going to be cool enough to get into the cliques.

OUT OF CONTROL

When your child was two, your biggest conflicts were about who had control over him, who decided when he'd go to bed, what he'd wear, when he'd eat,

want to be appreciated for their internal, personal qualities—who they are, as opposed to what they do.

Let me say right here that there is absolutely nothing wrong with the male way of expressing approval. It is simply different from the female way—not better, not worse. Of course it would be great if dads could pay a little more attention to what's on the inside as well as the outside. But it would also be great if mothers could also pay a little more attention to doing as well as feeling.

Besides all that, most fathers and daughters have fewer common interests than fathers and sons. She's probably into makeup, shaving her legs and armpits, and boys—not the kind of things most guys care much about, and not the kind of things most girls want to talk to their dads about anyway. And then, of course, there's puberty. Girls are sometimes scared and confused by what's happening to their bodies and their minds, and they naturally rely more on their mothers for support and understanding and to be their role models.

As a result, dads can feel pushed away by their teen daughters. They (the dads) miss the warm, close relationship and feel unloved and unappreciated. It's up to you as the grown-up to do something about this situation if it happens. Try to think of her rejection of you not as an actual rejection, but as a test, a way to get you to show her that despite all the physical changes she's going through, she's still beautiful to you, and you love her unconditionally.

To further complicate matters here, most dads are also puzzled and scared by what's happening to their daughters and to their budding sexuality. They may feel attracted to their daughters sexually and back off completely, afraid that they'll do something horrible. Remember this: it's perfectly normal to have those feelings; it's *not* normal to act on them. Girls whose fathers back off may get confused and feel rejected, thinking they did something to drive Dad away. Girls who get lots of attention from their fathers feel closer to them than girls who don't. And girls who don't often go looking for it elsewhere.

and where he could go. In most cases you won the arguments—in no small part because you were bigger. When he was two, you could pick him up or physically restrain him if you thought he was about to do something you didn't want him to, like run into the street.

Well, some things never change. The main theme of parent-adolescent arguments is control over the child's behavior, says researcher Dorothy Martin. But there are two big differences. First, your size isn't nearly as much of an advantage now as it was then. If your child wants to drive, drink, take drugs, have sex, get a tattoo, or wear completely inappropriate clothing, there's precious little you can do about it. Second, like it or not, you're going to have to learn to give up some of your authority.

That's not going to be easy. "Fathers, even more so than mothers, approach interactions with adolescents from a position of power," write Larsen and Richards, "and they are more disposed to use this power... fathers are more resistant to yielding their authority." Teens themselves rate their fathers as somewhat less sympathetic and more in need of being in control. One of the reasons dads have a harder time giving up authority is that mothers and fathers tend to be concerned about very different things. Mothers worry more about their kids' social lives and emotional issues. Dads worry more about areas where mistakes are harder to recover from: drugs, alcohol, car accidents, AIDS, and so on. Another reason that dads try to retain what power they have is that males in our society are socialized to view things in hierarchical terms, where power is linked to social standing and access to resources. That also explains a little more about father-son power struggles: of two males, one has the power and wants to keep it, while the other doesn't have it but wants it.

The bottom line here is that in much the same way as in the terrible twos, your child is struggling between relying on you and wanting to be completely independent. And, as it was back then, your role is to both set limits and support independence. But there's one important difference: at this point, you need to do your limit-setting and your supporting from a little further away, giving your teen more control over his life, letting him stretch his wings and figure out a few more things for himself.

BEYOND HIGH SCHOOL

Three of the major issues of the last couple of years of high school are whether, when, and where to go to college. When it comes to "whether," in my mind the answer is clear. Yes: sure, every once in a while you hear about some incredibly

"Good day, Madam. I'm working my son's way through college."

successful person who didn't go to college or who went but never finished, but they're by far the exception.

In the real world, someone with a bachelor's degree earns an average of about $15,000 per year more than someone with only a high-school diploma. Having a master's degree adds another $11,000 per year, and a doctorate kicks in $15,000 on top of that. People who have college degrees are more likely to have white-collar jobs, which means they're less likely to be working in some dangerous profession. People with degrees have better insurance, better benefits, live a more rounded lifestyle, have more transferable skills, and tend to live longer than those without.

So what about timing? Well, the traditional way to do things is to start college right after high school. The problem with that tradition, though, is that not too many eighteen-year olds—especially boys—are mature enough to be in college. The solution? Have your teen take a year off to broaden his horizons. He can take a backpacking tour of Asia, get a job, do volunteer work with Americorps, spend a few months stomping grapes in France, serve drinks on a cruise ship. It doesn't really matter what he does, just as long as it's something he wouldn't ordinarily do at home.

The disadvantage of taking a year off like this is that when your teen finally does start college, he'll be a year behind his high-school buddies and a year older than his college classmates. In my view, though, the advantages more than make up for it.

- ◆ This may be the last big block of responsibility-free time he'll have for a while.
- ◆ He'll be a more attractive candidate. When I interviewed admissions directors several years ago, most of them told me that they love to see kids who've taken some time off after high school. They're more mature, more well rounded, and more interesting.
- ◆ You might save some money. If your teen has already been accepted, see whether he can defer enrollment for a year. Some colleges actually give a tuition discount to those who do.
- ◆ He'll be more focused. Kids who've had some experience in the world are less likely to flounder around for a few years trying to figure out what to major in—on your nickel.

If you're interested in finding out more about year-off programs, Danielle Woods's *UnCollege Alternative* is a great resource. On the Web, you can get a comprehensive list of programs at *guidance.wwwcomm.com/alternatives.htm*. Another option is to get some professional counseling. For about $120 a year (or $80 for six months), you sign up at *www.whereyouheaded.com* and get access to their exhaustive database.

If your child is extremely self-directed and does a huge amount of research on his own, he may know exactly where he wants to go to college. But most kids aren't that way, which means that you and your partner will be getting involved in the decision. If you're lucky, you may get a little extra help from your teen's high-school guidance counselor.

Whether he's planning to enroll now or later, the first question to consider is how far away from home your child wants to be. If he's very mature and independent, living in a dorm 2,000 miles away might suit him just fine. But a lot of kids need or want to be closer to their friends and family, so you'll be wasting your time looking at faraway colleges. Once you've decided on the near/far decision, consider the following questions. The answers, of course, will depend on your teen. Even if your teen has already made up his mind, it's worth encouraging him to go through this process anyway—just to be absolutely sure.

- What does your child want to major in? The question is *not,* What do *you* want him to major in?
- What kind of weather does he like? If he's a skier, schools in Florida should probably be pretty low on your list.
- What kind of environment does he want—major metropolitan area or in the middle of nowhere?
- Does he want to go to a large college or a small, more intimate one?
- How important are extracurricular activities or having the opportunity to study abroad?
- Finances. Are you planning (or able) to pay for everything? Will your child be working? How much financial aid/scholarship money will you need?

Once you've got a pretty good grip on these basics, you can get down to considering some specific schools.

- Get a book. *Barron's, Peterson's, Princeton Review,* and others publish annual guides to colleges and grad schools. These books will include detailed information on majors offered, admission requirements, extracurricular activities, financial aid and scholarships, social life, and much more.
- Broaden your horizons. Despite the impression you get in the media, there are a lot more colleges out there than Harvard, Princeton, Yale, Stanford, Brown, and a few others with big names. These schools usually have more applicants than places and are extremely selective. Not getting into one of the Ivy League schools is *not* a failure. The truth is that there are hundreds of other colleges out there that offer a great education without a waiting list.
- Be reasonable. Apply to colleges that your child has the best chance of getting into. If he has a 2.5 GPA, and you know that a particular school admits only students with 4.0, cross that one off your list, or at least off the A list.
- Once you've narrowed your choices to a handful, do two things. First, call each one's admissions office and get the names of a few local alumni your child can meet with and talk to about what life is really like at that particular college. Second, pack your bags and go visit a few of the finalists.

As you go through this process, keep reminding yourself that your child is the one going to college, not you. You can have an opinion, and you can even express it, but ultimately the final decision—including whether to go at all—should be *his.*

Pass the Everything, Please: On Taking Care of Parents and Kids at the Same Time

Imagine this: Your aging mother can't take care of herself any longer and has just moved in with you; your four-year-old complains that you spend more time with Grandma than with her; and your teenager is angry about all the extra responsibilities he's had to take on around the house. And then there's you—exhausted, overworked, frustrated, and furious—stuck in the middle, juggling your teen's social obligations and your parent's medical appointments and trying to hold everything together.

Sound like a nightmare? Could be, but for those of us in the "sandwich generation"—the 9 million or so households where they're caring for an elderly person as well as young children—it's a harsh reality. The result? Stress, and lots of it. Your marriage can suffer, your job performance can slip, and you can end up feeling depressed, anxious, exhausted, and physically ill. Overall, about 70 percent of people in this situation are women (that still leaves a lot of men). But the ratio varies greatly by culture: in Asian families, for example, it's fifty-fifty.

Fortunately, there are some things you can do to reduce some of the stress involved in being caught in the middle.

- ◆ **Take care of yourself.** If you can't take care of yourself, you won't be able to take care of anyone else either. So make sure you eat right, exercise, get plenty of rest, and have some time left over for yourself. The healthier you are, the less likely you'll be to burn out, and the better you'll be able to keep up that hectic pace that so many people are counting on you to maintain.

THE PREFAB FAMILY

About half of all marriages are remarriages for at least one of the partners, many of whom have children. It's quite possible, then, that you may be starting your fatherhood experience with a teenager. Or your new wife might be the incoming stepparent. Either way, the most important thing to remember is to have reasonable expectations and be patient.

It's not easy being a stepparent. There's not a lot of social support out there, and the stepparent's role in the new family isn't always clear. Fortunately, you're not alone. In fact, there are over 2.5 million families (including more than 6.5 million kids) made up of a biological mother and a stepfather. Cyberparent.com (*www.cyberparent.com/step/*) is a good source of information and referrals.

- **Learn to accept—and ask for—help.** Being a martyr won't do you or anyone else any good. So instead of gracefully turning down those "If there's something I can do, just call" offers, assign specific tasks. And don't just wait around for the offers to come in. Sit down with your immediate family and divvy up the responsibilities. Everyone can chip in somehow—even your kids.
- **Find out about community resources.** Churches and social groups often have volunteers who can provide regular or as-needed assistance. The National Eldercare Locator, 800-677-1116, can refer you to the agency nearest you. And check out *www.careguide.com* for resources and referrals for child care as well as elder care.
- **Talk to your parents.** Have they written a will? Do they want to give you the authority to make health-care decisions if they're no longer able? It's hard to have these discussions, but it's important.
- **Don't hover.** Let your parents do as much as they can for themselves. Treating them like invalids (if they aren't) or helpless children will depress them and make your job even harder.
- **Talk to your employer.** At least half of caregivers make workplace accommodations such as passing up promotions and travel, leaving early, or even quitting, according to the National Alliance for Caregiving (*www.caregiving.org*). So ask your employer what kinds of workplace initiatives are already in place. You may, for example, be eligible for a leave under the Family and Medical Leave Act. Or you may be able to telecommute, use flextime, or change your shift.

Don't be offended if your stepchildren want to spend a lot of time with their biological dad. There's going to be some natural competitiveness between the two of you, especially if your ex tells you he isn't a particularly nice guy. But you absolutely must support the kids' relationship with their father. (If the situation is reversed, try to help your new wife to understand that your kids are going to want to spend a lot of time with their mother, and that she should try as hard as she can to support that relationship.)

An adolescent who's felt responsible for his divorced mother may feel relieved to have you step in and take over some of the burden, according to psychologist and researcher Mavis Heatherington. But for the most part, it's not easy for adolescents to accept a new stepparent. A lot of teens, just like younger kids,

Speak the Same Language

Sound's silly, but it's not. Some of the biggest communication breakdowns come because couples don't (or can't or won't) agree on the definition of some very basic words. For example, does the word *intimacy* mean the same thing to you and your partner? For women, intimacy usually involves emotional vulnerability. Some of the most intimate moments of my life, though, have involved playing catch with my father, fifty feet apart, not saying a word. And what about *love?* Do you and your partner express your love for each other in the same way? Probably not. Men commonly express love for their partners by *doing* things. Women, however, are more likely to express their love *verbally.* Unfortunately, most people want to be communicated with in their own language. Consequently, what you *do* may not be loving enough for your partner, and what she *says* may not be enough for you. Learning to understand and express love differently is like learning a new language. Granted, it's a little more complicated than high school French, but it can be done.

fantasize that their parents will get back together. Your marriage to his mother dashes that hope. In addition, your new stepchild probably had a lot of additional responsibilities around the house and was feeling very mature. But now that you're on the scene, he'll have to go back to being a kid again, which is something he may resent. He may also resent the intrusion of yet another grown-up to push him around just at the time when he's seeking autonomy, says sociologist Anne-Marie Ambert. He's trying to figure out who he is in life. Adding in "How do I fit into this new family?" may be more than he wants to deal with. Expect to hear a lot of "You're not my father, so I don't have to listen to you."

One of the most important factors in a child's adjustment to a stepparent is trying to maintain the one-on-one relationships he had with his natural parents. Kids often feel that they're losing their biological parent to the new stepparent. And the truth is that in a way they're right. Before, it was just them and you, but now they have to share you with some interloper. This brings up all sorts of loyalty issues for a lot of stepkids. They often feel that if they love their new stepparent they're somehow being disloyal to their biological parent (in other words, by loving you, your stepchild might feel that he's betraying his father). As a result, they may lash out at the stepparent for what seems like no reason at all. Even stranger, these explosions often happen just when you think your relationship with your stepchild is getting better. If (when) they happen, try to take them as a compliment.

It's also critical that you and your partner devote some time to keeping your relationship healthy and that you discuss the role she expects you to take in her children's life, or that you expect her to take in your kids' life. Don't be naive and think that everything will work itself out—it won't. Over half of remarried women and about two-thirds of remarried men get divorced again. Overall, remarriages that involve kids are five times more likely to fail than those without, according to Hetherington. Major problems include conflicts over child-rearing, the children's behavior, and the relationship between the stepparent and the stepchildren. So don't be afraid to get some couples therapy if you need it.

If you and your new wife both have kids from previous relationships, pay special attention to how the kids react, and don't underestimate the magnitude of the changes they're going to experience: new routines, a new house, new customs, new bedrooms—they may even have to share a room—and even a new birth order. A child who was once the oldest, and had all the privileges that went along with that, might resent being bumped by an older child. The opposite might happen to a child who gets displaced as baby of the family. Don't make the mistake of expecting that everyone's going to live as one big, happy family. Give the kids plenty of time to get used to each other and to their new stepparents. It's not going to be easy on any of you.

DEALING WITH YOUR OWN FATHER

No matter how old we get or what we've done in our lives, there's always a little part in every man that seeks his father's approval. It doesn't matter whether we had a great or a horrible relationship with him, or whether he was even there; the desire to prove ourselves to Dad lingers on. As we've talked about elsewhere in this chapter, by the time you have a teenager around the house, you're probably pretty well established in your life and in your routines. This is a time when you've earned a lot of successes and want to show off a little, says Gail Sheehy. It's a time when you want your own father's approval.

Unfortunately, it's also a time your father is getting older himself and is starting to lean on you—physically and metaphorically—relying on you for support. As you might guess, there can be problems, especially if you're not ready to be leaned on yet. (We'll talk about what it's like to be a father of a midlife son in a chapter 7.)

As complicated as the father-son relationship is while everyone's alive, it can actually get even more complicated when the father dies. For most men, especially those under forty, a father's death is his first major loss, says Neil Chethik, author of *Fatherloss*. The most common piece of advice offered by the

A Dad's (Brief) Guide to Puberty

"At no other time, except during infancy, does the human body change so dramatically as it does during puberty," says Chrystal De Freitas. And you remember what all those changes are about, right? Hormones raging through your child's body, preparing it to reproduce (isn't that an absolutely horrifying thought?). While puberty is going to be tough on your child, it may not be all that easy for you. So read on:

BOYS

WHAT YOUR CHILD MAY BE GOING THROUGH

- His penis and scrotum will get bigger, pubic hair starts appearing, his voice will change, he may start getting acne, and he'll grow hair under his arms.
- He may become obsessed with comparing his progress to that of his friends.
- He'll have his first wet dreams, which he may find anything from confusing to scary as hell. He may think he's wet the bed or that something is wrong.
- The process usually starts at age eleven or twelve (although the range is roughly from nine to fourteen) and can take 4–8 years to complete. If puberty hasn't started by the time your son is fifteen, tell his pediatrician.

HOW IT MIGHT AFFECT YOU

- On the one hand, you may be proud that your son is becoming a man.
- On the other, you may suddenly find yourself feeling competitive with him.
- You will most certainly have fond—and horrible—memories of going through puberty yourself. When I was eleven or twelve, I remember comparing pubic hair counts and penis measurements in the bathroom with my friends.

WHAT YOUR CHILD NEEDS FROM YOU

- Information, patience, and reassurance that what he's going through is normal. By the time girls reach puberty, they've been exposed to all sorts of magazine articles and books that have prepared them—at least a little—for what they're going through. But there's precious little out there for boys. You should make a point to ask your son whether he has any questions and set aside some time to answer them. You might also want to pick up a copy of Robie Harris's *It's Perfectly Normal: A Book about Changing Bodies* or *The What's Happening to My Body? Book for Boys* by Lynda Madaras.

GIRLS

WHAT YOUR CHILD MAY BE GOING THROUGH

- Her breasts will start to develop, she'll start growing hair on her genitals and under her arms, her skin may start breaking out, and she'll begin menstruating.
- She'll probably be quite concerned about how she's developing compared to her friends.
- The process can start as early as nine or ten (the range is typically eight–fourteen) and usually takes 18 months to 7 or 8 years to complete. If puberty hasn't started by the time your daughter is fifteen, make sure you tell her pediatrician.
- Girls may feel fat, embarrassed, and ill-at-ease in their new bodies. And girls who start developing early usually begin attracting boys' attention, and are often stereotyped as loose or easy.

HOW IT MIGHT AFFECT YOU

- Now, this can be awkward. Your daughter's puberty can be a very difficult time in your relationship. "Girls may become flirty with their fathers in much the same way they were when they were three," write Don and Jeanie Elium, authors of *Raising a Daughter*. "But now the fathers notice their daughter's developing hips and breasts and may get 'turned on.' Thinking that these feelings are abnormal and shameful, they push their daughters away to avoid their feelings and to protect their daughters from them."
- Besides being confused by your daughter's physical changes, it's not uncommon to feel embarrassed or slightly put off by the whole menstruation thing.

WHAT YOUR CHILD NEEDS FROM YOU

- Support. She's concerned about her changing body, and she wants to know whether it'll influence the way other people treat her. "Daughters need reassurance from the first man in their lives that these changes they are undergoing are okay, that their father still loves them," write the Eliums.
- Take it easy on yourself. To feel a sexual tingle around your teenage daughter is perfectly normal, but acting on it isn't. "When you hug your daughter, if it feels uncomfortable, continue," says Gordon Clay, who runs workshops for fathers and daughters. "If it feels wrong or inappropriate, stop. Most men know exactly what I am saying and what I mean." A word of advice: even though these feelings are normal, most people won't admit to having them; if you have them, keep them to yourself.

An extra note if you have a girl

It's fairly safe to assume that your daughter will have the necessary discussions on puberty and menstruation with her mother. But if you're a single dad, a widower, or just the kind of guy who wants to know how to handle these things, follow these three steps:

1. Pick yourself up a few books on adolescent child development and carefully read the sections on girls' puberty. Chrystal De Freitas's *Keys to Your Child's Healthy Sexuality, You and Your Adolescent,* by Laurence Steinberg and Ann Levine, and *The What's Happening to My Body? Book for Girls* by Lynda Madaras are excellent resources.

2. Ask your daughter if she has any questions about the ways her body is changing and let her know that you'll always be there for her if she wants to talk about anything. Chances are, though, that she'll be far too self-conscious to discuss those intimate details with you—a man. But making the offer in a loving, supportive way will let her know that you care—and that's what's really important.

3. Offer to put your daughter in touch with an adult female friend or relative with whom she may feel more comfortable talking about these things.

men in Chethik's study was to try to make peace with Dad any way you can. Resolve outstanding issues, clear up conflicts, say the things that need to be said. This kind of peacemaking is good for you and for your father. He needs to know that you appreciate him, or at least that you forgive him. And you need to say good-bye in some way.

Death is often too sudden, and in Chethik's study, only about half of men age thirty-three to fifty-five were actually able to make peace before their father died. But of those who did, 82 percent said it helped them cope with the loss. Those who were able to prepare for a terminally ill father's death found that getting involved in caring for him was extremely important. Ninety-three percent of those who did said it made coping easier. Nevertheless, Chethik found men who were thirty-three to fifty-five when their father died were more likely than men in any other age group (including those over fifty-five) to experience a rising concern about their own mortality in the first few years following the father's death.

Why Be an Involved Father at All?

Well, as we've discussed in previous chapters, being an involved father is good for everyone: your kids, your partner, and even yourself. Here are some of the specific benefits to being actively involved with your teenage child:

BENEFITS FOR YOUR CHILD

- **Less likely to have sex early.** Girls who perceived their biological father as more caring are more likely to postpone their first consensual sexual experience, have fewer male sexual partners before age nineteen, and are less likely to become teen mothers.
- **Increased autonomy and independence.** Since fathers tend to encourage their teens' independence more than mothers, this encourages kids to be more independent.
- **They'll go further in life.** Fathers who praise, compliment, and express pleasure over their children's achievements have children who set their educational goals higher, according to T. E. Smith. In addition, John Snarey found that strong father-child relationships were a big predictor of the child's (boy or girl) later academic and career success.
- **More secure gender identity.** When dads are warm and affectionate, boys grow up with a healthier sense of their own masculinity and girls with a more secure sense of their femininity. This is especially true in cases of divorce: boys who don't have contact with their fathers run the risk of becoming too dependent on their mothers, says researcher Neil Kalter. That can make them grow up doubting their masculinity. The consequences of this self-doubt are often devastating. A large percentage of boys in prison or involved in gang activity, for example, grew up without a father in the home.
- **Better mental and physical health.** The more their dads are positively involved in their lives, the better kids feel about themselves. Teens who have positive relationships with their fathers (whether they live with them or not) are less likely to have emotional or psychological problems, and are less likely to be sick overall.
- **Fewer behavioral problems.** Whether kids live with their father or not, a high level of paternal involvement is associated with fewer adolescent behavioral problems, according to Princeton University researcher Marcia Carlson. In addition, adolescents with less involved fathers (or those living

with no father at all) are nearly 2.5 times more likely to have used illegal drugs or alcohol.

- **Fewer eating disorders.** Girls with involved, supportive dads are less likely to be bulimic or anorexic. Fathers of women and girls who do have eating disorders tend to be a lot more concerned with their daughters' weight and body image than fathers of girls who don't have them.

BENEFITS FOR YOUR PARTNER, YOUR MARRIAGE, AND YOURSELF

- Fathers who have positive relationships with their adolescent children have less stress associated with midlife issues, have fewer marital problems, and are more emotionally expressive, according to researcher T. W. Julian and his colleagues.

Staying Involved during the Teen Years

This is going to be a time of great conflict for your child. Kids in this general age group are yearning for independence while still being controlled by their parents, teachers, and other adults, says Charlene Giannetti and Margaret Sagarese, authors of *The Roller Coaster Years*. They worry about their appearance while nature is wreaking havoc with their bodies; they are on the brink of adulthood, yet have trouble controlling their childlike impulses; they're fascinated by the world and want to explore it; they're learning to formulate their arguments; they're developing their individual skills, and they're putting together their own values and moral framework.

All sorts of things have an influence on your teen's behavior: you, his friends, the media, his teachers, and himself. Unfortunately, you have control over only one: yourself. Fortunately, though, how you treat and raise your child will have an influence over how much credence he gives to the other things in his life. Here's what you need to do to be the most involved parent you can, as well as to reduce the chances that your teen will engage in risky or dangerous behavior:

- **Be there.** As much as you can, as often as you can. Teens want to know that you care about them, and your physical presence is big. Having regular family dinners is a major sign of involvement. Be there when he comes home from school if you can—kids who are left alone after school are more likely to drink or do drugs than kids who have adult supervision. Be there in spirit too. Turn off the TV during dinner; read the paper later.

"They may be your grades, but they're the return on my investment."

- **Hug him often.** He still probably wants that reassurance, even if he's too embarrassed to ask for it.
- **Have high expectations.** High, yet reasonable—grades, music practice, homework. Again, this lets him know that you care, and that you want him to succeed.
- **Monitor your teen.** Do you know how much time he's spending watching television? Or surfing the Internet? What he's doing in school? Do you know what kind of CDs he's buying? This does not mean sneak around and shove your nose into everything; just pay attention.
- **Keep harmful and tempting stuff out of the house—drugs, cigarettes, alcohol.** Model the behavior you expect from them—your drinking, smoking, or doing drugs increases the chance that your children will. Seventy percent of teens say their parents have a lot of influence, compared to 26 percent who say their boyfriend or girlfriend does.
- **Encourage physical activity and good nutrition.** As big as your kids are, wrestling with them will not be as easy as it used to be. Thankfully, your kids

aren't going to be as interested themselves. But that doesn't mean that they shouldn't be active. They need to exercise for at least half an hour a day. Unfortunately, during the teen years exercise time declines while television/video game time increases. That, plus fewer meals, frequent snacking on high-fat snack foods, vitamin and mineral deficiencies, and eating too much pasta and other carbohydrates and not enough vegetables and fruits, explains why the prevalence of obesity has increased about 50 percent over the past two decades or so. Obese kids are more likely to be depressed, lonely, nervous, have low self-esteem, and smoke or drink alcohol. Encourage team sports. And set a good example by being physically active yourself. If they're interested, invite them to join your softball team, swim or run with you, play racquetball together, or even tag along to your yoga class. Another way to keep them (and yourself) interested is to coach a team they're on.

♦ **Read like there's no tomorrow.** Reading is an essential skill, and you should do everything you can to promote it. Encourage him to spend time reading every day, and make sure he sees you with a book in your hand. Take him to book readings at your local bookstore and talk about what you're reading—even if it's a critical discussion of a story from the front page of the newspaper. And encourage him to read on his own. Books expose adolescents to present and future possibilities that we can't give them. They can learn about cultures, find new role models as they move away from us, and start putting together their philosophy on life.

♦ **Support his interest in art and music.** Make sure he has the right equipment (including good-quality instruments) and the right teachers. Take him to concerts and gallery openings, and if he's interested but doesn't want to go with you, get him tickets and send him with a friend. If your teen suddenly rejects the music teacher who has been important for years, don't stop the lessons completely just yet: instead, take a short break and remind your child that all the adults in their lives (including you) have both positive and negative qualities.

♦ **Wake up, for God's sake.** There's a huge disconnect between what most parents think their kids are doing and what the kids are actually doing. For example, 63 percent of parents say their kids never cheat; 80 percent of teens say they have. Here are a few more examples taken from a recent poll of parents and teens conducted by the Partnership for a Drug-Free America:

◇ Ninety-five percent of parents say they talk with their teens about drugs; 77 percent of teens say parents have talked to them.

◇ Forty-three percent of parents believe their teens can find marijuana easily; 58 percent of the teens say it's readily available.

◇ Thirty-three percent of parents say their kids think marijuana is harmful; 18 percent of teens feels that smoking marijuana is risky.

◇ Twenty-one percent of parents think their teen has experimented with marijuana, and 45 percent think their child has a friend who smokes it; 44 percent of teens say they've tried pot, and 71 percent have a friend who uses it.

• **Encourage him to think creatively, especially with other people.** When dealing with any kind of problem, focus on these four steps: identify the problem, brainstorm about all the possible solutions—even the ones that sound silly—identify the best and the worst options, and implement the best one.

• **Capitate him.** No, not *decapitate*, although that will be tempting at times. John Whitcomb, author of *Capitate Your Kids,* suggests sitting down with your teen to chart out how much you expect to spend on clothes and so on over the next year. Then, give him one-twelfth of that amount every month and let him buy his own outfits. (If you're feeling particularly adventurous, give him three or six months' worth at a time.) The big catch is that he's on his own. If he blows the whole thing on a Gucci gym bag, he may end up wearing the same tattered jeans for the next six months. I've tried this with my kids, and it works incredibly well. It teaches them about money, gives them a lot of control, and reduces the amount of fights we have over who's paying for what or whether a particular item is really needed at all. This is also a good time to get your teen set up with a checking/ATM account and to encourage him to start socking away some of his allowance or lawn-mowing money for a car.

• **Give him more responsibility and encourage independence.** This can mean everything from letting your teen baby-sit for younger siblings or neighborhood kids, to letting him drive your car, to helping him investigate and plan overseas trips. Let him make his own decisions (within reason) and don't bail him out unless you really need to. Teens, like the rest of us, learn a lot from making mistakes.

• **Have clear, reasonable expectations and limits.** Certain things, such as cleaning up his bedroom, time spent with friends, television watching, curfew, and so on, may be negotiable. Other things, such as drugs, alcohol, R-rated movies, homework, or risky or self-destructive behavior, may not be. If you don't set limits, your child will go to his friends for support. The

Staying Involved for Long-Distance Dads

Some wise person once said that you can measure distance in miles or in tears. And when it comes to being a long-distance dad, truer words were never spoken. You might, for example, be one of the nearly 40 percent of single fathers who, according to the U.S. Census Bureau, have no court-ordered access to their kids at all. Or you might have a court order but still not be able to see your children because your ex kidnapped them or is interfering with your access in some other way. Or you might have joint custody, and things might be fine between you and your ex, but your child lives so far away that you're only able to see her for a few weeks in the summer and an occasional school holiday during the year.

Wherever you live, whether it's an entire continent away from your child or only a block, not being able to see him is going to be hard for both of you and will have an impact on your relationship. But don't confuse physical distance with emotional distance. Too many long-distance fathers think that since they can't see their children, the kids don't love them or need them anymore, or that they can't still play an important role in their lives or have any kind of impact on the kind of people they grow up to be, and they let communication fade or even die out. But nothing could be further from the truth: your kids will always love and need you— no matter how far away you are. It's also very important for them to know the stories and legends that make up the history of your side of their gene pool, and that's something they can't get anywhere else.

Maintaining an emotional bond between you and your children won't be easy.

problem with that is that in most cases the friends don't know any more than your child does. But because teens share a certain flock mentality with sheep, he's likely to go along with what "everyone else" seems to be doing. Get him involved in coming up with the rules and setting the consequences. You enforce them.

- ◆ **Choose your battles.** Some things just aren't worth arguing about, so don't be afraid to compromise. Who cares what your teen wears, just as long as it doesn't smell? And if he doesn't want to do his homework, great—just as long as he knows that he's responsible for maintaining his grades.
- ◆ **Support his friendships (unless he's hanging out with a truly bad crowd), and his interest in popular culture.** Kids this age are consumed with the notion of belonging and being accepted by their peers, and sometimes see-

But it's nothing you can't do, and it's everything you must. Here are a few things you need to do.

- **If your child can't come to you, go to him.** Fly or drive to his mother's house, check into a hotel, and spend a weekend doing things with your child there. If you and your ex are getting along, and you live within driving range of each other (and that could be more than a thousand miles), you might be able to convince him to meet somewhere in the middle. Denny's restaurants all over the country are being used for exactly this purpose. You might even be able to check into a nearby hotel and spend a weekend with your child. It's a lot of driving, but I've met several single fathers who drive five or six hours every weekend just to see their kids.

- **Stay up-to-date on your kids' lives.** If your ex won't help you, write your child's teacher and school principal. Ask him to send you copies of report cards, notices of school events, vacation schedules, and so on. You probably won't be able to attend any of these events, but at least you'll know what your kids are up to. Be aware, though, that teachers and principals are under no real obligation to comply with your request if you don't have at least some kind of joint legal custody. So if you do, be sure to enclose a copy of your custody order. If you don't, be sure to ask in the nicest, least threatening way possible.

- **Call and write as often as you can.** Expect that you won't be in contract with your child quite as often as you used to be, but don't let yourself—or your child—drift away.

ing the right movies, going to the right concerts, wearing the right clothes, and even an occasional ear piercing is what it takes to do that. Get to know his friends. We hear so much about the evils of peer pressure, but peers can be good too. One national survey found that kids think the following people understand them best: 42 percent friend, 28 percent parent. Keep up to date on what's cool, but don't get too involved: the last thing your child wants is to have a dad who acts like a teenager.

- **Encourage community involvement.** Volunteering at a recycling center and serving meals at a homeless shelter on Thanksgiving are important ways of reinforcing a sense that he's a citizen of a larger world. It's crucial that you set a good example by doing some of the same activities. I still remember as a ten-year-old sitting down with my father and going through the dozens of solicitations he received from charitable groups and watching him write check after check to ones we both decided were most worthy.

- **Respect his feelings.** A few years ago, when your kids were younger, they probably thought you were the coolest thing going. But now you're more of an embarrassment. If your son (or daughter) has four or five friends over to watch a video, don't even think about trying to hang out with them. If you're driving the carpool, and he wants you to pick him up or drop him off around the corner, do it (as long as it's safe). You might also want to cut back on hugging him in public. And don't get your feelings hurt if he stops wanting to go the movies with you. No self-respecting teen wants to risk being seen with his father.

- **Find some common interests—hiking, biking, board games, art, movies, music, sports, camping, and going to museums, for a start.** And take an interest in his activities, but don't fake it. Try arranging a date with him. Try to set aside one evening every week to spend time alone with each of your kids—especially the teens.

- **Don't take things too personally.** Your feelings are going to get hurt during this time. You'll be challenged, told that you're hated, and called an idiot. Fortunately, you aren't alone in trying to cope with a rude, cantankerous teen, writes Susan Kuczmarski. Getting together with other parents of teens may help. Eventually your child will come around. As Mark Twain put it, "When I was 14, I couldn't believe how ignorant my father was. By the time I turned 21, I was astounded at how much the old man had learned in just seven years."

- **Know when to listen and when to talk.** "If you want to discover who your teen really is, observe, listen, and don't ask questions," says Kuczmarski. Try not to preach or lecture or talk about when you were a kid and how perfect the world was then. You're a mentor now, so keep your unsolicited advice to a minimum. Your teen may get furious at you for a perfectly well-intentioned offer of help—not because he doesn't need the help, but because he doesn't want it rubbed in his face that he can't do without it. Exceptions to the advice rule are for certain tough topics like drugs, sex, and other nonnegotiable health and safety issues. And let him know he can always talk to you, and that you'll listen in a nonjudgmental way.

- **Keep in touch with your child's teachers, coaches, counselors, and others.** Chances are your child will hear that you've been snooping around, but deep inside he'll appreciate your concern.

The Middle-Aged Father

6

LETTING GO OF AND RECONNECTING WITH YOUR ADULT CHILD

Just because the kids have moved out doesn't mean that you're not a parent anymore or that you're not still evolving both as a father and as a man. In a sense you're entering a whole new phase of life. Unless your child has moved back home or hasn't left at all, the years of active parenting are pretty much behind you, the nest is empty, and it's just you and your partner now. This can be a period of great excitement, a second honeymoon of sorts, a peaceful interlude when you and your partner can spend time with each other, get to know each other again, and plan out your future. It can also be a scary period when you'll have to decide what to do with all the free time you have on your hands, an opportunity to wonder who this person is that you're married to and what the two of you have in common now that the children have left home. Most important, though, it's a time when you'll be reevaluating who *you* are. Your relationships with your children have changed, and you're no longer the most important adult in their lives. But you're still a father—it's just a question of figuring out what that means.

What's Going On with Your Emerging Adult?

PHYSICALLY

- When your young adult child was younger, her body developed along fairly predictable lines (see earlier chapters) all the way through adolescence. But by the time she graduates from high school, there are so many variables that it's almost impossible to chart. That said, most females reach their full height at about eighteen, males by twenty-one.
- In her twenties and thirties, your child's body will be in the best condition it ever will be. Barring any illness or chronic ailment, everything's working the way it's supposed to. She'll be stronger, faster, and quicker to heal than at any other time in her life.
- Unfortunately, the concept of mortality hasn't completely sunk in yet, and they don't see the connection between what they do now and the price they'll pay later. Young adults (especially young men) have the highest rates of sleeplessness, smoking, excessive drinking, under- or overeating, excessive dieting (bulimia, anorexia), drug abuse, and risk-taking. Young women should start doing monthly breast exams. Young men should do monthly testicular exams.
- Starting at about thirty, the aging process begins. There are two kinds of aging: *primary* aging is the physiological changes that you can't do anything about. Some of these, such as gray hair and early wrinkles, will be visible. Others won't be, such as a decline in sexual fertility (far more for women than for men), and slight decreases in lung capacity, stamina, and immune system function. The other kind of aging, *secondary*, is the result of environment and lifestyle. These can be changed, and the results can be significant. Exercise, nutrition, quitting smoking, drinking moderately, reducing stress, and practicing safe sex are all effective steps in reversing or preventing secondary aging.
- Your son is at far greater risk of dying prematurely than your daughter. Men are four times more likely than women to die in an accident, five times more likely to commit suicide by twenty-five (four times more by thirty-five), four times more likely to get murdered, twice as likely to develop heart disease by twenty-five (three times more by thirty-five), and seven times more likely to die of AIDS.

MENTALLY

- Fortunately, her brain function is quite safe for another few decades. That's why athletes are usually over the hill at thirty-five, an age when scientists and academics are just coming into their intellectual prime.

- There is, however, a major shift in the way she thinks. The first twenty years or so of a child's life are devoted to acquiring information, according to psychologist Warner Schaie. The next twenty are what Schaie calls the achieving stage, when the young adult starts using all that acquired information to establish herself in the world. To sum it up, she moves from What do I have to know? to What do I do with what I know?
- When she was an adolescent, your child's world was black and white, and things were either right or wrong. Now, though, she's learning that the world is made up of infinite shades of gray and that she has to adapt her thought process to the different—and constantly changing—situations in her life.
- She knows that she's entering a stage where she's responsible for making her own decisions and dealing with the consequences, and she's finding the world to be a complicated and often contradictory place. It's also a precarious one—outside of your protective nest, she could lose her job, her spouse, her place in her community.

EMOTIONALLY/SOCIALLY

- You've probably figured out by now that her relationship with you and your partner is no longer the major one in her life. Hopefully you'll still be friends, but she—and you—will have to learn to deal with each other as peers and adults, rather than as parent and child.
- At this point in her life, your child has a number of major issues to deal with:
  - ◇ Separating from you and the rest of her immediate family
  - ◇ Figuring out where she stands and taking her place in the larger world
  - ◇ Learning marketable skills and getting a job
  - ◇ Defining her life goals and dreams
  - ◇ Creating a new community of friends and coworkers
  - ◇ Finding her life partner and starting (or not starting) a family of her own
- Over the next 10–15 years, your child will gradually become more autonomous and more assertive, and take more charge of achieving her own goals.
- College can give your child a structure for her life and can help her with some of her choices. Kids who don't go to college don't have that structure and may have a harder time figuring out what they want to do with their life and whom they want to do it with.
- Twenty-first century or not, mate selection tends to happen along what's called "the marriage gradient:" men tend to marry women who are younger, shorter, and make less money than they do. Women do exactly the opposite.

◆ At about thirty she may have a mini midlife crisis as she takes stock of where she is in life and makes comparisons between her fantasies and reality. Major changes—especially in career and relationships—are common at this time.

Meanwhile, What's Going On with You?

FIRST OF ALL, YOU'RE NOT THE MAN YOU USED TO BE, PHYSICALLY ANYWAY

In your forties, you may still feel almost the same as you did when you were in your twenties and thirties, but as you cruise into your fifties and sixties, you're going to notice some physical changes. No matter what shape you were in—even if you were a professional athlete—your body is going to show some deterioration. To start with, a lifetime of compression on your spinal disks has probably knocked up to an eighth to a quarter of an inch off your height. Chances are you're ten to twenty pounds heavier than when you were at your trimmest. You may also be the proud owner of a belly that refuses to go away. As if that weren't enough, your immune system is slowing, and you're more susceptible to colds and minor infections. And your vision is changing too: it takes you longer to get used to the dark, and holding small print at arm's length to read may not be enough anymore, so you'll most likely make the transition to bi- (or tri-) focals. Oh, yeah, and you've lost some high frequencies in your hearing and some hair from your scalp.

In your fifties the creases around your eyes will deepen, your body-fat percentage will rise a little, and your sense of taste won't be as sharp as it used to. Your voice may change too, getting a few tones higher as your vocal cords stiffen and vibrate at a higher frequency. And no matter how much you've worked out in your life, by the time you're sixty, you'll have lost about 10 percent of your strength.

Fortunately, as with your child, there's a difference between primary (physiological) and secondary (environmental) aging, and many of the ravages of time can be avoided or minimized by doing regular exercise, eating right, maintaining a strong social network, getting regular physicals, and keeping the stress in your life to a minimum.

The good news is that your brain is fine. You may see a slight decline in your ability to learn new things, but your long-term memory will be sharp for another decade—longer if you get up from the TV and exercise it by doing and learning and reading things that challenge you.

The one thing that won't change much as you age is your basic personality. What psychologists refer to as your "big five" traits (neuroticism, extroversion,

Go to the Doctor—Before It Kills You

When it comes to health care, most men (myself included) are idiots. We don't get regular checkups, don't do much in the way of preventative care, ignore symptoms, and don't get medical attention until the pain is unbearable (or, more likely, until a woman in our life insists). Overall, men are 66 percent less likely to visit a doctor than women, and we make only about one-fourth the number of physician visits for diagnosis, screening, or test results. Twenty-five percent of us say we'd wait as long as possible before seeking help for pain or illness, according to a recent study by the Commonwealth Fund. Nearly 40 percent would hold off for at least a few days, and 17 percent would wait a week. When (if) we finally do seek medical attention, we frequently sabotage our doctors' effectiveness by canceling follow-up appointments and not finishing prescriptions.

The results of all this negligence are startling: for every 100 women who die between forty-five and sixty-four, 170 men die. Men are twice as likely to die from heart or liver disease, 18 percent more likely to die of a stroke, and 45 percent more likely to die of cancer. And the situation is getting worse. In 1940, women outlived men by an average of 4.4 years. Today, that difference is nearly 7 years.

And once you get to the doctor, will he actually save you? Not necessarily. Almost 70 percent of men over forty who visit the doctor aren't even asked whether they have a family history of prostate cancer, despite the fact that prostate cancer kills about as many men every year as breast cancer kills women. In the past year, 40 percent of men over 50—who should be getting a prostate exam every single year—weren't even screened by their doctors, 60 percent weren't screened for colon cancer, and half had neither a physical nor a blood cholesterol test. Going to the doctor also won't do much about the fact that four times as many men commit suicide as women, that the victims of violent crime are 75 percent male, that 98 percent of the people who work in the most dangerous jobs in this country are men, and that 94 percent of people who die in the workplace are men. And going to the doctor won't help men discuss private medical issues such as sexual dysfunction, which is often a symptom of a far more serious physical condition such as clogged arteries, high blood pressure, or diabetes.

Bottom line? Go to the doctor. You should be having a complete physical at least every two years, and should be screened for prostate and colon cancers every year.

openness to experience, agreeableness, and conscientiousness) probably haven't changed much since you were about thirty or so. Actually, your fundamental temperament probably hasn't changed since you were a toddler!

How you cope with aging is largely a function of how you see yourself in general. Most people accept aging as a natural part of life. But some people—especially those whose self-image is tied up in how they look or how they perform physically (models, actors, athletes, for example)—may have a tougher time.

CHANGES IN THE WAY YOU THINK

When our adult children leave home (at least for a while), we end up with a lot more time on our hands to reflect on things, soul-search, review our life, and make adjustments. "We cannot live the afternoon of life according to the programme of life's morning," wrote Carl Jung, one of the fathers of modern psychoanalysis. "For what was great in the morning will be little in the evening, and what in the morning was true will at evening have become a lie."

The idea that life has changed and that we have to change along with it seems simple enough. And most of us do okay with it, gracefully taking on more responsibility in the community, transforming our relationships with our children, adjusting to the process of aging (as it affects us, as well as our elderly parents).

Many midlife fathers find themselves redefining themselves and what it means to be a man, according to Gail Sheehy. When we were younger, it was about "making it" and proving ourselves—attracting women, working hard, playing hard, and so on. At this point in life, says Sheehy, midlife men become less concerned with performance and money, and more concerned with emotional nourishment. We know that our time is limited, and we want to feel—right now—that our lives have had meaning.

We want to reassure ourselves that we've been good fathers, set a good example, prepared our children to survive and thrive in the world, and made a positive impact on them (if you aren't sure of that last one, go back and reread the "benefits" sections in all the previous chapters). Most of all, we want to be remembered for all that. In short, the focus now is on our legacy.

One very positive side effect of all of this is that a lot of men become more tolerant of the strengths and weaknesses of others, according to pioneering psychologist George Vaillant. As we mature, we put ourselves and others in perspective, becoming less defensive about who we are and more willing to accept differences. But those who are rigid, says Vaillant, become increasingly isolated from others. There's also a shift from inward to outward. "Caring behaviors and activities that promote the well-being of others begin to overtake previously more narcissistic pursuits," writes Kyle Pruett. Dads at midlife tend to be better children to their adult parents. They're also better parents to their young adult kids, at least in part because most dads have gotten past their need to be in control, and they take great pleasure in their children's independence. Men who haven't been the fathers they could have (or should have) been often reach out to their adult children, trying to reconnect with them. Sometimes this reaching out is a result of a man's increased ability to identify with his adult child.

You'll also find yourself being more selective about your friends—you'll have fewer friendships, but they'll be more fulfilling. Interestingly, you're more likely to say that your partner is your best friend than she is to say that you're hers.

YOUR EVER-CHANGING RELATIONSHIP WITH YOUR CHILD

One of these days, the moment you've hoped for and dreaded is finally going to come. Your child is going to move out. Some researchers have called this the beginning of the "postparental stage," but I think that's a mistake. Yes, your child is leaving, but that doesn't mean you're going to stop being a parent. In fact, you're just getting started on the longest phase of your fathering experience.

You're going to miss her, and it'll probably take you some time to adjust to your newly empty nest (unless you're in what Craig Roberts and Kaye Zuengler call the "quasi-postparental stage," which is when you've launched some but not all of your children). It'll also take you some time to get used to your new relationship with your child and with your partner (see below for more). If you were a very hands-on, involved dad up till now, it may be hard to adjust to your child being gone. If you weren't around that much, having her leave home might be even harder because it's unlikely that you'll ever be able to develop that close a relationship.

Overall, having your child leave home will be a good thing for you. "With departure of the offspring, fathers worry less about their children's welfare and their own finances," write Roberts and Zuengler. "In most cases, both fathers and mothers recognize the postparental period as a time of relative freedom from worry and responsibilities." (Of course, this could be a case of what you don't know won't worry you. Either way, it's going to be a relief not to have to worry about so much so often.)

As in every other stage of your child's development, her struggle for independence is central. But there's a difference between independence at this stage and independence at any other stage. One of the biggest changes in your relationship with your child is that the relationship itself has gone from involuntary to voluntary; as long as she was living under your roof, your child had to live by your rules, and she had to have contact with you, whether she wanted to or not. Now she doesn't. Interestingly, once your child has successfully proven to herself that she doesn't need you, she may feel that it's safe to turn to you for advice again. Asking when she was a teen would have been an acknowledgment of her dependence on you. Now, though, she can do it on her own terms.

"Until now, our parents have been the producers, directors, and scriptwriters of our lives while we've been the lowly actors, with limited opportunity for improvisation," writes Roger Gould. Before, no matter what happened, she could always come home and be dependent again—eat your food, sleep in your house, drive your car, use your Internet connection, and so on. But now she's on her own. Now she has unlimited opportunity to improvise, and she has to actually take care of herself. Sure, you'll be there to catch her if she really falls, but she knows that it's time to start taking responsibility. And that can be one hell of a scary thought.

Ideally, your relationship should gradually evolve from a hierarchical, parent-child one to something more adult. (But keep in mind that some aspects of the parent-child dynamic won't ever change. No matter how much like peers you treat each other, you'll probably never take your child out for a beer and talk about sex—and you shouldn't. It's also going to be a long time before she gives you as much help as you give her.) Watching your child stretch her wings and take her place in the world can be a wonderfully rewarding thing. Developing a genuine friendship with her and being open to learning things from her can be even more wonderful, says psychologist Mary Lamia.

Not everyone can do this, though. Some midlife dads come down with what researchers Bryan Robinson and Robert Barret call "postparental distress syndrome." Symptoms include an inability to acknowledge that the parent-child relationship has to change and feeling powerless and not needed in the marriage—often because the breadwinner role isn't as important as it used to be (see "Hey, I'm Rich!" page 255). "Husbands experiencing such discomfort typically shift from alarm to anger and entreat their wives and children to come back by promising gifts," write Robinson and Barret. "The successful midlife father accepts his children's separateness and individuality but maintains regular contact with them."

Remember how you used to complain that your teenager never lifted a finger around the house? Well, you may end up eating those words once she's gone and you're left with taking out the garbage, making meals, cleaning the bathrooms, washing dishes, running errands, and all the other chores you never noticed that she was doing.

And finally, get ready for another shocker when your child gets married. All of a sudden you'll find yourself bumped out of closest-relative status, replaced by the child's spouse.

How Your Divorce Impacts Your Children

If you were divorced a while ago, you may only now be seeing the results. Ten years after their parents' divorce, young women who are now nineteen to twenty-three are afraid of intimacy with a male, afraid of betrayal, and/or afraid of losing love, says clinical psychologist Clay Tucker-Ladd. Young men the same age have many of the same issues. Ten years after the divorce, 40 percent of them are drifting in school, and don't have any real sense of self-direction. There's a pretty good chance that you're still suffering too. According to Tucker-Ladd's research, 30 to 50 percent of divorced couples are still bitter after the divorce ten years after the fact.

Your divorce, whether it happened a while ago or right now, is going to have a big impact on your relationships with your adult children. Later in life, divorced fathers get less care from and are less likely to live with an adult child, according to a study conducted by Barbara Steinberg Schone, Ph.D., of the Agency for Health Care Policy and Research, and Liliana Pezzin, Ph.D., of the Johns Hopkins University School of Medicine.

If you thought that getting remarried would make things better, you'd be wrong. Remarried parents get less care from their children—and provide less cash assistance to them—than parents who are either in intact marriages or haven't remarried, according to Schone and Pezzin.

For stepfathers there's an interesting double standard. Although dads' ties with their stepkids are not typically as strong as they are with their biological children, adult children get along better with stepfathers than with stepmothers, according to Harvard sociologist Constance Ahrons. About half of adult children whose mothers had remarried consider their stepfathers parents and were happy about the new marriage. But only about a third of adult kids whose fathers had remarried liked the idea of having a stepmother and considered her a parent.

If you think about this, it actually makes sense. In cases of divorce, more mothers get custody. That means that when Mom remarries, the kids have a chance to establish a good relationship with their new stepfather. Since they don't spend as much time with their biological father, it's natural that the kids wouldn't bond nearly as well with his new wife.

"Hi, Dad. Investment banking wasn't that great after all."

I'm Baaaack: When Adult Children Come Back Home

One of the biggest risks to adjusting to a child's leaving is that your young adult might come back. (The title of a book by Stephen Bly, *Just Because They've Left Doesn't Mean They're Gone,* quite well says it all.) All of us have certain preconceived notions about when major life events are supposed to take place, and we have a social clock that rings at the appropriate time. If the clock doesn't go off at the right time, we're likely to feel some stress. Moving out of the house is one of those events, and for most of us, the clock is set for eighteen, which is when the majority of American kids move out.

If a child is going to college at eighteen, we're perfectly content to hit the snooze button and let her hang out at home for a few more years. (You may even be secretly—or not-so-secretly—thrilled to have someone around again who's dependent on you. Or you may be thrilled to have someone around you can be dependent on.) But if she's still home at thirty-five, you're not going to be as happy. If you had plans to retire or to sell your house and spend two years on the road living out of an RV, you may resent her for interfering with your new, more independent lifestyle and for making you be an active parent longer than you wanted to. And you might see her moving back (or never leaving) as a sign of some failure on your—or her—part. In contrast, if the clock goes off too early, say fourteen or fifteen, you might feel that you've done something wrong, that you weren't a caring enough father.

(For fathers of disabled kids, the child's twenty-first birthday can be especially hard, for several reasons. In the abstract, twenty-one is the age at which, according to our social clocks, we instinctively expect our children to be able to take care of themselves on their own pretty well—work, vote, pay taxes. Having a disabled twenty-one-year-old at home brings up issues of disappointment at the child's lack of independence as well as concern about what she's going to do after the parents are no longer able to take care of her. There may be some concrete hardships as well, as many government-provided services terminate at age twenty-one.)

In the United States, almost 60 percent of twenty-two- to twenty-four-year-olds are living at home. For the twenty-five to twenty-nine set, it's about 30 percent, and it's down to one in four thirty- to thirty-four-year-olds. Ninety percent of adult children living at home are single, but that still leaves plenty of married kids coming home to roost with Ma and Pa for a while. The most common reasons are housing costs, debt, unemployment, and divorce. Unfortunately, we're a downwardly mobile society. It used to be that children almost always had a better life than their parents. But with housing costs rising a lot faster than salaries, many young adults feel that there's no way they'll ever get ahead. In addition, young adults are waiting longer before getting married. Between 1970 and 2000 the average age at first marriage for women increased from 20.8 to 25.1; for men, it went from 23.2 to 26.8 years.

About twice as many young men as women live at home. Why? Well, first of all, because women get married younger, they tend to leave home sooner. They're also more likely to have a husband or boyfriend to support them (which is much more uncommon for young men), say researchers Paul Glick and Sung-ling Lin. Second, there's an attitude issue. Young men tend to have the idea that parents have an obligation to house their children. They're also less likely to think that children should pay for the privilege, say Constance Shehan and Jeffrey Dwyer. Third, men living at home are more likely to be unemployed than women, although it's not clear whether they're home because they aren't working or they aren't working because they're home and they don't have to.

Interestingly, researchers William Aquilino and Khalil Supple found that most parents whose adult children (ages nineteen to thirty-four) live at home are happy with things the way they are. There were, however, two important factors that caused problems. First, the child's being unemployed or financially dependent on the parent increased the chances of parent-child conflict. Second, having a divorced or separated child—especially one with a baby in tow—move back home reduced the parents' satisfaction with the entire living arrangement.

If your child does move back home (or doesn't leave in the first place), resist the urge to shout, "This is not a hotel!" and set up a lot of ground rules—doing so is the fastest way to create conflict. Adult kids don't want a hotel either. They want a home, independence, and self-respect. If your young adult child had responsibilities as a teen, and she had a respectful relationship with you and your wife, it's pretty safe to assume that nothing will change. She knows that coming home is a temporary solution—something to help her over the hump—and she's looking forward to getting out there on her own.

In general, adult children don't feel very good about living at home and being dependent on their parents again. They worry that they'll be stuck there forever, and some respond to their own fears by behaving irresponsibly. Laying down the law and treating your child like a, well, child, will be counterproductive. If she's not being responsible, sit her down and start a conversation with, "It must be hard for you to be living at home. How can we make things easier for all of us?" That's the time to gently raise issues such as how long she'll be staying, whether she'll be paying rent or contributing financially, whether she'll have any responsibilities or chores to do, and if it's okay to borrow the car. It may also be a time to go over your domestic policies, which will probably be pretty similar to the ones you had when your child was living at home the first time around. Do you have a curfew? What's your philosophy on bringing lovers home (of course she's not a virgin, but, hey, it's your house, so you make the rules)? Do you want her to call home if she's going to be late (if only to keep you from worrying)? How about smoking or doing drugs (Is it okay at home? Okay out of the home? Neither?)? If necessary, establish some milestones. If she's unemployed, you might expect her to have a certain number of interviews or send out a certain number of résumés per week. If she's at home because of a drug or alcohol problem, you might set a timetable for finishing a rehab program.

Whatever you do, make sure that you establish some boundaries and agree to respect each other's privacy. That means that you don't pry into her personal life, and she stays off your favorite chair. Don't expect her to be interested in par-

"Your friend is more than welcome, dear, but we just want you to know that your father and I didn't do anything funny till after we were married."

ticipating in all your activities, and don't expect to be invited to participate in hers. And if your child moves home with her family, get clear up front how often you'll be available for baby-sitting duty. Don't let yourself get treated as a live-in nanny in your own home.

The purpose of all this is to help your child become more independent. It's also to keep you from building up a huge amount of resentment at being taken advantage of. You need to strike a good balance between allowing your adult child the freedom she needs, asking her to take on a reasonable amount of adult responsibility, and your own sanity. Remember, though, that the more rules you have, the greater the potential for conflict. So try to keep them to a minimum and bring them up only if you really need to.

When Your Child Refuses to Grow Up

Despite all your attempts to help your child achieve the independence she needs to make it in the world, some kids just don't want to leave home. She may be afraid of becoming independent and having to take responsibility for her own life; she may be afraid of failing; she might be lazy; she might need more love and attention; she might not want you to stop being the parent, because if you do, then she has to stop being the child; or she may be angry and trying to punish you by forcing you to care for her.

This kind of adult clinginess can play out in a number of ways. Dropping by to do laundry and raid the refrigerator a few times a week, or relying on you to handle her finances, pay her bills, and make big decisions for her, seem fairly mild. Sometimes, though, there's a self-destructive element, such as dropping out of school, mismanaging her budget, getting fired from her job, developing a drug or alcohol problem, or anything else that might give her an excuse to move back home, or never leave in the first place.

It's essential that you nip this kind of thing in the bud before you get completely steamrollered. Allowing your child to stay a kid forever will feed her lack of confidence and make it even harder for her to grow up. At the same time, having an eternal adolescent around the house can be tremendously stressful for you. You may blame yourself or your partner for having done something wrong, or you might feel angry and resentful that your child has created a financial crisis for you, or that she's keeping you from doing the things you want to do with *your* life.

The solution? It's not easy, but you need to show her the door. Don't change the locks right away, but gradually start helping her build essential survival skills. See "I'm Baaaack: When Adult Children Come Back Home," above, for some suggestions on establishing ground rules and limits. Be prepared: while some kids will, deep down, appreciate being helped to achieve independence, others won't. You may find yourself facing a furious young adult who feels that you "owe her" and that she's entitled to freeload for an unlimited time, and she may berate you or try to make you feel guilty or inadequate as a parent. Stand your ground. You don't have to take that kind of crap from anyone.

When Your Child Needs Help

In the chart at the beginning of this chapter, we mentioned some of the major issues that young adult child are dealing with in their lives:

- Separating from you and the rest of her immediate family
- Figuring out where she stands and taking her place in the larger world
- Learning marketable skills and getting a job
- Defining her life goals and dreams
- Creating a new community of friends and coworkers
- Finding her life partner and starting (or not starting) a family of her own

As a full-fledged adult, you're in a position to help your child with almost all of these things. You've grown up, gotten married (maybe more than once), started a family, had a few jobs, bought a few houses. You've also made all sorts of difficult and important decisions in your life; some have turned out well, others not so well. All in all, you can be an excellent resource for your child, especially in one or more of the following areas:

- **General advice.** Things like finding a house or apartment, getting the best deals on cars or computers, and so on.
- **Education and career.** Choice of major, what classes to take, evaluating job prospects, deciding whether to go to grad- or post graduate school, proofreading and sending out résumés, practicing for job interviews, evaluating job opportunities, using your contacts to grease the wheels.
- **Money.** See below.

But before we go on, here are a few advice- and help-giving guidelines.

- You do not have to fix everyone's problems. It's okay to say, "Gee, that's too bad." Even if you wanted to fix everyone's problems, you couldn't anyway.
- Your child may not want or even need your help or advice. Before you jump in, find out.
- Offer once. Don't be offended if your advice isn't taken. And banish the words "I told you so" from your vocabulary.
- Keep your unsolicited advice to a minimum. If you really think your child needs help, ask. She may not want to call out of fear that you'll think she wants something from you, or she may really need something but be too embarrassed to ask for it. The only exception to this is if she's having a real crisis. See below for more.
- Keep away from manipulative phrases such as, "You're an adult and you're going to do whatever you want, but I think you should . . ." Instead try, "Here's my opinion," and leave it at that.

- Be reasonable. If she doesn't want to change the oil in her car every 3,000 miles, or she doesn't eat as much protein as you think she should, it's none of your business.
- Ask for help or advice if *you* need it. Your doing so might make your child more receptive.

MONEY, MONEY, MONEY

It used to be that becoming financially independent was a sure sign of adulthood. Well, if that's true, there are a lot of thirty- and thirty-five-year-olds running around who aren't adults yet.

The list of things your child might need money for is endless: a car, an engagement ring, a rent deposit, the down payment on a house, school tuition, a once-in-a-lifetime trip, and so on.

If you don't have the money, there's not much you can do besides help your child put together a budget and encourage her to pay off her credit cards and

"Dad, the dean has gone over your financial statement, and he doesn't think you're working up to your full potential."

start socking some money away. But if you do have the money, you've got a lot to think about, starting with the question of whether making the requested financial assistance is going to actually help your child move toward financial independence, or whether it's going to keep her dependent on you.

Because money issues are so sticky, it's probably best to wait for your child to ask for financial help if she needs it. But if she's too embarrassed to say anything, and you see that she really needs help, go ahead and bring it up yourself. Be careful, though. Your child might interpret your offer as a statement that you don't think she can take care of herself. And if you have more than one child, keep the others in the loop. Sometimes the one(s) you're not helping will feel slighted—even if they don't need the help in the first place. So just make sure the rest of the kids know you'll be glad to help them if they ever need it.

And then there's the question of gift vs. loan vs. investment. If it's a gift, make sure your child really wants it and don't use money as either a carrot or a stick. Are you offering to pay for college tuition, but only for a major you want instead of what your child really wants? Are you willing to pick up the tab for the wedding, but only if things get done your way? Are you secretly hoping to get something in return for your gift besides a hug and a thank-you note? If so, stop.

If you're making a loan, do everyone a favor and make it a real loan, complete with a repayment schedule. It's all very tempting to keep everything informal, but a formal schedule does two important things. First, it tells your child that you have confidence that she can do what it takes to repay a loan. And second, it's a good way to build up her money-handling and budgeting skills.

Investments are perhaps the toughest parent-child financial transactions. The critical thing here is to try very hard to treat buying into your child's business venture the way you'd treat any other investment. Okay, cut your child a little slack if you can afford to, but don't go overboard. Start by reading the business plan. If there isn't one, get one. If you don't know how to read a business plan, find someone to help you. Does the idea seem reasonable? What are the tax consequences? Can your child answer your questions to your satisfaction? Determine up front exactly what she wants from you. Are you to be a silent investor, or will you have a say in how the business is run? Get everything in writing, including return and payout time, just so there's no confusion. And make absolutely sure that your child has something at stake—she's lot more likely to take things seriously if she does. Finally, never make an investment if you can't afford to lose the whole thing. If things head south, you may end up resenting or at least not trusting your child. And she's going to feel awfully guilty if you're living out of the back seat of your car.

OFFERING HELP WHEN BAD THINGS HAPPEN TO GOOD KIDS

Despite everything I've said about moderation in offering help, when something goes seriously wrong, you may need to jump in, invited or not. The one problem here is figuring out exactly when that is. Clearly, immediate action is required if there's a sudden health crisis, a death in the family, your child unexpectedly loses her job, or her house is destroyed by a tornado. In these cases, you do everything you can. But what about ongoing problems like depression, drug abuse, a lousy marriage, or chronic money problems? Well, in some cases you act, in others you don't.

If your child and her spouse are fighting all the time, for example, your job is to stay on the sidelines without taking sides. But if your daughter or son is getting beaten up by a spouse, you have to get her or him out right away. If your child drinks more than you think she should, there's not much you can say or do. But if she starts putting herself or others in danger, you've got to help. In any true crisis situation, start by talking the situation over with your child. If you can't resolve things that way, be prepared to call in some professionals—lawyers, doctors, psychiatrists, clergy, someone to liberate her from a cult, or whatever.

Perhaps the hardest thing for dads about dealing with their adult child's serious problems is how helpless it makes them feel. If your child declares bankruptcy, goes to jail, gets a divorce, or anything like that, the temptation to blame yourself is almost overwhelming, as is the temptation to look at the child's bad behavior as a reflection on you. Actually, it's hard not to look at *any* of the child's behavior as a reflection of you. Your successful plastic surgeon child might decide one day to chuck everything and sell scented candles at a flea market, or she might be gay or living a lifestyle you don't approve of. But don't give in to either temptation. Your child is a grown-up and responsible for herself. Torturing yourself with a bunch of "If onlys" and "I really should haves" won't do either of you any good. Her success and her failures are her own, and she has to learn how to deal with both.

THE MATING GAME

By the time your child is old enough to move out of the house, she's (hopefully) had a few romantic relationships—some serious, others less so. One of these days, though, she's probably going to find herself a life partner and settle down. Whom your child ultimately gets involved with is really none of your business. But, for better or worse, you actually play a major role in the decision.

There's an old Russian proverb, "Love is cruel; you could fall in love with a goat," which basically means that there's no accounting for chemistry. And there's

*"Everything I have, son, I have because your grandfather
left it to me. I see now that that was a bad thing."*

A Family Affair

About two-thirds of all the companies in this country are family businesses. If one
of them is yours, you could find yourself in the position of having your child join—
or even replace—you. Bringing a child into the family business can be a wonderful
thing, making the family closer than ever. It could also be a disaster, destroying
both the business and the family.

One of the first things you need to consider is whether the business can support another person at all. If it can't, does bringing your child in mean you have to
retire? Regardless of the size of the business, it's essential that everyone involved
agrees on what's expected. Are you planning to stay on, and if so, in what capacity? Will your child start in the mailroom and work her way up, or will she start at
the top or somewhere in the middle? Will she need any specialized education
or training?

(continued on following page)

(continued from previous page)

A business should be run like a business, not like a family. That doesn't mean you manage the company like a tyrant, ignoring everyone else's input. But at some point decisions have to be made, and you (if you're running the show) have to make them, which means everyone—including your child—has to respect your authority. The fact that your child may be sporting a brand-new MBA and has some great ideas about how to run things doesn't necessarily offset your twenty years of real-world experience.

Keep in mind that having your child join the firm will probably have an impact on any employees you might have. Adding another family member, particularly one who comes in at the top of the organizational chart, adds a layer of bureaucracy that could bog down decision making and the flow of information. In addition, your child is going to have to earn their respect—some long-term employees may resent taking orders from some young whippersnapper. So before you hand over the keys and give your child the corner office, make sure she's got the practical and interpersonal skills to do the job.

And finally, spend some time thinking about how you're going to resolve two common conflicts. First, two siblings may fight over the same position, or none of your children may want to go into the business at all. Only between a third and half of family businesses survive into the next generation. Some go under because of financial pressures, some because the owner's kids have no interest in taking over, and some because the family members can't resolve their squabbles. The second common conflict is between you and a child or children who are pressuring you to retire sooner than you want to. You may resent their lack of confidence in your ability to take care of yourself and run the business, or (what you might perceive to be) an attitude of caring more about your money than about you.

very little you can do to overcome thousands of years of genetic programming: no matter how enlightened we like to think we are, men tend to look for physical attractiveness, intelligence, and loyalty in a mate. Women aren't quite so picky about looks, but they tend to give a lot of weight to a prospective partner's financial status, ability to provide her with status, intelligence, and height (80 percent of women claim they prefer a man six feet or taller.) Unfortunately, love, money, looks, and the relationships they spawn don't always last as long as we'd like.

If your child actually asks you for advice, great. But one big warning: Be absolutely sure that when you're talking to her you keep *her* happiness in mind,

*"Well, young fellow, my daughter tells me you're
a survivor. I'm not sure if I like that."*

not yours. And after you've said your piece—once—stop. If she doesn't ask for
your advice, you still may be able to slip a little bit of logic into the whole mate-
selection process by subtly suggesting that she consider the points below, which
may help avoid some problems later.

- **Philosophical similarities.** How do your child and prospective mate feel
  about things like abortion, the death penalty, and other social and political
  issues?
- **Money, lifestyle, leisure activities.** Someone who spends money lavishly
  and loves to go on extended Caribbean cruises may butt heads with someone who likes a strict budget and enjoys camping in snow caves.
- **Other similarities.** Humans may be a lot more evolved than sheep, but we
  still have a tendency to stick with the flock. That means that we're generally
  happier with people from our own group, whatever that means—religious,
  economic, social, educational, employment, racial, ethnic, or anything else.
- **Balance of power at home.** Do they have the same attitudes about gender
  role expectation, children, and division of labor?

- **Relationship with extended families.** A little tension is normal between prospective spouses and their future in-laws, particularly if they haven't spent a lot of time together. But major conflicts—hate, lack of respect, threats of being disowned, and so on can weaken a young couple's marriage even before it starts.
- **Premarital counseling.** More and more clergy are meeting with prospective couples to discuss the issues raised above and many, many more. This helps couples get to know each other better and gets potential problems out into the open before it's too late. A startling number of couples avoid bringing up sensitive issues because they're afraid of starting a fight. Unfortunately, that's only a short-term solution. In a few years the problem will come up anyway, and the resulting fight will be even bigger. Churches and synagogues report that couples who marry after going through this kind of premarital counseling have a far lower divorce rate.
- **Slow down.** People who get married very young (say under twenty) don't stay married as long as those who are a little older.
- **Don't live together first.** Sure, it's tempting to give the relationship a test before making it "official," and it sounds like living together would give both people a chance to see whether they're really compatible. But in reality, couples who've lived together before getting married have a higher divorce rate than those who don't.
- **Keep using birth control.** It's just good sense to make sure the relationship is solid before complicating things with a baby.

Again, it's important to make sure that you're putting your child's needs before your own. That can be pretty tough. When your child gets married, your role in her life will change. Sure, you'll still be a father, but in most cases you'll no longer need to be the provider and protector, roles that have probably figured prominently in determining how you see yourself. Besides that, your new in-law has become your child's next of kin, legally as well as practically.

This impending role change can be especially tough if you have a daughter, according to Jungian analyst Maureen Murdock. That she's not "Daddy's little girl" anymore can make you feel older, and you may actually feel threatened by the man you feel has replaced you in your daughter's heart. Some fathers actually consider a daughter's decision to get married as a kind of betrayal, says Murdock. This reminds me of a female friend who once told me that when she was eighteen, her extremely rich father gave her a huge diamond ring, along with the admonition, "Never marry a man who can't do better than this."

Hey, I'm Rich!

Okay, "rich" might be an exaggeration, but there's a pretty good chance that you'll see a bump in your disposable income once your young adult child finishes college. No more adolescent expenditures, no more private-school tuition, no more extra auto and health insurance to pay for. At the same time, your wife may choose this time to go back to work, which will bring in even more money. All this might allow you to cut back your own work schedule, which would free up some time for you to develop some of those other interests that have been simmering on the back burner for a while.

That's the way it should be—in a perfect world. But in the world as we know it, things might turn out differently. Your child might move back—or never move out at all. And while it would be great if she'd kick in a little financially, she probably won't. Even if she does move out, you'll probably be picking up some of her expenses for a while.

It's very important at this point to start building some financial boundaries between you and your child. I'm not saying that you should cut her off completely. But I *am* saying that you should help her take charge of her own expenses (actually, "charge" is not a good word here—putting everything on a credit card is a horrible solution—but you know what I mean). Encourage her to get a job and to take out some student loans. Help her set up a budget if you both think it's necessary. If she's making good money, it's not unreasonable to ask her to pay some rent. If she's not making much money, she should still pick up some groceries once in a while. Above all, don't offer her money if she really doesn't need it. It may be easier to come to you for loans (which may or may not ever get repaid), but if that happens too often, she'll never develop the confidence she needs to keep her head above water. (See "I'm Baaaack: When Adult Children Come Back Home," pages 242–45.)

Of course, all this can change if you happen to retire. As we've discussed earlier, work plays a central role in most men's lives, giving us an identity. It also gives our lives a structure around which we build (and schedule) everything else. Losing that identity and that structure can be a big shock. The change in your income (on average, income drops 50 percent upon retirement) will probably require a change in lifestyle—perhaps less travel, less eating out, fewer movies. And if you don't take quick steps to fill up your free time with something productive—volunteering, spending time with your grandchildren, teaching, mentoring—you could end up feeling depressed and useless.

In a perfect world, you'd love your new daughter- or son-in-law as your own, and in most cases parent/in-law relationships are pretty civil. But what if you just can't stand the person your child is with? Well, the first step is to figure out why. Are you thinking of your child's happiness or of your own? You might resent your child's partner for taking her away from you. You might, as mentioned above, see the marriage as an act of disloyalty or betrayal. You might hate your new in-law's culture, religion, race, educational background, social status, job, or family. Or you might be embarrassed about what your friends will think of your child's choice. And then there's the possibility that your child really and truly picked a jerk. Regardless of your reason for not liking your child's partner, keep your mouth shut. Your job is to remember that your child's new relationship is the primary one in her life and support it. In Zen Buddhist terms, it goes like this: the partner you don't like but your child loves is better than the partner you love but your child doesn't like.

There is, of course, one exception to all of this: if your child's partner is in an abusive or dangerous relationship. In this kind of situation you absolutely must share your worries and fears with your child and offer to help. If she refuses your help, and you're genuinely worried about her health or safety, it's your obligation to step in any way you can. If that means calling the police, do it. If it means helping your child pack her bags and sneak off in the middle of the night, do it.

OTHER RELATIONSHIPS

Your relationship with your child isn't the only one that changes at about the same time as your child moves out of the home. Your relationships with your partner and your parents will also evolve. Let's take a look at each of these separately.

- **You and your partner.** As part of your overall life assessment, you're going to spend a lot of time reassessing your relationship with your partner. And it won't take you long to figure out that having said good-bye to your child (for a while, at least) will change that relationship in a big way.

    You're likely to discover that a lot of your relationship with your spouse was dependent on your child—what she did, where she went, who her friends were, her health, her grades, her accomplishments, her feelings, and so on. And so many of your joint activities and conversations and plans and dreams revolved around your child. If that's all there was to your marriage, your home may truly become an empty nest—"empty of interesting activity and interaction," as Craig Roberts and Kaye Zuengler put it.

    Most couples make it through this jarring transition just fine. In fact, if you were to look at a graph of the average couple's marital satisfaction over time, you'd see a big U. Satisfaction starts dropping not long after marriage and bottoms out after the kids are born. Once the kids leave home, though, it starts creeping back up.

You're going to have to make a special effort to work on your empty-nest marriage, concentrating on things like plans for retirement, travel, living arrangements, and even your sex life. The more satisfied you are with your marriage, the more satisfied you'll be with other areas of your life. (Also, the more satisfied you are with the other areas of your life, the more satisfied you'll be with your marriage.). Fine-tuning your relationship is good for your adult kids, too. Dissatisfied parents tend to spend less time with their children, something that the kids themselves find very distressing, according to researchers Elizabeth Fishman and Steven Meyers.

About 11 percent of all divorces end marriages that have lasted twenty years or longer. Just as with young children, the divorce of parents of adults lowers the quality of the parent-child relationship and reduces the contact parents and adult children have with each other. Divorce is especially damaging to father-child relationships. Dads who get divorced later in life are less likely to rely on their adult children for support, according to researchers Teresa Cooney and Peter Uhlenberg.

• **You and your aging parents.** More than three-fourths of older adults who have adult children live within an hour of at least one of them. Half live within ten minutes. And that's just the way they want it—over 90 percent of older adults don't want to live with their kids, and most are pretty content with the amount of contact they have together.

We talked a little in the previous chapter about the sandwich generation—the group of people who are trying to balance caring for an aging parent with being an active parent. As your own children leave home, this will be less of an issue. However, taking care of an aging parent will still compete with your job, and could compete with your grandparenting time as well. Generally speaking, if your mother and father can't take care of each of other, the next most likely person to do the hands-on caregiving is your sister (if you have one). As you get older, though, this gender gap decreases.

A few things to watch out for:

◇ **Don't force your help on your aging parents.** Being able to do things for themselves will make them feel more competent, which in turn will make them feel happier and make life more enjoyable. And let them help you out too. Elderly parents accept help more readily when they can contribute something in return, writes Anne-Marie Ambert. Overall, the more help aging parents get, the more depressed they tend to be.

257

On Death and Anniversaries

The death of a father when the son is over fifty-five is considered the most "normal." Midlife men, according to Neil Chethik, are the least likely to cry after their loss, and only 17 percent said that the father's death affected them more than any previous death. (Contrast with 58 percent of men thirty-three to fifty-five, and 80 percent of sons younger than thirty-three, who said it had.) In most cases, says Chethik, the pain of the loss is offset by the recognition that Father has lived a long-enough life. Few midlife men felt cheated by the loss of their father or more concerned with their own mortality.

But the grieving process is often a long and complicated one. One fascinating thing about how people deal with the death of a parent is what psychotherapist Martha Gabriel calls the "anniversary reaction." Some surviving adult children get sick or horribly depressed around the anniversary of the parent's birth or death or illness. And in some cases they worry that they will die at the same age and sometimes even of the same cause as the parent. Besides bringing up feelings of grief and sadness, the anniversary reaction can sometimes trigger a bout of self-destructive behavior such as drug or alcohol abuse. Sometimes it goes further than that. Winston Churchill died on the same date and at the same age his father did. And Elvis, who was extremely close to his mother, died at the same age and in the same month as his mother did.

The anniversary doesn't always have to be the death of a parent or relative. Timothy J. McVeigh blew up the Murrah Federal Building in Oklahoma City on April 19, 1995—the date the Revolutionary War started, as well as the date of the FBI's raid on the Branch Davidians in Waco, Texas. And Janis Joplin committed suicide on the anniversary of the death of Bessie Smith, her idol.

◇ **If you're caring for a disabled or chronically ill parent, try not to do it alone.** Burnout is a major problem for caregivers, but it can be reduced by having a strong social support network and getting adequate breaks. This is especially true if your parent has Alzheimer's or another type of dementia. According to Ambert, adult children who care for elderly parents are more stressed when the parent suffers from cognitive problems than from physical ones. Having a parent with Alzheimer's is like losing the parent before he or she actually dies.

♦ **Congratulations, you're a grandfather!** Given that about 90 percent of adults become parents, there's a pretty good chance that you're going to be a

"All right, now. I want you and Grandpa to run along and interact."

grandfather one of these days. You can laser away wrinkles and tuck your tummy and make yourself look twenty-five again, but no matter what you do, there's still one thing that's going to remind you—and everyone else— that you're getting older: it's that cute little kid following you around in the supermarket shouting, "Hey, Grandpa, buy me some ice cream!"

Becoming a grandfather is something you have absolutely no control over. Your kids make the decision, and you deal with it. It seems like the first sign of the coming decrease in control that accompanies getting older. At the same time, your new grandchild is a living, breathing opportunity for you to be a parent again, an opportunity to do all the things that you didn't or couldn't do with your own kids. It's also a chance to have all the fun of fatherhood without any of the responsibilities. (We'll talk a lot more about grandfatherhood in the next chapter.)

Be prepared, though: your child may resent the easy, casual, loving relationship that you have with your grandchild. I remember watching my father with my daughters—taking them to museums, reading stories, telling jokes, playing games, taking them on out-of-town trips—and wondering where all of that was when I was a kid. On the other hand, your grandchild may provide you with the perfect excuse to develop and deepen your relationship with his parents. Seeing you with your grandchild might help your child remember that you were, in fact, a warm, loving, caring dad. (We'll talk a lot about the father-son-grandchild dynamics in the next chapter.)

Whether you're hot to be a grandparent or not, there's no doubt that once it happens, your life will change in some pretty significant ways. Here are some things you can do to make the transition a little easier:

- **Practice saying no.** If your children are counting on you to help out with the baby, you may have to make some significant changes in your schedule—and find yourself with a lot less free time. So be sure to leave yourself enough time for your own interests.

- **Don't compete.** Too many grandfathers try to outdo their sons and sons-in-law. It's less about looks, which might be the source of competition between your wife and your daughter or daughter-in-law (gray hair and crow's feet can be distinguished on a man), and more about stamina and earning power. So don't give in to the urge to work longer hours or run faster or shoot more baskets.

- **Don't fight over turf.** It used to be that grandparents were respected and revered as the senior people in the family. But today, with people living longer, there's a good chance that your own parents are still in the picture. It can be pretty hard to be a respected patriarch when your eighty-year-old father is showing you up every chance he gets. On the other hand, just think about how lucky your kids are to have four generations around at the same time.

- **Embrace the changes.** Let's face it, you're getting old, whether you want to or not. But if you're like most people, you'll agree that being a grandfather just may be the best thing you've ever done.

- **Be aware of the grandfather-child-grandchild dynamics.** Although your relationships with your grandchildren are separate from your relationship with their parents, there can be plenty of connection and overlap. If you're young (say in your late forties or early fifties), your natural concern for your child (which is completely normal at this stage) may make it hard for you to establish a bond with your grandchild. In addition, no matter how old you are, if you have a son, you may feel jealous of his fertility and sexual potency at a time when yours are starting to decline.

MIDLIFE CRISIS

Just the words *midlife crisis* conjure up images of middle-aged men speeding around in brand-new red Corvettes, getting hair implants, and trying to bed younger women they met at the gym. But let's dispense with the cliché now. First of all, most men don't go through a midlife crisis, at least not of the red-sports-car variety. Yes, as we've discussed, they do some soul-searching and may make some major changes. But most men don't feel the need to go to such extremes to recapture their youth. If they did, sports cars would outsell SUVs ten to one.

But sometimes all that soul-searching and introspection can open up some unpleasant emotional doors. When that happens, the more clichéd midlife crisis can become a reality. It's hard to come to terms with your own aging, or with not being as physically or sexually active as you'd hoped, or with not having accomplished what you wanted to in life. It's hard to admit to yourself that your children may have disappointed you. And it's hard (and scary) to hear about other men your age who dropped dead.

And then there's what's going on with your wife. In a lot of more traditional homes—where Dad is the breadwinner and Mom is at home with the kids—mothers often return to the workforce when their kids move out of the house. On the one hand this can be great—adding to the family income and taking some of the breadwinner pressure off you. On the other hand, you and your wife are going to be in very different places: she's just starting a new career, while you're winding down. It's easy to slip into feeling depressed. "No one needs me anymore," you might say to yourself. "My kids have moved out, my wife is making plenty of money—who am I, anyway?" Suddenly the idea of dumping everything—job, friends, wife—and starting all over (but twenty years older) somewhere else becomes incredibly attractive.

Of course most men don't leave their wives or even their jobs. They do, however, experience mood disturbances, sexual difficulties, and a lot of physical complaints that are similar to women undergoing menopause, according to Craig Roberts and Kaye Zuengler.

Work itself can sometimes trigger a midlife crisis. Some men, particularly those who started working when they were very young, or those in "helping" professions such as doctors, civil rights lawyers, social workers, psychologists, and so on, simply burn out (although this tends not to happen to people who love their work). Worse still is getting laid off. As we talked about in chapter 5, men's identities are, to a great extent, reflections of our jobs. Losing a job, then, may feel like losing an identity, which can be depressing, particularly if you weren't ready—financially or otherwise—to retire. It's also hard for midlife guys to find jobs out there. But your skills may need updating, and too many employers don't want to hire "older" workers anyway. The fact that age discrimination is illegal doesn't seem to stop a lot of people. Most guys—at this age, anyway—aren't going to be truly fulfilled working behind the counter at McDonald's or being a greeter at Wal-Mart.

Regardless of what causes it, a midlife crisis is usually invigorating and at least temporarily exhilarating. Despite the stereotypes, challenging yourself in midlife doesn't necessarily involve doing anything that's destructive to your marriage, family, or job. Change and even risk-taking behavior can be healthy and fulfilling (at any age) if the choices you make are positive and productive.

Why Be Involved?

Most of the benefits of fathering that your adult child is enjoying now were planted in earlier years. Still, there are some specific benefits to being actively involved with your adult child.

- **Better mental health.** Adult kids who have good relationships with their parents report having better mental health and higher self-esteem.
- **It helps the next generation.** If you've been an active, involved father, your son will want to be one too, and your daughter will want to have one around when she's ready to start her own family. No matter how much we swear we won't, almost all parents eventually find themselves doing some of the things their parents did. In most cases, though, children usually improve on their parents' parenting skills in much the same way that they improve their lives in other ways—educationally, professionally, and so on.
- **Better marriages.** "Teenagers who have grown up feeling close to their fathers in adolescence also go on to have more satisfactory adult marital relationships," according to researchers Eirini Flouri and Ann Buchanan.
- **Better job prospects and chances for success.**

Staying Involved with Your Adult Child

The best way to be involved at this stage is to do it from a short distance. Give her the autonomy she needs to grow and develop on her own, but make sure she knows that the door's always open if she really needs you.

"We're really bonding now, aren't we, Dad?"

* **Don't sell the house just yet.** She may be gone, but she may be back in a year or two. And even if she isn't planning to come back, her new place may not be big enough for all the stuff you're going to want her to get out of your basement and attic.
* **Keep in touch.** If you live nearby, try to get together regularly. If you're farther away, set up regular times to talk or e-mail. Either way, make a serious attempt to create a one-on-one relationship with your child that is separate from the one that you and your wife have with her.
* **Ask for advice.** It may seem like a terrible role reversal, but the truth is that your adult kid knows a lot of stuff that you don't. Listen up, and you'll learn a lot.

263

- **Be a consultant.** If your child gets herself into trouble, whether it's divorce, bankruptcy, losing a job prospect, dropping out of school, or going to jail, it's going to be incredibly tempting to try to take care of the situation. Don't— at least not right away. There's nothing you can do to keep your child from making mistakes, and if you jump in too quickly and keep her from suffering the consequences of her bad decisions, she'll never grow up. (See pages 247–48.)

- **Offer—and let it go at that.** You can't force her to live her life the way you want her to. If she needs your help, give her advice, contacts, or whatever she needs. But don't do it too often—you don't want her to become (or stay) too dependent on you. Actually, a bigger risk is that if you give too much and are too available, your child may feel that you don't have any confidence that she can do things for herself. So ask a lot of questions and encourage her to come to her own conclusions. And whether you agree with the final decision or not, be supportive, not judgmental.

The Grandfather Years

7

BECOMING THE ELDER STATESMAN

Well, it's come to this, the final stage that ends your journey through father-hood, and your transition from man to husband to father to grandfather, maybe even great-grandfather. To a large extent the relationships you have with your children and grandchildren, and what happens during your grandfather (and great-grandfather) years, will be a reflection of everything that's happened during all of the other stages of fatherhood. But the focus will be a little different. Whether you're going to be a good father or not isn't going to be as important as whether you've actually been one. Instead of worrying about things like how your kids are going to turn out and whether they'll be able to take care of themselves, you'll think instead about the more distant future, the one that doesn't include you.

So did you raise decent human beings, people who will do the right thing when they have to? Are you confident that your financial and psychological legacies are safe in the hands of the future generations? Will they remember you after you're gone? If so, you've achieved a certain level of immortality. But what if things—and your children—didn't turn out the way you expected or hoped? Will you be able to accept the choices they made, rejoice at their successes, and not feel responsible for their failures?

The issues of separation and independence and control will be as powerful now as they were when you changed your first diaper. The only difference is that the players have changed. You tried to raise your children to be independent and establish their own identity, but the irony is that now that you're older, you need them more and more, and they need you less and less. And now that they have their own lives, your identity as a parent—which is one of the main ways you've defined yourself for the last forty-five years or so—is dependent on maintaining a connection with them.

When your child was growing up—learning to talk, walk, read, ride a bike, drive a car, be an adult—you frequently battled over who was in control of his life. But now that you're older, the battles are more likely to be over who has control over *your* life. It wasn't all that long ago that he complained that you were treating him like a child, not letting him think for himself. Now you may find yourself saying those same words.

What's Going On with Your Adult Child?

PHYSICALLY

- In one of the strangest human feats of all time, your no-longer-spry midlife child is expanding and contracting at the same time. In his mid- to late thirties, he'll be an eighth inch or so shorter than he was in his twenties. Over the next few decades he'll keep shrinking. And as if to make up for his loss, he's ten to twenty pounds heavier than at his fighting best, and what used to be a charming little belly just isn't going away.
- Other signs of aging include gray hair (assuming there's any left at all), wrinkles, and some hearing loss, particularly at higher frequencies. His voice may gradually be getting higher as his vocal cords lose their elasticity. Oh, and to add insult to aging, he's probably about 10 percent weaker by the time he reaches sixty.
- Now that his immune system isn't working as well as it used to, meaning he's more susceptible to minor infections or colds, his prostate is probably getting bigger (please do encourage him to get regular physicals), testosterone production drops with age, and so does the sperm count. Women, meanwhile, are in menopause.
- The only blessing here is that he may not notice all of this himself because of his worsening vision, which also makes it harder to see in the dark and to perceive depth.

MENTALLY

- Overall, you may have the impression that he's mellowed with age. Hopefully this is true.
- On the other hand, it might just be further decline of his perception, inductive reasoning, and spatial-orientation skills, which started slipping in his late twenties. Thankfully, his facility with numbers and words won't start dropping off until his forties. So if he takes you out for dinner, he'll still be able to figure out the tip without using a calculator. At about sixty, everything pretty much levels off.
- You may notice a slight decline in his ability to process and learn new information, but long-term memory should remain sharp at least through age sixty or sixty-five—longer if he exercises it by reading, doing puzzles, experiencing new experiences, and challenging himself. If you never bought him that set of encyclopedias he wanted as a child, there's still time.
- Now that he's reviewing his life and realizing that time is limited, he may lose some interest in his job but get more interested in his family. (See "What's Going On with You" in chapter 6 for more.)

EMOTIONALLY/SOCIALLY

- Despite all his physical and intellectual changes, his personality is basically the same as it's been since birth.
- Careerwise, he's at the top of his game. People this age—in the middle years—are the ones who run society. People this age are also the ones most likely to experience career burnout or midlife crisis (see "Midlife Crisis," pages 261–62, in chapter 6).
- At some point during his middle years he'll probably become a grandparent himself, which means he'll be going through all the same stuff you did not all that long ago. And that means you get to lord it over him.

What's Going On with You?

Okay, so you're getting older—but at least you're not alone. The percentage of Americans over sixty-five grew from only 6 percent in the 1900s to 17 percent in the 1990s, and some experts estimate that it will reach 25 percent by 2030. On the one hand this could cause some real problems for us and our society. An increasing percentage of older people means fewer younger workers out there to support us as we retire. On the other hand, as the number of older people grows, so does our political and economic clout, some of which we'll need to deal with ever-increasing health-care costs (and the ever-more-callous youth of today).

How You're Aging

Gerontologists (people who study aging) divide old age into two periods. The *young-old* period lasts roughly from sixty to seventy-five or eighty. Then the *old-old* kicks in. On average, the young-old tend to be healthy and active, not all that much different from the way they were in midlife. Most old-old also do pretty well, though some get frail and weak.

The differences between primary aging (inevitable decline) and secondary aging (disease, atrophy, lifestyle) that we talked about in the previous chapter are even more heightened here. Since you were about thirty-five, your body and almost all its organs, functions, and abilities have been losing about 1 to 1.5 percent of their capacity each year. That gradual decline may have been only barely (or not at all) noticeable for the past few decades, but it is now. Although women age more visibly than men, men are typically more susceptible than women to disease, mostly because we don't take care of ourselves, we ignore symptoms, and we refuse to go to the doctor unless we're bleeding to death (see "Go to the Doctor—Before it Kills You," page 237). But it's not too late to break those habits; doing so could even add years to your life.

The following chart will give you a good overview of what the natural aging process looks and feels like. But as you're looking through it, keep in mind these two critical points:

- Few, if any, of the natural changes that go along with aging should prevent you from leading a perfectly normal, fulfilling life.
- At this point in the life span, aging is really much more a function of attitude, abilities, capacity, and interests than of actual chronological age. Sure, there are some genetic factors that keep some older people looking and feeling younger than others the same age. But a lot of it is in your head. "Some people age so gracefully, they have been considered *gerontocrats,*" writes psychiatrist and aging expert Stanley Cath. "Others find the last third of life so painful they may be regarded as *gerontophobes.* Most of us range somewhere in between."

PHYSICALLY

WHAT'S GOING ON

- As your cardiovascular system slows down, your blood flow decreases, and your blood pressure goes up.
- Lung capacity is as much as 50 percent less than it was, which will probably make you a little short of breath.
- Risk of cancer and other diseases increases as your immune system continues to slow down.
- Also, you'll have more digestive and stomach complaints as your gastrointestinal system becomes less efficient.
- At sixty, the typical man is about one-eighth inch shorter than he was at the height of his height, just twenty years before. He's also about 20 percent heavier.
- As if to offset these losses, your nose and your earlobes have probably picked up somewhere from a quarter to a half in length.
- Starting at age fifty, you'll also notice a major decrease in muscle flexibility. (The process actually started when you were ten—really—but the gravity of it doesn't fully hit you until now.) It'll be harder to get dressed and undressed, climb or go downstairs, sit down or get up, turn your head around to look at something behind, and—for the celebrities among us— sign autographs.
- Your sense of balance gradually deteriorates, which means you might start walking like a toddler again, taking shorter steps, not raising your feet as high, and using handrails.
- Falling down, not skydiving, is the biggest cause of injury among the elderly.

WHAT YOU CAN DO ABOUT IT

- Remember! Older adults who have strong social networks and get lots of affection have lower risk of getting cancer and other diseases.
- Keeping independent and maintaining as much control over your life as possible also protect against disease, injury, smoking, alcohol abuse, overeating, and especially depression.
- Eat right.
- Getting plenty of physical activity, especially exercises that increase strength and flexibility, is the best way to reduce the fear of falling and increase the muscle control that will keep you on your feet. A lot of physical problems are the result of not using your muscles.

SENSORY

WHAT'S GOING ON

- You're going to need a lot more light to read than you used to. It also takes longer to adjust when going from light to dark or vice versa, and you're probably a lot more sensitive to glare than you used to be. So no more staring into the sun.
- You'll undoubtedly experience some hearing loss and may find that it's harder to focus on individual sounds. That means it's harder to concentrate on a conversation if there's any other background noise.
- Only about a third of your taste buds still function, and your sense of smell is way off, so eating's not as much fun. Risk of food poisoning goes up a lot here, since you might not be able to taste the difference between something that's fresh and something that's gone bad.

WHAT YOU CAN DO ABOUT IT

- Not much you can do to prevent these gradual, natural changes besides getting hearing aids and new glasses.

COGNITIVE

WHAT'S GOING ON

- Your brain takes a little longer to process information, which means that it takes you longer to respond to almost everything.
- Cognitively, you may experience some memory problems, and losing your car keys will start to scare you and bring up fears of Alzheimer's.
- Reaction time slows down, meaning that the possibility of traffic accidents goes up. Driving at this stage can be dangerous—for you and everyone else on the road.
- You're losing axons, which send information out of your brain cells, but gaining dendrites, which enable the cells to receive information.
- Thankfully, crystallized intelligence (the knowledge you've accumulated over your lifetime) is always increasing.
- Fluid intelligence (your ability to process information and come up with strategies) has been decreasing since your twenties or thirties.

WHAT YOU CAN DO ABOUT IT

- See your doctor. Eighty percent of dementia is caused by disease and isn't reversible. But at least 20 percent may be caused by factors such as depression, alcoholism, injury and drug misuse, all of which are reversible.

- Good health and a good marriage contribute to higher intelligence scores.
- Practice. This can bring back lost skills and abilities.
- Stay sharp. Get plenty of mental exercise—do puzzles, take classes, learn new things.
- Physical exercise reduces the stress that can decrease memory.

REVIEWING YOUR LIFE—DÉJÀ VU ALL OVER AGAIN?

As you move into old age, it's natural to spend some time considering the past, revisiting old memories, and thinking about the events, relationships, and choices that made you who you are. You've done mini versions of this kind of life assessment at various other points in the past. But this time it's a little different. This time you aren't going to be looking back at individual elements or events or decisions. You're now in what psychologist Warner Schaie calls the "reintegrative stage," the time in late adulthood when we sit down with ourselves and do a major personal appraisal—not only of the things we've accomplished in our life but of our life as a whole.

Most of the time it's a positive experience. We can look back contentedly on a life that, overall, was pretty good. Sometimes, though, reviewing a life can bring up guilt, memories that were better off forgotten, and horrible regrets.

Okay, so that takes care of the past. But how we function in the present and the future depends a lot on whether we can adapt to the changes that aging demands of us. According to psychoanalyst Robert Peck, to age successfully, a person must be able to:

- value wisdom over physical power
- socialize instead of sexualize
- be emotionally and mentally flexible rather than rigid and stagnant

Just so you know, most men make these gradual transitions without any problem. Let's take a look at them in a little more detail:

- **Valuing wisdom over physical power.** As your strength, stamina, and good looks fade, you'll probably make up for the loss by getting wiser, and possibly more spiritual. (After all, what's left?) You'll become less interested in the rewards offered by society and more interested in utilizing your own inner resources, says Daniel Levinson. However, if you emphasize physical attributes (what your body can do) over personal qualities, you'll have a harder time coping with aging.
- **Socializing instead of sexualizing.** As you become less sexually active, you'll see people more as individuals than in terms of sex (i.e., women as potential

The Blues

One emotion it's essential you watch out for is depression. Occasional bouts of sadness are perfectly normal. But in the old-old years (over seventy-five) severe depression gets more and more common. And since suicide risk increases with age, major depression at this stage is increasingly dangerous.

Depression sometimes comes on the heels of retirement or the death of a spouse or close friend, and can reappear on or around the anniversary of the deceased person's death or illness. Depression is also often the result of disease or a side effect of medication you're taking for something else, and it arises naturally if you're having problems with your memory, your hearing, or your vision (all of which you may be able to do something to improve). It's especially frustrating not to know what the people around you are doing or saying, which means it becomes easier to assume that they're plotting something against you.

Getting plenty of exercise and eating right can go a long way toward curing the blues or mild depression. If your feelings of sadness have lasted for more than just a few weeks, if you've lost your appetite or are having trouble sleeping, if you're feeling worthless or like a failure as a man or a father, if you're having trouble making decisions or getting motivated to do anything, if you've lost interest in friends or activities you used to enjoy, or if you're been thinking of suicide, get yourself to a physician or mental health professional right now. It is not a sign of weakness, and it could save your life.

sex partners, and men as potential competition). This will help you to form deeper, more fulfilling relationships with people of both genders and enable you to enjoy life more. This can actually be a very nice development.

- **Emotional and mental flexibility over stagnation and rigidity.** Over the course of your life you've formed emotional attachments—with parents, friends, spouse, children, coworkers, and others. But you have to be able to let these attachments go, or at least allow them to change. You also have to be able to form completely new relationships. Many men "express deep regrets over having maintained the primacy of their work or their attachments to sports or to art over human connectedness," writes Stanley Cath. Children leave home; you retire and leave your coworkers or move to a new home; your parents, friends, spouse, or even a child die; and you have to prepare for your own inevitable death. Besides emotions, how flexible are you in other areas? Are you open to new ideas, or are you still doing and thinking about things the way you always have? Most older men are actually quite open to new experiences and ways of looking at things, despite ye olde can't-teach-an-old-dog-new-tricks stereotype.

YOUR RELATIONSHIPS WITH YOUR CHILDREN

Your relationship with your adult child has changed over the years, and now that he's fully grown, it's a lot different than when he was a kid. But chances are that your relationship hasn't changed a whole lot over the past few years. Researchers Gayle Kauffman and Peter Uhlenberg studied elderly parents and their adult children over a four-year period and found that during that time one-fifth of the parent–child relationships got better, and one-fifth got worse. The rest didn't change at all.

But whether your relationship with your child has changed much or not, one dynamic has probably remained constant: the hierarchy of the parent–child connection. Your children may have children (and even grandchildren!) of their own, but you're still the parent, and they're still the kids. You're still trying to help them succeed in life, and you probably don't depend on them much to help you out with domestic chores, which is a good thing because on average (shock of all shocks!), older parents still help their kids more than the kids help them.

The same applies to financial help: at any point in time, only 5 percent of adult children have given money to their parents in the previous five years, says

Well, Dad, I'll tell you: Every time I face a dilemma about parenting, I ask myself, "What would Dad do?"... And then I do the opposite.

SIPRESS

273

Susan Eisenhandler. Over the same period, though, 20 percent of adult children have received money from their parents. (And that doesn't count the free room and board given to adult children who are still living at home.)

The who-cares-for-whom scales will start evening out only when you're in your mid-seventies and your children are in their forties, according to researchers Glenna Spitze and John Logan. But if you're hoping for a major change, don't hold your breath: Spitze and Logan also found that older mothers receive more help than older fathers.

Of course giving or receiving help isn't all there is to parent-child relationships, but it's a metaphor. In Eisenhandler's study, the older adults who had the best relationships with their kids tended to be in the best health and were active and independent. In other words, they didn't need a thing. And the factors that strain parent-adult child relationships the most are the parents' divorce and health problems, both of which necessitate the child paying attention to the parents.

This creates a bit of a loop. Parents like to give (especially to their sons, for some reason) more than they like to receive—partly because it makes them feel independent and useful. And when they're able to give and be independent, they feel better and have the best relationships with their kids. But that doesn't completely explain why adult children don't help their parents out more than they do. Interestingly, a recent poll conducted by the American Association of Retired Persons (AARP) found that 36 percent of elderly parents over sixty-five say they haven't gotten help from their grown children during times of need. Only 16 percent of grown children, however, say they haven't helped a parent when it was needed. The answer that makes the most sense to me is that once it's in place, you just can't shake the old parent-child relationship.

Keeping things friendly between you and your children—and getting help from them—may even be a matter of life and death. A group of researchers found that elderly parents who felt above-average closeness with their grown children were less likely to become depressed or disabled and were 40 percent less likely to die than those with below-average closeness. Actually, keeping things friendly with just about *anyone* is good for you. A different group of researchers found that elderly people who go out to eat, play cards, go to movies, and do other social activities live 2.5 years longer than people the same age who aren't quite the social butterflies.

YOU AND YOUR ADULT DAUGHTER

As we've seen throughout this book, fathers tend to have different relationships with their daughters than with their sons. When Gail Agronick studied adult women's relationships with their fathers, she found that the women felt a little closer to their mothers but were calmer with their fathers. They were also less likely to take on the role of emotional caretaker for their fathers.

Jane Roiter-Eash also studied fathers' relationships with their adult daughters. She found that adult daughters felt that their relationships with their fathers had changed more over the years than the fathers felt they had. Daughters also *wanted* more change in the relationship, including more emotional expressiveness from their fathers. Dads also wanted more involvement with their daughters and thought they *were* actually more available to them than the daughters realized.

This miscommunication is indicative of the problem of defining certain terms—such as *availability* and *intimacy*—too narrowly. In our society we tend to define both these words in a female way, which means that men's availability and intimacy don't count. It would be great if fathers could be more expressive to their daughters. But it would be great if daughters could learn to accept their fathers' love, even if it isn't expressed the way the daughters want it to be.

YOU AND YOUR ADULT SON

Your relationship with your adult son is going to be at least as complicated now as it has been since he was born. Competitiveness and the need for each of you to prove himself still dominate. However, with mortality staring you in the face, there's an inevitable—and painful—shift in the power balance, says Gail Sheehy.

"The father of a midlife son has his own inner battle," writes Sheehy. "He is being required to relinquish his role as the strong, all-knowing one. As the younger man struggles to assume mastery of his own life, the older man is left feeling weak, passive, and even helpless in relation to another man, his own son, his guarantor of immortality."

At the same time, the son may feel a little uncomfortable about becoming more affluent or more successful than his father. "The adult child still feels very loyal to the parent," says psychotherapist Mary Lamia, "but he ends up feeling as though he's abandoning the parent by surpassing them." And as he watches his father decline with age, he has to confront his own mortality, imagining himself right where his father is in a few years.

What makes this even worse is that both father and son need each other's emotional support and each other's approval and confirmation that what they're doing and what they've done with their lives are okay. Unfortunately, neither one usually gets enough of what he so desperately craves.

When You Live with Your Adult Child (or He Lives with You)

Fifteen percent of parents over sixty-five live with one of their adult children. You might think that most of these adult children are living with their parents so they can help them out. But you'd be wrong. The truth is that most adult children who share a residence with their parents do so because they—not their parents—need it. Thirty percent of adults twenty-five to fifty-four who had never married and 13 percent of those who had divorced live in their parents' home, according to Anne-Marie Ambert. And the more children the parents have, the greater the chances that at least one of them will live at home. Younger elders (those under seventy-five) are more likely to live with a son, while older elders (over seventy-five) are more likely to live with a daughter, according to Carl Schmertmann, Monica Boyd, and their colleagues.

What's truly amazing about all of this is that as a rule, the elderly parents get little if any help, financial or around the house, from their adult children. Sons do even less than daughters. Miraculously, despite the one-sided nature of the relationship, the level of conflict between parents and cohabiting adult children actually tends to be pretty low.

Nevertheless, as we discussed on pages 242–45, it's important to try to establish some ground rules when you live with an adult child—particularly if that child arrives with his own children in tow. What kind of role does your child

WHEN THE FATHER BECOMES THE CHILD

For older adults—especially older men—independence is the key to physical and mental health. Walking, for example, is something we've almost always taken for granted. It was one of our first big steps toward independence when were babies, and even as adults we rely on it for the ability to come and go as we please. In a lot of ways, the same can be said about driving. Losing either of those abilities—which can happen gradually as the result of normal aging, or suddenly after a stroke or other illness—can be a terrible blow.

If you're getting lost a lot, driving too slowly, or have been in an accident recently, it's time to consider handing over your car keys. And if you're having trouble with basic tasks, such as walking, getting dressed, eating, paying bills, using the bathroom, and cooking, you're going to need some help.

As a man, you may resent being dependent on others and embarrassed to have them see you that way. For that reason you'll probably put off asking your

"Big date tonight, Dad. Can I borrow the cardigan?"

expect you to have with your grandchildren? Are you going to be an occasional baby-sitter, or is your child expecting you to be a full-time day-care provider while he works or goes back to school or goes out to paint the town red?

children for assistance as long as possible. It's hard enough to get used to being cared for by a wife, but it's a lot worse to be cared for by a child—especially a son. When elderly parents require a lot of help from their children, they tend to be less satisfied with their relationships with those children, according to Anne-Marie Ambert. Part of the reason is that parents understand that their children are helping because the parents need it, not because they (the children) truly want to. Adult children can also be a little overzealous. In a recent study conducted by the AARP, 27 percent of elderly parents said they thought they'd need help from their adult children, but 54 percent of the children expected that their help would be needed. A third of adult children also suspected that their parents really needed help but weren't asking for it. What this all adds up to is that, in their well-meaning attempts to assist, your children may underestimate your abilities and take over too much decision making, leaving you feeling weaker and more useless than before.

At this point in your life you've probably spent a lot of time thinking about getting older, and about how aging will affect your level of independence. So have your adult children. In fact they may actually have thought about it more than you have. Sixty-nine percent of elderly parents think about getting older and how long they'll be able to stay independent, while 75 percent of children think about their parents' aging and possible need for help, according to the AARP.

Most of these families go beyond thinking and actually sit down with each other to talk about aging and independence. (Interestingly, children are a little more likely to talk to their mothers than to their fathers, and parents are a little more likely to talk to their daughters than to their sons.) But a quarter of the children and nearly a third of the parents don't. That's a big mistake; you're getting older whether you think about it or not.

Of course, there's no law that says that you have to turn to your kids for anything, but if you need something, ask for it. Programs like Meals on Wheels (*www.projectmeal.org/*) can help you on the food front if you're having trouble getting out, and there are all sorts of push-button emergency radio-transmitter devices out there that you can use to call the paramedics if you need medical help. In addition, a lot of churches, synagogues, and social groups have volunteers who visit homebound people. If you do ask your children for help, expect to see your daughter (or daughter-in-law) more than your son. Daughters tend to do the bulk of the caregiving, even when it's their husband's parents, perhaps because they're less likely to be working full time. According to Ambert, sons are more likely to assist with transportation and money.

What happens if you're no longer able to take care of yourself on your own? Unfortunately, most families deal with this question only in the midst of a crisis such as a fall or an unexpected illness, before they have a chance to fully investigate their options. Most children feel guilty about putting a parent in an assisted care facility or a nursing home, and most parents find the idea terrifying. Moving in with one of your children, however, may not be geographically or financially practical, and the "we won't put you in a home" promise may be a hard one to keep.

So do yourselves a favor and start talking about all this stuff now. It may be difficult and even uncomfortable to broach the subject, but elderly parents and adult children alike say that these are critical discussions to have. They'll give you both some peace of mind and help you come up with a plan that works for everyone.

How Your Kids' Troubles Affect You

All of us have problems now and then. As parents, our instinctive response to our children's problems is to try to step in and help—even if those children are grown up and have kids of their own. Fortunately, most of the problems our adult children face in their life are fairly minor, and the children can take care of them on their own. But 26 percent of older adults say that at least one of their children is experiencing serious physical or mental health problems or a high level of stress, according to psychologist Anne-Marie Ambert.

As you might guess, our children's problems have an impact on us, and parenting in the later years of life is no exception. The only difference is that we're older now, and we want to be—and should be—focusing more on ourselves. Having to care for our adult children at this point in our lives can be stressful. In fact, parents whose adult children experience serious problems are more depressed than those whose children's problems are less serious, according to Karl Pillemer and Jill Suitor, who did a study of over 1,400 elderly parents (age sixty-five to one hundred).

Unfortunately, many adult children are so fixated on their own problems that they don't see how it's impacting their parents, says Ambert. The result? Even more stress, along with feeling exploited and underappreciated.

Nevertheless, fathers remain involved and interested and helpful in their adult children's lives, even if those children are severely disabled. The old stereotype that fathers of adult children with mental illness are distant, for example, turns out not to be true at all, according to researcher Jan Greenberg. Interestingly, another researcher, Elizabeth Lehr, found that fathers' feelings of closeness with adult retarded children living at home were influenced by two things: the quality of the father's marriage, and the retarded child's behavior.

GRANDFATHERHOOD

More than 90 percent of parents over sixty-five have grandchildren, and about half of those have at least one adult grandchild. What this means is that with life expectancies getting longer all the time, you're going to be a grandfather for a long—maybe a *very* long—time. Most grandfathers love being able to add the title of "grandpa" to their list of identities (father, husband, brother, uncle, worker). Here are some of the reasons why:

- **It's a second chance.** You may not have had the chance, or the opportunity, or the desire to be as good a father as you would have liked, but

*"Do you remember any of those things people
said we'd tell our grandkids someday?"*

grandfatherhood gives you a chance to look back and to try to "do it right" this time. It may also be more fun. "Since they do not have the responsibility for raising the child toward that unconscious goal, their love is not as burdened by doubts and anxieties as it was when their own children were young," writes Therese Benedek. "Relieved of the immediate stresses . . . and the responsibilities of fatherhood, grandparents appear to enjoy their grandchildren more than they enjoyed their own children."

- **It links you to the past and the future.** Your grandchildren are your assurance that your biological line will continue for at least one more generation. At the same time, becoming a grandfather may help you repair, deepen, or reestablish relationships with your children. "When your kids have kids of their own, you suddenly have an area of shared experience," my dad told me recently. "And that leads to tolerance and forgiveness on both sides."
- **It makes you feel important.** Your children are grown, everything seems to be taking care of itself okay, and it's been a long time since anyone really

needed you. But having a grandchild gives you the chance to teach, give advice, tell stories, be a financial and emotional resource, and contribute to their lives. As a result, you'll feel valuable again. It's that "second lease on life" you always hear people talk about.

- **It may make you lighten up a little.** Time is short at this stage of life, and it's just not worth the energy to demand perfection from everyone—especially young children. It also gives you the chance to shamelessly spoil someone without being accused of being a bad father.
- **It can be payback.** Remember all those times when your kid told you how much he hated you and how he would never, never, ever be as horrible a parent as you were? Well, chances are that now that he's a parent, your child has become a lot more sympathetic to the errors you made when you were the dad and he was the kid. As my own father often tells me, "It's a great comfort to me that you're not a perfect parent."
- **It brings back the past.** "Grandparents get to relive the memories of the early phase of their own parenthood in observing the growth and development

"That's right, Timmy—once upon a time Grandpa was part of the target audience, just like you."

of their grandchildren," writes Benedek. Grandparenthood may also bring back some memories of your relationship with your own grandparents.

YOUR RELATIONSHIP WITH YOUR GRANDKIDS

There's no question that the grandfather-grandchild relationship can be wonderful for both. In fact, it "has even been advocated by scholars as being second only in emotional importance to that of the parent–child bond," says grandparent researcher Alan Taylor.

You'll probably like being able to share activities with your grandchildren, watching them grow, and feeling important and useful. Grandparents also enjoy being able to play different roles, including being a family historian or link to the past; a mentor and teacher; a role model for the family and society; a nurturer of emotional and physical well-being; a playmate; a wizard and magician to provide imagination experiences; and finally, a hero who can be looked up to, according to Arthur Kornhaber, a psychiatrist and president of the Foundation for Grandparenting.

Grandchildren, in turn, enjoy spending time with their grandparents because they like the grandparents' personalities, like sharing activities with them, like the individual attention and the sense of appreciation they get, and see the grandparents as role models and sources of inspiration, according to researcher Gregory Kennedy.

Keep in mind that grandfathers do things differently than grandmothers, in the same way that fathers do things differently than mothers. Grandfathers, for example, do their grandfathering pretty much like they did their fathering, paying more attention to physical, outdoor, and community activities, while grandmothers lean more toward the social and family-oriented. Grandfathers also tend to be more lenient than grandmothers.

In 1986, researchers Andrew J. Cherlin and Frank F. Furstenberg identified three basic grandparenting styles. Chances are your style is a combination of one of the following:

- **Remote grandparents** don't have a lot of direct contact with their grandchildren, and they behave in an unattached and distant way.
- **Companion grandparents** are relaxed and friendly, but take very little direct responsibility for the grandkids.
- **Involved grandparents** do take an active role. They have a lot of influence over how the grandchildren turn out, and they express definite expectations for their behavior.

"Feel free to take notes."

Also remember that just as your relationship with your child changes over time, so will your relationship with your grandchildren. Some grandparents just have a hard time connecting with their grandchildren, says grandfathering expert Stanley Cath. "They say that their activity is too intense, their language degrading, their logic appalling." A particularly close relationship with a school-age grandchild may cool when he gets close to adolescence and focuses more on establishing bonds with people outside the family. But that relationship may warm again when the child becomes an adult and establishes a friendship with you that's based on mutual desire rather than family obligation, according to Karen Roberto and Johanna Stroes, authors of *Grandchildren and Grandparents*.

Three more important factors may influence your relationships with your grandchildren:

- **Distance.** If you don't live near them, you're obviously not going to have the kind of relationship you would if you did. And the less contact, the less satisfying the relationship is for both sides.

283

On Not Becoming a Grandfather

We've been talking so far about the 90 percent of older dads who have grandkids. But what if you're in the 10 percent that doesn't?

For some, it may come as a blessing. If you hated fatherhood (and some men do—there's nothing wrong with that), for example, you may be relieved at not having to hold another yowling baby or, God forbid, change another diaper. Ditto if your child is disabled or irresponsible or otherwise unfit or unable to take care of a child of his own.

Most of the time, though, not being a grandfather is a major disappointment. Most guys, regardless of whether they liked being a father, would like a shot at being a grandfather. Several studies have found that many mothers become depressed if their adult daughters have repeated miscarriages. They feel that they're being deprived of grandmotherhood. Although there haven't been any similar studies of men, my guess is that the results would be about the same: fathers could become depressed and feel deprived if their adult children (sons or daughters) don't reproduce.

Besides that, not having the opportunity to be a grandfather may raise some other issues, including fear and disappointment that the family line won't continue on, and a feeling of being punished by your child and deprived of your one shot at immortality. If you really do want to have grandchildren, consider putting yourself in situations where you can interact with children, such as becoming a volunteer tutor in a local school. There are plenty of kids out there who don't have a grandfather around and who would benefit enormously from being with you.

- **Parental gatekeeping.** Your grandchildren's parents control your access to your grandchildren. The better your relationship to your own kids, the more time you'll be able to spend with the younger generations. This is especially true in cases of divorce. (See pages 296–98.)
- **Gender.** Grandfathers tend to favor boys over girls, especially the paternal line (your son's son will probably be your closest grandchild). And no, you're not the only sexist in the family. Grandmothers do basically the same thing, preferring girls, especially their daughter's daughter. Stanley Cath points out something fascinating that may influence your relationship with your son's son: "They (grandchild and grandparent) are linked in their common resentment of the father whom they both have cause to envy." Your grandson envies his father's strength and prowess and status—and so do you.

Your Changing Sex Life

Let's start with this. The prevailing myth that older people can't (or don't) have sex is just that—a myth. Having said that, there's no question that your sex life has changed since your teens.

Almost 90 percent of men (and about 85 percent of women) in their thirties have sex at least once a month. In the forties it slips to about 85 percent for men, 75 percent for women. In the fifties, it's 79 percent and 65 percent; in the sixties, it's 70 and 40; in the seventies, 44 and 15. In the eighties and above, it's about 18 percent for men, 3 percent for women. The reason women's numbers drop so sharply starting at about sixty is that half of women that age are widowed (vs. only 15 percent of men). Three-quarters of women over seventy-five are widowed, vs. 30 percent of men.

The natural aging process has certainly caused some changes. None of your basic senses (sight, hearing, taste, smell, and touch) are quite as sharp as they used to be, which means that it will probably take you longer and require a lot more direct stimulation of the penis to achieve an erection (what might have taken two seconds when you were seventeen may take five to ten minutes now). When you do have an erection, it probably won't be as firm as it used to be, thanks to your reduced cardiovascular capacity, which also makes it harder to engage in any kind of strenuous activity. Ejaculation won't be as forceful, and you'll notice a lengthening of the refractory period, the time your body takes to recover between orgasms. The good news is that you'll be able to last a lot longer, which your wife won't complain about, since it will enable you to give her more stimulation.

Sexual problems, including occasional bouts of impotence, at this age are perfectly normal. So don't panic. Many of the causes of impotence are often curable. Enlargement of the prostate, for example, can often be reduced by massaging it or through surgery. All sorts of other things may interfere with your sex life: diuretics and drugs for cardiovascular conditions, which a lot of elderly people take, contribute to erection problems. So do drugs for hypertension, alcohol, and some antidepressants. Diabetes and heart conditions, as well as hormone and circulation problems, can also cause trouble.

Responding to an inability to have an erection by worrying that there's something wrong with you will only lead to performance anxiety next time around. And given that most of what happens sexually is in our heads, the problem will probably repeat itself.

(continued on following page)

(continued from previous page)

There are four important steps you can take to keep your sex life going for as long as possible.

1. **Talk to your doctor.** Don't be embarrassed to tell him if you've had sexual problems. And be sure to ask about the side effects from any medication you're taking.

2. **Don't stop having sex.** Stopping in your fifties or sixties means you'll have a greater chance of becoming impotent later.

3. **Be creative.** It doesn't have to be all about penetration. There are lots of other things you and your wife can do to please each other sexually. Just relax and use plenty of lubrication.

4. **Talk to each other.** Researchers have found that having a close relationship with a spouse and feeling comfortable about discussing sexual feelings (and problems) is what separates couples who don't have sexual problems from those that do.

YOUR RELATIONSHIP WITH YOUR WIFE

About 65 percent of Americans sixty-five to seventy-four are married and living with a spouse. Strange as it sounds, elderly couples are happier with their marriages than couples of any other age, and divorce is almost unheard of. Couples who've been together for a very long time may stay together because they realize that they need each other's support—physical and emotional. It could also be that they realize that at this stage of life, it's going to be relatively hard to start a new relationship (although marriages that take place during these years are much less likely to end in divorce than those that occurred years ago). But whatever the reason, one thing is for sure: having a good marriage in old age—however a couple defines "good"—makes people happier in all other areas of their lives.

A lot of grandfathers I spoke with said that having grandchildren has made their relationships with their wife closer. Others said that closeness wasn't an issue, but that grandparenthood had given them and their wives something new to share.

OTHER RELATIONSHIP CHANGES DURING THE OLD-OLD YEARS

As you get older, you'll find that your relationships with just about everyone else in your life will change. Besides your wife, you'll create new kinds of relationships with your children, your friends, and even your coworkers (or former coworkers). We'll talk about your changing relationships with your kids and grandkids elsewhere in this chapter, but first let's take a look at how your friendships and other nonfamily relationships may change.

YOUR MENTORING RELATIONSHIPS

When you think about leaving a legacy, the inclination is to think of biological and financial legacies, the ones you leave to the younger generations of your family. But if you've been doing mentoring at work, taking one of the younger people under your wing and grooming him for bigger and better things, you're leaving behind another kind of legacy. Earlier, mentor-mentee relationships could have been a little tense, especially if the mentor felt that he was being overshadowed by his protégé (sure, that's what mentoring is supposed to be about, but it still hurts when it happens). At this stage, though, you'll probably be a lot more selfless, and you won't have any qualms about using your position and your power and your influence to help the people you most want to help.

RELATIONSHIPS WITH FRIENDS

You may find yourself with more casual friends than you had before, more guys you say "howdy" to every morning on the way down to get your newspaper. But your inner circle of close friends will shrink. You'll be more selective, and the friends you do keep will be very strong. Interestingly, even though your family members will be the biggest source of physical and emotional support for you, your friends will have a bigger influence in determining your overall well-being, according to Reed Larson and his colleagues.

That may be why many men say that losing a close friend can be almost as hard as losing a wife. Don't underestimate how hard it is to lose a friend. Psychotherapist Mary Lamia says that loss is the main thing that elderly people talk about in therapy, largely because there's so much of it. Losing your best friend, the one you played dominoes with twice a week for the past twenty years, can be devastating. And the pain and feelings of emptiness may return every year, on the anniversary of the friend's death or a date that was especially meaningful to him.

For the most part, you'll do the same kinds of things with your friends that you always have—socializing, hanging out, helping each other. But some of the specifics will vary, depending on where you live. Men who live in urban areas lean toward recreation activities that involve spending money, say gerontologists Karen Roberto and Jean Scott. Urban men also drop in on their friends more often than rural men, and they spend more happy occasions, like birthdays, together. Rural men do more of their socializing and recreation outdoors or at home. They also help each other make important decisions more than urban men.

FACING THE END

LOSING A SPOUSE

As mentioned above, about 15 percent of men over sixty, and about 30 percent of those over seventy-five, are widowed. Losing your wife will undoubtedly be the most significant change in your later years; it can be especially hard if you're dealing with your own physical problems. But the hardest issue is loneliness. Replacing your best friend, companion, sexual partner, and confidante will be impossible—no matter how many friends or family members you have around.

For what it's worth, older widowers tend to cope with their loss better than younger ones. Still, the loneliness can trigger a major, long-lasting depression (see "The Blues" sidebar on page 272). Support groups for widowers and widows are often helpful. But if you're finding yourself too despondent to function, or if you're thinking seriously either about suicide or throwing in the towel, please get some help.

DEATH

Back on pages 197–203, we talked about Elizabeth Kubler-Ross's five stages of grief as they apply to coping with the trauma of divorce. Let's talk about them again, but in their original context: death. Kubler-Ross did extensive interviews with terminally ill patients, and she found that almost all of them went through a similar psychological journey. Family members who are faced with the death of a loved one also go through the same five stages:

- ◆ **Denial.** As irrational (and vain) as it sounds, many people refuse to acknowledge that they will eventually die. Family members can also be in denial. Death isn't always a bad thing, at least according to novelist Paul Theroux, who wrote, "Death is an endless night so awful to contemplate that it can make us love life and value it with such passion that it may be the ultimate cause of all joy and all art."
- ◆ **Anger.** You might be angry at not having enough time to finish the things you want to finish, at not getting the respect or recognition you think you deserve, or any number of other things, and you may lash out at everyone around you. Your family might be angry that you're being taken from them

before they're ready to let you go, or that you're not getting the care they think you should have, or that they have unresolved issues with you, and so on.

- **Bargaining.** This might be a prayer not to die, or it might be an expression of regret—if only you had made a different choice at some point, things might be different, or you wouldn't have to die so soon.
- **Depression.** Facing an unpleasant reality—especially one you have absolutely no control over—can be enormously depressing. You might withdraw into yourself and be too gloomy to be around. Your family may be in the same state.
- **Acceptance.** Eventually, hopefully, you and everyone else will get to this point. It's nice if your family can get to this stage, but your acceptance is by far the most important. You need to be at peace with yourself before you can be at peace with everyone else.

Although these five stages provide a useful guide to understanding what's going on toward the end of life, it's critical to remember two things. First, not everyone goes through the steps in order, and not everyone spends the same amount of time on each one—it could be days, weeks, even years. Acceptance, if it's reached at all, does tend to be the last one, although a lot of people feel that it never completely happens—instead, you just keep cycling through the stages. Second, you and your family and friends will probably not all be in the same place at the same time. This can cause a lot of tension.

Also keep in mind the "anniversary reaction" that we discussed in chapter 6. Although this isn't true for everyone, you may have more control over your death than you might think. Mark Twain, for example, was born in 1835, the year Halley's Comet appeared, and he firmly believed that he would die when the comet returned in 1910, which is exactly what happened. Elderly people are frequently able to "hold off" their death until certain milestones are achieved, such as passing a birthday, outliving a parent or other relative, making it through one more holiday, or seeing the birth of a grandchild.

While preparing for one's own death is never easy, having gone through the shifts we talked about above (feeling satisfied that you've lived a good life and that you've made a contribution to your family and to society) can make it a little less hard. When you've taken care of your psychological and philosophical legacies, what's left are your physical and financial ones.

Hopefully you did all this long ago, but if not, spend some time talking to your attorney or tax adviser about whether a will or trust is best for you. You should also think about a durable power of attorney, what you want to happen to your body (burial, cremation, donation to science), and your preferences for a funeral service. Either collect or tell someone where to find important documents such as life and burial insurance policies, veteran's and social security benefits, wills, financial statements, and so on. If you need guidance for some of this, you might want to check out *www.finalthoughts.com/*. The American Association of Retired Persons (AARP) also has a tremendous amount of information on these and related topics at *www.aarp.org*.

Is There Such a Thing as a "Good Death"?

With very few exceptions, death isn't something anyone looks forward to— either their own or anyone else's. But the prospect is looming larger every day. And as you enter the old-old years, you'll probably have lost a number of friends and relatives.

Sudden or unexpected deaths are hard to deal with. They offer the "advantage" of not causing the deceased extended pain and suffering, but they also make it impossible to say good-bye, make peace, or achieve closure. Sometimes that's harder to deal with than the loss itself.

A more expected death, whether it's the end result of a long illness or simply the end of a long life, is very different, often allowing for final good-byes and reconciliations. But that doesn't necessarily make it any easier. So is there anything that can make death more bearable? Quite possibly.

Dr. Keith Meador, a researcher at Duke University, conducted an extensive study designed to identify the factors that the dying, the survivors, and doctors would say make for a "good" death. Most agreed that managing pain and symptoms, being able to make clear decisions, being able to adequately prepare for death, and completing a life review are critical.

Two more factors were especially important to patients themselves:

• **Being able to make a contribution to the well-being of others.** This shows how central the mentoring role is to people—especially fathers. Even in their final moments, they're concerned with making other people's lives better.

• **Needing to be affirmed and treated as a "whole person."** While nearly everyone agreed that this last point is important, patients and doctors defined "whole person" very differently. Here are the factors, along with the percentage of patients and doctors who cited each one.

	PATIENTS	DOCTORS
Being mentally aware	92 percent	65 percent
Being at peace with God	89 percent	65 percent
Not being a burden	89 percent	58 percent
Being able to pray	85 percent	55 percent
Planning a funeral	82 percent	58 percent
Feeling one's life is complete	80 percent	68 percent

I'm fascinated by how important "not being a burden" is to patients. You'd think that if there's one time in your life when it should be okay to be completely self-centered, it's when you're near death.

One thing that's clear from Meador's study is that doctors need to do a better job figuring out what's important to their patients. The simplest solution seems to be assertive and to tell your family and your doctor exactly what you want.

The deceased person isn't the only one affected by death, and a good death can help the survivors deal with their loss. Families, for example, aren't satisfied with end-of-life care when their dying relative is subject to pain and social isolation, according to Susan Pierce and Karin Kirchoff. And researcher Gregory Hinrichsen and his colleagues found that even though caring for a dying person puts a lot of emotional and physical strain on caregivers, it's far outweighed by the rewards, such as increased closeness. For surviving relatives and friends, one important factor of a "good death" is being there at the moment of death. Those who are find it easier to cope with the death than those who aren't, according to psychologists Kate Bennett and Steph Vidal-Hall.

Surviving spouses generally better adjust to their loss when they are able to spend time with their spouse before the death, resolving unfinished business and achieving closure. Sometimes, though, spending this time together has the exact opposite effect. Couples may become closer than ever before. That's usually a good thing, but in this case it can make the death even harder to deal with.

NURSING HOMES

Not surprisingly, the proportion of people in nursing homes rises sharply with age: only 1 percent of those between sixty-five and seventy-four live in homes. It goes up to 4 percent by age eighty-four, and 20 percent after that.

Moving into a well-managed home has the advantage of ensuring that you'll be comfortable and get the medical care you need. While those things are very important, there are also some big negatives that you may face. Leaving the neighborhood you lived in, with its familiar neighbors and activities, can be incredibly hard. So can facing the facts that you aren't able to take care of yourself, that your family can't or won't, and that almost no one ever moves *out* of a nursing home.

Perhaps the worst part about nursing homes (besides the food) is the social life. One study found that only half the people who entered a long-term care facility made new friends. Over a third of residents had no friends at all in the home. Being lucid, speaking well, and having pretty good eyesight all helped reduce social isolation and made it easier to make or keep friends, according to gerontologists Joan Retsinas and Patricia Garrity, but the longer people stayed in homes, the fewer friends they had, "suggesting that the home was an asocial place where long-term residents lost the ability to socialize."

Why Be an Involved Father?

At this point, you've had about as much influence on your adult child as you possibly can. Your grandchildren, however, are another story—your influence over them is just beginning. In the next few pages we'll talk about some of the specific ways.

"The country Grandpa came from was a stinking hellhole of unspeakable poverty where everyone was always happy."

BENEFITS TO YOUR GRANDCHILDREN

- **All-around success.** Kids who have close relationships with their grandfathers do better in school, have higher self-esteem, and are more successful at forming and keeping up friendships than kids whose relationships with their grandfathers aren't as close.

- **You can make up for deficits.** If your grandchild's father has abandoned his family or isn't the kind of father he should be, you can provide your grandchild with a positive male role model and teach him—through your own behavior—what it means to be a man in our society.

- **A stronger identity.** As an older person, you have access to your family's history in a way that your grandchild's parents don't. By passing on your family's lore, traditions, and rituals, you're giving your grandchild a link to the past as well as a stronger connection to who he is, where he came from, and his role in the family and the world. This can be tremendously valuable to adolescents during their quest for self-identity.

- **Values and beliefs.** Grandfathers play a key role in transmitting religious beliefs and core values such as the importance of academic and workplace achievement. And by simply being who you are, you'll be teaching your grandchild lessons about things like friendship, loyalty, honesty, and family— lessons he'd ignore if they had come from his parents.

- **A refuge from Mom and Dad.** When your grandchildren hit adolescence, chances are they're going to have a pretty rocky relationship with their parents, which means they'll feel safer talking to you about things they're too embarrassed or angry to ask their own parents. Just by being there, you allow your grandchild to reject and rebel against his family while still maintaining an important ally. This is good for the grandkids, says Therese Benedek. It "gives the child a sense of security in being loved without always deserving it."

- **Creating respect for the elderly.** Watching you age (hopefully gracefully) gives your grandchild a great opportunity to see that older people can be smart, active, and engaged. In addition, if you're not divorced or widowed, you're a model to your grandchild of how it's possible to maintain loving relationships over a lifetime.

BENEFITS TO YOUR CHILDREN

- **Support.** Researchers Barbara Tinsley and Ross Parke found that "geographically close grandparents are involved, appreciated, and active members of the support network of parents with young infants, as well as positive stimulatory agents for babies."

- **Closeness.** Children love being able to make their parents into grandparents, and most of those new grandparents are delighted about the additional identity. The presence of a grandchild is often the one thing that can restore strained parent-child relationships.
- **Life path.** Numerous studies of adults have found that closeness with the father during childhood is a good predictor of future academic and occupational success. Adult children who had good relationships with their parents as kids are also less likely to be homeless as adults.
- **Better mental health.** Father involvement protects adult children (especially daughters) against later mental and psychological problems. This is particularly true when the parents divorced when the children were younger. In adulthood, a good father-daughter rapport is linked to lower negative emotions for women, according to researcher Gail Agronick.
- **Time and advancement.** Your being available to do some child care once in a while can give your adult child the invaluable gift of time—to relax, to strengthen his relationship with his spouse, to go to school, or to work.
- **Role modeling.** All your years of being an involved dad have increased the chance that your own son or son-in-law will want to do the same. That, of course, will give him, his kids, and his partner all the benefits we've talked about in previous chapters.

BENEFITS TO YOU

- **A second chance—but with less downside.** A lot of men see grandfathering as a way to compensate for their own guilt over their inadequacies as fathers, says psychiatrist and grandfather expert Stanley Cath. Being a grandfather also gives you a chance to have all the fun of parenting but few of the responsibilities.
- **A source of pride.** It feels damned nice to know that who your child is and how successful he is in life (and all the other good stuff—none of the bad, of course) is at least partly thanks to you. And it'll feel just as nice to see your child being a good father and passing along the family values and ideals—just like you taught him.
- **A connection to the future.** Your grandchild is, in a sense, your legacy. He's your link to the future, the one who will keep a little bit of you alive after you're gone by passing on your philosophy, values, and genes to the next generation.
- **Reconnecting with your emotions.** Back when your kids were a lot younger, you experienced all sorts of emotions you had never felt before. In

the years since then, those emotions have changed and evolved, just as you have. But having a grandchild can reignite those feelings of unconditional love that you haven't felt since your own child was young. You also get a chance to be on the receiving end of unconditional love—something else you haven't felt for a long time. As psychiatrist Kyle Pruett's father once told him, "By this point in my life, I have either made it or not made it, and my grandchildren couldn't care less. They love me without judgment, and I return the favor without a second thought."

Staying Involved as a Father and a Grandfather

Here are some excellent ways to continue to be an active, involved part of your child's and grandchild's life. In addition to the points below, I highly recommend that you go to the "Staying Involved" sections of the previous chapters for suggestions appropriate to your grandchild's age.

- **Stay connected.** Call, write, e-mail, fax. Do whatever you have to do to keep in close (but not too close) contact with your grandchild. You might be able to facilitate communication by buying your grandchild (or his parents) a computer, sending a prepaid calling card, or getting yourself a toll-free number.
- **Watch the unsolicited advice.** Part of what makes the grandchild-grandparent relationship so satisfying for the grandchild is that it doesn't include a lot of the natural conflicts inherent in his relationship with his parents. Remember, if you act like a parent, you'll be treated like one—and get rejected.
- **Be there.** If you live nearby, mark as many of your grandkids' special occasions as possible: birthdays, soccer games, school plays, music recitals, graduations, performances, and so on. If you don't live close by, at least try to mark those special occasions with a call or a card.
- **Expose them to a wide variety of things.** Take them to museums and concerts, share your hobbies with them, read to them, or better yet, tell them about your childhood and the "good old days" (even if you have to make some up).
- **Get to know them.** Learn about what they're interested in—the kind of music they listen to, the books they read, their hobbies. At the very least you'll learn a lot about popular culture. You'll also get a ton of great birthday-present ideas.

Staying Involved in Special Circumstances

When it comes to divorce and custody, there's so much focus on the conflict between the mother and the father that almost no one pays any attention to grandparents. That means that if your child is the noncustodial parent and has limited access to the children, you will too. And if he has no access at all, or visitation is supervised, or his ex decides to punish him by not letting him see the kids, you're going to get punished too. And if your child's ex never liked you anyway, this is the perfect opportunity for her (or him, in the rare cases where the father gets primary custody) to make you miserable. That's really a shame, because you, as a grandparent, can do a lot to help the kids cope with the divorce.

So what are your options if your child is divorced and you want more time with your grandchild? To start with, do everything you can to keep things civil between you and the custodial parent, who controls your access to your grandchildren. If you hate her, never let that show, and never say anything remotely negative about her in front of the kids. Here are some other important things to do:

- Set her mind at ease. Try to convince your child's ex that you have no intention of turning the kids against her or of using them as a weapon.
- Let her set the ground rules—and live with them. The goal here is to get some time with your grandchildren. If your child's ex wants you to wear one green sock and one red one, do it.
- If that doesn't work, call, e-mail, and send packages or letters. If your grandchildren have moved to another state or are too far away to visit, this may be your only option.
- Suggest mediation. It's usually cheaper and more effective than going to court.
- Go to court—but only as a last resort. A number of states have laws protecting grandparents' rights to have access to their grandchildren. Be careful, though. Let the dust settle after the divorce before you even consider this. Your taking this step could rekindle resentment and hostility.
- Never give up. No matter what happens, keep trying to establish or maintain contact with your grandchildren.

Sometimes divorce disrupts grandparent-grandchild relationships. Other times it creates them. Given the incredible number of breakups and remarriages, there's a good chance that you could wake up one day to find yourself an instant stepgrandfather.

"It's your grandparents, claiming their visitation rights."

In this kind of situation, the most important thing you can do is take a deep breath and relax. It's tempting to jump right in and try to make everyone into one big happy family—especially if your stepgrandkids are your first grandkids. But it'll never happen.

Everyone needs time to adjust to the new situation. Coming on too strong, acting too grandfatherly, or trying to "buy" the kids' love with presents could create more problems than it solves, in addition to the ones outlined in "Don't be a Disneyland grandpa" (page 299). Your new stepgrandchildren may treat you with suspicion. Even worse, you might stir up a lot of resentment among the biological grandparents, especially if they don't get to see their grandkids as much as you do.

Your role can be quite important. Simply being warm, accessible, understanding, and accepting can help the kids with their transition by making the new stepfamily seem a lot less scary.

(continued on following page)

(continued from previous page)

Here are some important things to do if you become a stepgrandparent:

- ◆ Make friends with the grandkids' biological families and reassure them that you're not trying to displace them.
- ◆ Let the kids know it's okay not to love you, and that relationships take time to build. They also need to be reassured that you're not trying to displace any of their existing grandparents.
- ◆ Encourage the kids' relationships with their biological grandparents and the rest of their relatives. This may not be easy to do, but it's essential, because it shows the children (and their families) that your first priority is the kids and their happiness.
- ◆ Do the same kinds of things you'd do (or you already do) with biological grandkids. See "Staying Involved as a Father and a Grandfather," pages 295–300.
- ◆ Don't expect smooth sailing. Your relationship with your stepgrandchildren will get better and closer over time. But there may be some bumps in the road. You and the grandkids might be getting along wonderfully, and then they could blow up and lash out at you over what seems to be nothing. One explanation (besides typical teenage irrationality) is that the kids might suddenly be seized by feelings of guilt, believing that if they like or even love you, they are betraying their other grandparents.

- ◆ **Get to know them one at a time.** If you have more than one grandchild, you'll probably spend most of your time together in groups. But try to log some one-on-one hours too. This has a number of advantages, starting with not having to waste time breaking up fights between siblings or cousins. More important, it will give you and your grandchildren a wonderful chance to truly get to know each other a lot better. It'll also give your grandchild's parents a great opportunity to spend some individual time with their other children, which is something all of them secretly wish they could do more often.
- ◆ **Get to know their friends.** Know their names and what your grandkids see in them. Asking about the friends, having them over to dinner or inviting one or two along on an outing, and otherwise supporting the friendships shows your grandchildren you're interested in them.

"Watch closely. This is how you write checks."

♦ **Don't be a Disneyland grandpa.** The term *Disneyland dad* usually applies to noncustodial divorced fathers who try to fill every second of time with their kids with fun and games and treats. Plenty of grandparents do the same kind of thing, buying the grandkids extravagant gifts, eating every meal out, taking them on expensive trips, giving in to their every whim, throwing discipline to the wind, and generally treating them like visiting royalty instead of children. Falling into this trap is easy, but you won't be able to keep it up for very long. Sooner or later you'll run out of money or ideas. And when that happens, your grandkids will have gotten so spoiled that they'll do one of two things (maybe even both): resent you for not giving them "their due," or think you don't love them any more. The solution is to try to make their time with you a little more normal. Of course you're going to indulge them a little—that's what grandparents are for. But don't go overboard.

299

- **Be patient.** Preteens and teens may back away from you during their I-must-reject-everything phase. Don't judge; just be there and let them know they have a safe place to land if they need anything.
- **Don't take sides.** Never, ever get in the middle of an argument between your children and theirs. And never, ever tell your grandchild anything negative about either of his parents.
- **Support their parents.** No matter what you think, never undermine your grandkids' parents in front of them. If you really disagree with something either one is doing, save it for later.
- **Back off.** The bottom line here is that you need to let your adult children live their own lives. Yes, you're interested in their job prospects. And sure, you want to make sure their finances are in order, that they aren't drowning in credit card debt, and that they're putting aside enough money to put your grandchildren through college. And you probably want to make sure they're happily married to the right person. But the truth of the matter is that none of that is your business. It's fine to clip out an occasional article on a topic you think your child might find interesting. But aside from that, unless there's real danger to life or limb, keep your advice (including telling your child that he or she married an idiot) to yourself unless it's specifically asked for.

Conclusion

As we've seen throughout this book, the influence of fatherhood goes far beyond the father himself. When a man is involved with his family and his children, his children are physically and mentally healthier and more successful. Their mother is usually happier, more satisfied, more fulfilled, and has more opportunity to grow and develop as a person. He also influences the world around him, constantly striving to make it a better and safer place for his children and grandchildren.

What's especially interesting is that the size of his world keeps growing over time. Before having children, most of us are concerned largely with ourselves—getting an education, establishing ourselves in a career, finding a mate, getting settled. We still care about others, but the focus is mostly on the things that concern us. When we become fathers, though, our world expands. A lot of things that used to be fairly abstract—crime, drugs, school vouchers, war, and so on—suddenly hit closer to home. Looking out for ourselves isn't enough anymore—there are future generations to worry about too. Changes need to be made, and sitting back, waiting for someone else to take care of things, is no longer an option. We become coaches, mentors, community leaders. And as we take on a greater role, we become better citizens, better people, better men.

For most fathers, being a dad is one of their defining features. There probably isn't a single aspect of their lives that fatherhood hasn't shaped, at least in some small way. Having children influences where they live, who their friends are, their education and hobbies, their jobs, where they go on vacation, their overall health, their marriages. In short, everything.

Being a father gives many men inspiration, hope, joy, and a reason to live—in some cases quite literally. In her book *Parenthood: Its Psychology and Psychopathology,* Therese Benedek talks about the role fatherhood played in the lives of many men who served in World War II. In their letters home to their families, many of these soldiers described how their thoughts and fantasies of their children helped them overcome hardships and deprivation, and made them more resourceful when they were in actual danger. Each man knew he might not be able to see his wife or child again for years, if ever. But his sense of responsibility for his family kept him going.

Naturally, being a father has plenty of downs to go with all those ups. Not all the changes fatherhood brings are positive or even welcome. Fathers and their children exist in a kind of symbiotic relationship, each influencing and adapting to the other, each growing and changing, struggling to find their bearings in a constantly shifting landscape. It's a never-ending developmental process for both, lasting from expectant fatherhood through grandfatherhood, and even beyond.

Although the overall path through fatherhood takes men through some fairly predictable terrain, every man's trip is a little different. Some get started the "traditional" way, having the first of their 2.5 children in their mid- to late twenties, putting the kids through college, marrying them off, becoming grandfathers and possibly even great-grandfathers. Some start earlier, in their teens, while others don't start their families until they're in their forties or fifties. Their experience of the early years of fatherhood will be much different than younger dads', and they'll probably miss out on the grandfather years entirely.

Some men skip the early developmental stages—their own and their babies'—and get introduced to fatherhood stepfathering someone else's children. Some get divorced and raise their kids on their own, while others get cut off from their children's lives. Some adopt, others are widowed; some are married, others not. For a lot of men the process isn't linear at all; they start off on one trajectory but may skip and repeat some steps along the way, perhaps even combining two or more at the same time.

That's my story in a nutshell. Things started off "normally"—marriage, two kids—but then I got divorced. Years later I remarried and became a dad again at forty-four. And I can assure you that being a father this time is much different—

for me, my wife, my baby, my parents, my friends—than it was the first time around. And then, of course, there's the way that having a new baby sister is affecting my older kids. They're excited about being big sisters and at the prospect of earning some baby-sitting money. But they're worried that the new baby will change my relationship with them. And the one who's now the middle child resents having had to give up her coveted spot as the baby in the family.

All in all, every father—and everyone around him—has a completely unique experience. But whether it's good, bad, or indifferent, one thing is guaranteed: he'll be a father for life, and it will truly be a journey of joy, challenge, and change.

Bibliography

ADOPTION

Brodzinsky, D., and M. Schechter, eds. *The Psychology of Adoption.* New York: Oxford University Press, 1990.

Dehaan, Gayle Hoekstra. "Parent–Adolescent Communication: Differences between Adopted and Biological Adolescents." Ph.D. diss., University of Minnesota, August 1998.

Finley, G. E. *Adoptive and Biological Fathers' Enjoyment of First-time Fathering.* Minneapolis, Minn.: National Council on Family Relations, 1999.

Hoopes, J. L., and L. M. Stein, *Identity Formation in the Adopted Adolescent: The Delaware Valley Study.* Washington, D. C.: Child Welfare League of America, 1985.

Lindholm, B. W., and J. Touliatos. "Psychological Adjustment of Adopted and Nonadopted Children." *Psychological Reports* 46 (1980): 307–10.

Nickman, Steven L., M. D. "Losses in Adoption: The Need for Dialogue." *Psychoanalytic Study of the Child,* 40 (1985): 365-97

ADULT DEVELOPMENT, GENERAL
Books

Akhtar, Salman, and Selma Kramer, eds. *The Seasons of Life: Separation-Individuation Perspectives.* Northvale, N. J.: Jason Aronson, 1997.

Austrian, Sonia G., ed. *Developmental Theories through the Life Cycle.* New York: Columbia University Press, 2002.

Buchmann, Marlis. *The Script of Life in Modern Society: Entry into Adulthood in a Changing World.* Chicago: University of Chicago Press, 1989.

Colarusso, Calvin A., and Robert Nemiroff. *Adult Development.* New York: Plenum Press, 1987.

Featherman, David L., and Richard M. Lerner, eds. *Life-Span Development and Behavior.* Vol. 12. Hillsdale, N. J.: Erlbaum, 1994.

Gould, Roger. *Transformations: Growth and Change in Adult Life.* New York: Simon & Schuster, 1978.

Hoare, Carol Hren Erikson. *On Development in Adulthood: New Insights from the Unpublished Papers.* London: Oxford University Press, 2002.

Levinson, Daniel. *The Seasons of a Man's Life.* New York: Ballantine, 1978.

Newman, Barbara M., and Philip R. Newman. *Development through Life: A Psychosocial Approach,* 6th ed. Pacific Grove, Calif.: Brooks/Cole Publishing, 1994.

Noller, Patricia, Judith A. Feeney, and Candida Peterson. *Personal Relationships across the Lifespan.* Philadelphia: Psychology Press/Taylor & Francis, 2001.

Sheehy, Gail. *Understanding Men's Passages: Discovering the New Map of Men's Lives.* New York: Random House, 1998.

Tucker-Ladd, Clayton. *Psychological Self-Help.* Mental Health Net, 2000. Not available in print. Can be downloaded at *http://mentalhelp. net/psyhelp/download/.*

Vaillant, George. *Adaptation to Life.* Cambridge, Mass.: Harvard University Press, 1998.

———. *The Wisdom of the Ego.* Cambridge, Mass.: Harvard University Press, 1993.

Wolman, B. B., ed. *Handbook of Developmental Psychology.* Englewood Cliffs, N. J.: Prentice Hall, 1982.

Articles

Bozett, Frederick W. "Male Development and Fathering throughout the Life Cycle." *American Behavioral Scientist* 29, no. 1 (1985): 41–54.

Caspi, Avshalom. "The Child Is Father of the Man: Personality Continuities from Childhood to Adulthood." *Journal of Personality and Social Psychology* 78, no. 1 (2000): 158–72.

Cath, Stanley. "Loss and Restitution in Late Life." In *The Seasons of Life: Separation-Individuation Perspectives,* edited by Salman Akhtar and Selma Kramer. Northvale, N. J.: Jason Aronson, 1997.

Christiansen, Shawn L., and Rob Palkovitz. "Exploring Erikson's Psychosocial Theory of Development: Generativity and its Relationship to Paternal Identity, Intimacy, and Involvement in Childcare." *Journal of Men's Studies* 7, no. 1 (1998): 133–56.

Kramer, Selma, LeRoy J. Byerly, and Salman Akhtar. "Growing Together, Growing Apart, Growing Up, and Growing Down." In *The Seasons of Life: Separation-Individuation Perspectives,* edited by Salman Akhtar and Selma Kramer. Northvale, N. J.: Jason Aronson, 1997.

Palkovitz, Rob. "Parenting as a Generator of Adult Development: Conceptual Issues and Implications." *Journal of Social and Personal Relationships* 13, no. 4 (1996): 571–92.

Parke, Ross D. "Families in Life-Span Perspective: A Multilevel Developmental Approach." In *Child Development in Life-Span Perspective,* edited by E. Mavis Heatherington et al., 159–90. Hillsdale, N. J.: Erlbaum, 1988.

Peck, Robert C. "Psychological Developments in the Second Half of Life." In *Middle Age and Aging,* edited by B. L. Neugarten, 88–92. Chicago: University of Chicago Press, 1968.

Vaillant, George. "Natural History of Male Psychological Health." *Archives of General Psychiatry* 33 (1976): 535–45.

———. "The Evolution of Defense Mechanisms during the Middle Years." In *The Middle Years,* edited by J. M. Oldham and R. S. Liebert, 58–72. New Haven, Conn.: Yale University Press, 1989.

FATHERHOOD
General

Biller, Henry, and Robert Trotter. *Father Factor: What You Need to Know to Make a Difference.* New York: Pocket Books, 1994.

Birks, Stuart, and Paul Callister, eds. *Perspectives on Fathering.* Issues paper no. 4. Palmerston North, New Zealand: Centre for Public Policy Evaluation, College of Business, Massey University, 1999.

Carnoy, Martin, and David Carnoy. *Fathers of a Certain Age: The Joys and Problems of Middle-Aged Fatherhood.* Minneapolis: Fairview Press, 1997

De Luccie, Mary. "Predictors of Paternal Involvement and Satisfaction. *Psychological Reports* 79, no. 3 (1996): 1351–59.

Hanson, Shirley, and Frederick W. Bozett, eds. *Dimensions of Fatherhood.* Beverly Hills, Calif.: Sage, 1985.

Levine, Suzanne Braun. *Father Courage: What Happens When Men Put Family First.* New York: Harcourt, 2000.

Lewis, R., and C. Roberts. "Postparental Fathers in Distress." In *Men in Transition,* edited by K. Soloman and N. Levy. New York: Plenum, 1982.

Parke, Ross. *Fatherhood.* Cambridge, Mass: Harvard University Press, 1996.

Parke Ross, and Armin Brott. *Throwaway Dads: The Myths and Barriers That Keep Men from Being the Fathers They Want to Be.* Boston: Houghton Mifflin, 1999.

Pruett, Kyle. *Fatherneed: Why Father Care Is as Essential as Mother Care for Your Child.* New York: Free Press, 2000.

Tiedje, L. B., and C. Darling-Fisher. "Fatherhood Reconsidered: A Critical Review." *Research in Nursing and Health* 19, no. 6 (1996): 471–84.

Wilson, Melvin N., Anthony Chambers, and Karen M. Schmidt. "Exploring Relationship Satisfaction Using Item Response Theory: A Fathers' Perspective." Working paper #01-09-FF, Center for Research on Child Wellbeing, 2001.

ADULT CHILDREN

Agronick, Gail Susan. "Do Fathers Matter? Women's Relationships with Their Fathers and Mothers in Adulthood." Ph.D. diss., University of California, Berkeley, 2001.

Aquilino, William S., and Khalil R. Supple. "Parent-Child Relations and Parent's Satisfaction with Living Arrangements When Adult Children Live at Home." *Journal of Marriage and the Family* 53, no. 1 (1991): 13–27.

DiGeronimo, Theresa Foy. *How to Talk to Your Adult Children about Really Important Things.* San Francisco: Jossey-Bass, 2002.

Farb, Mary Lou. "Adult Women's Perceptions of How the Father-Daughter Attachment Relates to Their Current Levels of Self-Esteem: A Phenomenological Study." Ph.D. diss., Saint Louis University, 1999.

Frain, Betty, and Eileen Clegg. *Becoming a Wise Parent for Your Grown Child: How to Give Love and Support without Meddling.* Oakland, Calif.: New Harbinger, 1997.

FATHERHOOD *(continued)*

Genuchi, Marvin Charles II. "The Father-Daughter Relationship and Selected Intimate-Related Outcomes in Adult Females." Ph.D. diss., Texas A&M University, 1997.

Kaufman, Gayle, and Peter Uhlenberg. "Effects of Life Course Transitions on the Quality of Relationships between Adult Children and Their Parents." *Journal of Marriage and the Family* 60, no. 4 (1998): 924–38.

Maisel, Roberta. *All Grown Up: Living Happily Ever After with Your Adult Children.* Gabriola Island, Canada: New Society, 2001.

Nydegger, Corinne N., and Linda S. Mitteness. "Fathers and Their Adult Sons and Daughters." *Marriage and Family Review* 16, nos. 3–4 (1991): 249–56.

Pillemer, Karl, and J. Jill Suitor. " 'Will I Ever Escape My Child's Problems?': Effects of Adult Children's Problems on Elderly Parents." *Journal of Marriage and the Family* 53, no. 3 (1991): 585–94.

Roiter-Eash, Jane E. "An Exploratory Study of Fathers' and Adult Daughters' Perceptions of Their Relationship." Ph.D. diss., Institute for Clinical Social Work, 1997.

Schmertmann, Carl P., Monica Boyd, William Serow, and Douglas White. "Elder-Child Coresidence in the United States: Evidence from the 1990 Census." *Research on Aging* 22, no. 1 (2000): 23–42.

Shehan, Constance L., and Jeffrey W. Dwyer. "Parent-Child Exchanges in the Middle Years: Attachment and Autonomy in the Transition to Adulthood." In *Aging Parents and Adult Children,* edited by Jay A. Mancini, 99–116. Lexington, Mass.: Lexington Books/D. C. Heath and Company, 1989.

Spitze, Glenna, and John R. Logan. "Helping as a Component of Parent–Adult Child Relations." *Research on Aging* 14, no. 3 (1992): 291–312.

Suitor, J. Jill, and Karl Pillemer. "Explaining Intergenerational Conflict When Adult Children and Elderly Parents Live Together." *Journal of Marriage and the Family* 50, no. 4 (1988): 1037–47.

CHILD CARE, GENERAL

Bernadette-Shapiro, Susan, Diane Ehrensaft, and Jerrold Lee Shapiro. "Father Participation in Childcare and the Development of Empathy in Sons: An Empirical Study." *Family Therapy* 23, no. 2 (1996): 77–93.

Blair, S. L., and C. Hardesty. "Paternal Involvement and the Well-Being of Fathers and Mothers of Young Children." *Journal of Men's Studies* 3 (1994): 49–68.

Hawkins, A. J., S. L. Christiansen, K. P. Sarent, and E. J. Hill. "Rethinking Fathers' Involvement in Child Care: A Developmental Perspective." *Journal of Family Issues* 14 (1993): 531–49.

McKeering, Helen, and Kenneth I. Pakenham. "Gender and Generativity Issues in Parenting: Do Fathers Benefit More than Mothers from Involvement in Child Care Activities?" *Sex Roles* 43, nos. 7–8 (2000): 459–80.

Radin, Norma. "Primary Caregiving and Role-Sharing Fathers." In *Non-Traditional Families: Parenting and Child Development,* edited by M. E. Lamb, 173–204. Hillsdale, N. J.: Erlbaum, 1982.

———. "Primary Caregiving Fathers in Intact Families." In *Redefining Families,* edited by A. E. Gottfried and A. W. Gottfried. New York: Plenum Publishing Corporation, 1994.

Williams, E., and N. Radin. "Effects of Father Participation in Child Rearing: Twenty-Year Follow-up." *American Journal of Orthopsychiatry* 69, no. 3 (1999): 328–36.

CHILDREN, GENERAL

Amato, Paul R. "Father-Child Relations, Mother-Child Relations, and Offspring Psychological Well-Being in Early Adulthood." *Journal of Marriage and the Family* 56, no. 4 (1994): 1031–42.

Biller, H. "Fatherhood: Implications for Adult and Child Development." In *Handbook of Developmental Psychology,* edited by B. B. Wolman, 702–25. Englewood Cliffs, N. J.: Prentice Hall, 1982.

———. *Father, Child, and Sex Role.* Lexington, Mass.: D. C. Heath, 1971.

———. "The Father and Personality Development: Paternal Deprivation and Sex-Role Development." In *The Role of the Father in Child Development,* edited by M. E. Lamb, 104. New York: Wiley, 1981.

Cath, Stanley, A. R. Gurwit, and J. M. Ross, eds. *Father and Child: Developmental and Clinical Perspectives.* Boston: Little, Brown, 1982.

Dollahite, D. C., A. J. Hawkins, and S. E. Brotherson. "Fatherwork: A Conceptual Ethic of Fathering as Generative Work." In *Generative Fathering: Beyond Deficit Perspectives,* edited by A. J. Hawkins and D. C. Dollahite, 17–35. Thousand Oaks, Calif.: Sage, 1997.

Futris, Ted. "The Developmental Trajectories of Teenage Males Who Become Fathers Compared to Those Who Delay Fatherhood." Ph.D. diss., University of North Carolina at Greensboro, 2000.

Hardesty, Constance, DeeAnn Wenk, and Carolyn Stout Morgan. "Paternal Involvement and the Development of Gender Expectations in Sons and Daughters." *Youth and Society* 25, no. 3 (1995): 283–97.

FATHERHOOD *(continued)*

Hawkins, Alan J., and David C. Dollahite, eds. *Generative Fathering: Beyond Deficit Perspectives.* Thousand Oaks, Calif.: Sage, 1997.

Imbesi, L. "When the Father Is Passive: His Impact on the Development of Masculinity." *Journal of Analytic Social Work* 4, no. 4 (1997): 1–19.

Lamb, Michael, ed. *The Role of the Father in Child Development.* 3d ed. New York: Wiley, 1997.

Pleck, Joseph. "Paternal Involvement: Levels, Sources, and Consequences." In *The Role of the Father in Child Development,* edited by Michael Lamb, 66–103. 3d ed. New York: Wiley, 1997.

Snarey, John. *How Fathers Care for the Next Generation: A Four-Decade Study.* Cambridge, Mass: Harvard University Press, 1993.

Whitcomb, John. *Capitate Your Kids: Give Your Kids a Financial Head Start.* New York: Penguin, 2002.

CHILDREN, SPECIAL SITUATIONS

Essex, Elizabeth Lehr. "Mothers and Fathers of Adults with Mental Retardation: Feelings of Intergenerational Closeness: Family Relations." *Interdisciplinary Journal of Applied Family Studies* 51, no. 2 (2002): 156–65.

Greenberg, Jan S. "Differences between Fathers and Mothers in the Care of Their Children with Mental Illness." In *Men as Caregivers: Theory, Research, and Service Implications,* edited by Betty J. Kramer and Edward H. Thompson, 269–93. New York: Springer, 2002.

Margalit, Malka, Yona Leyser, and Yakov Avraham. "Classifications and Validation of Family Climate Subtypes in Kibbutz Fathers of Disabled and Nondisabled Children." *Journal of Abnormal Child Psychology* 17 (1989), 91–107

Meyer, D. J. "Fathers of Children with Handicaps: Developmental Trends in Fathers' Experiences over the Family Lifecycle." In *Families of Handicapped Children: Needs and Supports across the Lifespan,* edited by R. R. Fewell and P. F. Vadasy, 35–73. Austin, Texas: Pro-Ed, 1986.

Vadasy, P. F., R. R. Fewell, D. J. Meyer, and M. T. Greenberg. "Supporting Fathers of Handicapped Children: Preliminary Findings of Program Effects." *Analysis and Intervention in Developmental Disabilities* 5 (1985): 151–64.

DAUGHTERS, GENERAL

Eicher, Terry, and Jesse Geller. *Fathers and Daughters: Portraits in Fiction.* New York: Plume, 1991.

Kelly, Joe. *Dads and Daughters.* New York: Broadway Books, 2002.

Marone, Nicky. *How to Father a Successful Daughter.* New York: Fawcett Columbine, 1988.

EDUCATION

Grolnick, Wendy, and Maria Slowiaczek. "Parents' Involvement in Children's Schooling: A Multidimensional Conceptualization and Motivational Model." *Child Development* 65 (1994): 237–52.

Levine, James, Dennis Murphy, and Sherril Wilson. *Getting Men Involved: Strategies for Early Childhood Programs.* New York: Scholastic, 1993.

National Center for Education Statistics. *Fathers' Involvement in Their Children's School.* Washington, DC: National Center for Education Statistics, 1998.

Nord, Christine Windquist, DeeAnn Brimhall, and Jerry West, *Fathers' Involvement in Their Children's Schools.* Washington, D. C.: U. S. Department of Education, National Center for Education Statistics, 1997.

Radin, Norma. "The Influence of Fathers upon Sons and Daughters and Implications for School Social Work." *Social Work in Education* 8 (1986): 77–91.

———. "The Role of the Father in Cognitive, Academic, and Intellectual Development." In *The Role of the Father in Child Development,* edited by Michael Lamb, 379–428. New York: Wiley, 1981.

Smith, T. E. "Mother-Father Difference in Parental Influence on School Grades and Educational Goals." *Sociological Inquiry* 59 (1989): 88–98.

U. S. Department of Education, Office of Educational Research and Improvement. "Nonresident Fathers Can Make a Difference in Children's School Performance." Issue brief, June 1998.

Wagner, B. M., and D. A. Phillips. "Beyond Belief: Parent and Child Behaviors and Children's Perceived Academic Competence." *Developmental Psychology* 63 (1992): 1380–91.

Weinberger, J. "Childhood Antecedents of Conventional Social Accomplishment in Midlife Adults: A 26-year Prospective Study." *Journal of Personality and Social Psychology* 60 (1991): 586–95.

EXPECTANT FATHERS AND THE TRANSITION TO FATHERHOOD

Brott, Armin. *The Expectant Father: Facts, Tips, and Advice for Dads-to-Be.* 2d ed. New York: Abbeville Press, 2001.

Hart, John. *Becoming a Father: The Real Work of a Man's Soul.* Deerfield, Fla.: Health Communications, 1998.

May, Katherine A. "Three Phases of Father Involvement in Pregnancy." Nursing Research 31 (November–December 1982): 337–42.

FATHERHOOD (continued)

Neville, B., and R. D. Parke. (1997). "Waiting for Paternity: Interpersonal and Contextual Implications of the Timing of Fatherhood." *Sex Roles* 37 nos. 1-2 (1997): 45-61.

Roopnarine, Jaipaul, and Brent Miller. "Transitions to Fatherhood." In *Dimensions of Fatherhood,* edited by Shirley Hanson and Frederick W. Bozett. Beverly Hills, Calif.: Sage, 1985.

Shapiro, Jerrold Lee. *The Measure of a Man: Becoming the Father You Wish Your Father Had Been.* New York: Delacorte Press, 1993.

Zapp, Rosanne. "Paternal Engrossment in Early-Timed and Later-Timed Fatherhood." Ph.D. diss., California School of Professional Psychology–San Diego, 1998.

FAMILIES, GENERAL

Biller, Henry. *Fathers and Families: Paternal Factors in Child Development.* Westport, Conn.: Auburn House, 1993.

Cath, Stanley, Alan Gurwitt, and Linda Gunsberg, eds. *Fathers and Their Families.* Hillsdale, N. J.: Analytic Press, 1989.

Jordan, Pamela L. "The Mother's Role in Promoting Fathering Behavior." In *Becoming a Father: Contemporary Social, Developmental, and Clinical Perspectives* edited by J. L. Shapiro, M. J. Diamond, and M. Greenberg, pp. 61–71 New York: Springer Publishing Co., 1995.

Speicher-Dubin, B. "Relationships between Parent Moral Judgement, Child Moral Judgement and Family Interaction: A Correlational Study." Ph. D. diss., Harvard University, 1982.

INFANTS

Brott, Armin. *The New Father: A Dad's Guide to the First Year.* New York: Abbeville Press, 1997.

Fein, Robert. "Consideration of Men's Experiences and the Birth of a First Child." In *The First Child and Family Formation,* edited by Warren Miller and Lucile Newman, 327–39. Chapel Hill, N. C.: Carolina Population Center, 1978.

Feldman, Shirley, S. C. Nash, and B. G. Aschenbrenner. "Antecedents of Fathering." *Child Development* 54 (1983): 1015–24.

Greenberg, M., and N. Morris. "Engrossment: The Newborn's Impact on the Father." In *Father and Child: Developmental and Clinical Perspectives,* edited by S. H. Cath, A. R. Gurwit, and J. M. Ross. Boston: Little, Brown, 1974.

Jordan, Pamela L., et al. "Supporting the Father When an Infant is Breastfed." *Journal of Human Lactation*—Vol 9, no 1 (1993): 31–34.

May, Katherine A. "First-Time Fathers' Responses to Unanticipated Caesarean Birth: An Exploratory Study." Unpublished report to U. C. S. F., 1982.

Palm G., and Bill Joyce. "Attachment from a Father's Perspective." Unpublished manuscript, 1994.

Pedersen, Frank, and Kenneth Robson. "Father Participation in Infancy." *American Journal of Orthopsychiatry* 39 (April 1969): 466–72.

Yogman, M. W., D. Kindlon, and F. Earls. "Father Involvement and Cognitive/Behavioral Outcomes of Preterm Infants." *Journal of the American Academy of Child and Adolescent Psychiatry* 34 (1995): 58–66.

PRESCHOOLERS

Brott, Armin. *The New Father: A Dad's Guide to the Toddler Years.* New York: Abbeville Press, 1998.

Crockett, L. J., D. J. Eggebeen, and A. J. Hawkins. "Fathers' Presence and Young Children's Behavioral and Cognitive Adjustment." *Journal of Family Issues* 14 (1993): 355–77.

Easterbrooks, M. A., and W. A. Goldbert. "Toddler Development in the Family: Impact of Father Involvement and Parenting Characteristics." *Child Development* 53 (1984): 740–52.

Fox, R. A., and P. Solis-Camara. "Parenting of Young Children by Fathers in Mexico and the United States." *Journal of Social Psychology* 137, no. 4 (1997): 489–95.

Giveans, David, and Michael Robinson. "Fathers and the Preschool-Aged Child." In *Dimensions of Fatherhood,* edited by Shirley Hanson and Frederick W. Bozett. Beverly Hills, Calif.: Sage, 1985.

PRETEENS AND TEENS

Ellis, Bruce J., Steven McFadyen-Ketchum, Kenneth A. Dodge, Gregory S. Pettit, and John E. Bates. "Quality of Early Family Relationships and Individual Differences in the Timing of Pubertal Maturation in Girls: A Longitudinal Test of an Evolutionary Model." *Journal of Personality and Social Psychology* 77, no. 2 (1999): 387–401.

Gabel, S., M. C. Stallings, S. Schmitz, S. E. Young, and D. W. Fulker. "Personality Dimensions and Substance Misuse: Relationships in Adolescents, Mothers and Fathers." *American Journal on Addictions* 8, no. 2 (1999): 101–13.

Harris, K. M., F. F. Furstenberg Jr., and J. K. Marmer. "Paternal Involvement with Adolescents in Intact Families: The Influence of Fathers over the Life Course." *Demography* 35, no. 2 (1998): 201–16.

Julian, T. W., P. C. McKenry, and M. W. McKelvey. "Mediators of Relationship Stress between Middle-Aged Fathers and their Adolescent Children." *Journal of Genetic Psychology* 152 (1991): 381–86.

Martin, Dorothy. "Fathers and Adolescents." In *Dimensions of Fatherhood,* edited by Shirley Hanson and Frederick W. Bozett, 170–95. Beverly Hills, Calif.: Sage, 1985.

FATHERHOOD *(continued)*

Paulson, S. E., and C. L. Sputa. "Patterns of Parenting during Adolescence: Perceptions of Adolescents and Parents." *Adolescence* 31 (1996): 369–81.

Shulman, Shmuel, and W. Andrew Collins, eds. *Father-Adolescent Relationships.* San Francisco, Calif.: Jossey-Bass, 1993.

Shulman, Shmuel, and Moshe Klein. "Distinctive Role of the Father in Adolescent Separation-Individuation." In *Father-Adolescent Relationships*, edited by Shmuel Shulman and W. Andrew Collins, 41–57. San Francisco, Calif.: Jossey-Bass, 1993.

SCHOOL-AGE CHILDREN

Bradley, Robert. "Fathers and the School-Age Child." In *Dimensions of Fatherhood,* edited by Shirley Hanson and Frederick W. Bozett. Beverly Hills, Calif.: Sage, 1985.

Duncan, Greg, Martha Hill, and Jean Yeung. "Fathers' Activities and Children's Attainments." Paper presented at the NICHD Conference on Father Involvement, Washington, D.C., October 10–11, 1996.

Radin, N., E. William, and K. Coggins. "Paternal Involvement in Childrearing and the School Performance of Native American Children: An Exploratory Study." *Family Perspectives* 27 (1993): 375–91.

Wentzel, K. R., and S. S. Feldman. "Parental Predictors of Boys' Self-Restraint and Motivation to Achieve at School: A Longitudinal Study." *Journal of Early Adolescence* 13 (1993): 183–203.

SONS, GENERAL

Goldblatt, Mark, "The Burden of Proof: The Story of a Father and Son." *National Review Online,* June 14, 2002.

Johnson, Stephen George. "The Effect of the Adult Son's Fatherhood on the Hierarchical Structure of the Father-Adult Son Relationship." Ph.D. diss., Texas Woman's University, 1995.

GRANDFATHERS AND OLDER ADULTS
Books

DiGeronimo, Theresa Foy. *How to Talk to Your Senior Parents about Really Important Things.* San Francisco: Jossey-Bass, 2001.

Kornhaber, A. *Contemporary Grandparenting.* Thousand Oaks, Calif.: Sage, 1996.

Kornhaber, A., and K. L. Woodward. *Grandparent/Grandchildren: The Vital Connection.* Garden City, N.Y.: Doubleday, 1981.

Articles

Barrett, Linda L. "Can We Talk? Families Discuss Older Parents' Ability to Live Independently. . . . or Do They?" *AARP,* April 2001.

Boon, S. D., and M. J. Brussoni. "Young Adults' Relationships with Their 'Closest' grandparents: Examining Emotional Closeness." *Journal of Social Behavior and Personality* 11 (1996): 439–58.

Cherlin, A. J., and F. F. Furstenberg. "Styles and Strategies of Grandparenting." In *Grandparenthood,* edited by V. L. Bengtson and J. F. Robertson, 97–116. Beverly Hills, Calif.: Sage, 1985.

Hinrichsen, Gregory A., Nancy A. Hernandez, and Simcha Pollack. "Difficulties and Rewards in Family Care of the Depressed Older Adult." *Gerontologist* 32 (1992): 486–92.

Kennedy, Gregory E. "Shared Activities of Grandparents and Grandchildren." *Psychological Reports* 70, no. 1 (1992): 211–27.

Kennedy, Gregory E. "Grandchildren's Reasons for Closeness with Grandparents." *Journal of Social Behavior and Personality* 6, no. 4 (1991): 697–712.

Larson, Reed, Roger Mannell, and Jiri Zuzanek. "Daily Well-Being of Older Adults with Friends and Family." *Psychology and Aging* 1, no. 2 (1986): 117–26.

Reisman, John M. "An Indirect Measure of the Value of Friendship for Aging Men." *Journals of Gerontology* 43, no. 4 (1988): 109–10.

Retsinas, Joan, and Patricia Garrity. "Nursing Home Friendships." *Gerontologist* 25, no. 4 (1985): 376–81.

Roberto, K. A., and J. Stroes. "Grandchildren and Grandparents: Roles, Influences, and Relationships." *International Journal of Aging and Human Development* 34, no. 3 (1992): 227–39.

Roberto, Karen A., and Jean P. Scott. "Friendships in Late Life: A Rural-Urban Comparison." *Lifestyles* 8, nos. 3–4 (1987): 16–26.

Roberto, K. A., and R. R. Skogland. "Interactions with Grandparents and Greatgrandparents: A Comparison of Activities, Influences, and Relationships." *International Journal of Aging and Human Development* 43, no. 2 (1996): 107–17.

Robertson, J. F. "The Significance of Grandparents: Perceptions of Young Adult Grandchildren." *Gerontologist* 42 (1976): 137–40.

Taylor, Alan C. "Perceptions of Intergenerational Bonds: The Comparison between Grandfathers and their Adult Grandchildren." Ph. D. diss., Virginia Polytechnic and State University, 1998.

Thomas, J. L. "Gender Differences in Satisfaction with Grandparenting." *Psychology and Aging* 1, no. 3 (1986): 215–19.

———. "Older Men as Fathers and Grandfathers." In *Older Men's Lives,* edited by E. H. Thompson Jr., 197–217. Thousand Oaks, Calif.: Sage, 1994.

Tinsley, B. R., and R. D. Parke. "Grandparents as Interactive and Social Support Agents for Families with Young Infants." *International Journal of Aging and Human Development* 25 (1987): 259–77.

GRIEF AND DEATH

Bennett, Kate M., and Steph Vidal-Hall. "Narratives of Death: A Qualitative Study of Widowhood in Later Life." *Ageing and Society* 20 (2000): 413–28.

Blauner, Robert. "Death and Social Structure." *Psychiatry* 29 (1966): 378–94.

Chethik, Neil. *Fatherloss: How Sons of All Ages Come to Terms with the Deaths of Their Dads.* New York: Hyperion, 2001.

Gabriel, Martha A. "Anniversary Reactions: Trauma Revisited." *Clinical Social Work Journal* 20, no. 2 (1992): 179–92.

Kirchhoff, Karin T., Vicki Spuhler, Lee Walker, Ann Hutton, and Beth Vaughn-Cole. "The Vortex: Families' Experiences with an ICU Death." *American Journal of Critical Care* 11 (2002): 200–209.

Pierce, Susan Foley. "Improving End-of-Life Care: Gathering Suggestions from Family Members." *Nursing Forum* 34, no. 2 (1999): 5–14.

Steinhauser, Karen E., Elizabeth Clipp, Maya McNeilly, Nicholas Christakis, Lauren McIntyre, and James Tulsky. "In Search of a Good Death: Observations of Patients, Families, and Providers." *Annals of Internal Medicine* 132: 825-32 (2000).

Turvey, Carolyn, Yeates Conwell, Michael P. Jones, Caroline Phillips, Eleanor Simonsick, Jane L. Pearson, and Robert Wallace. "Risk Factors for Late-Life Suicide: A Prospective, Community-Based Study." *American Journal of Geriatric Psychiatry* 10 (2002): 398–406.

Yeates, Conwell, Paul R. Duberstein, Kenneth Connor, Shirley Eberly, Christopher Cox, and Eric D. Caine. "Access to Firearms and Risk for Suicide in Middle-Aged and Older Adults." *American Journal of Geriatric Psychiatry* 10 (August 2002): 407–16.

MEN, GENERAL

Garfinkel, Perry. *In a Man's World: Father, Son, Brother, Friend, and Other Roles Men Play.* Berkeley, Calif.: Ten Speed Press, 1992.

Sandman, David, Elisabeth Simantov, and Christina An. *Out of Touch: American Men and the Health Care System.* New York: Commonwealth Fund, 2000.

PARENT DEVELOPMENT
Books

Ambert, Anne-Marie. *The Effect of Children on Parents.* New York: Hayworth Press, 2001.

Anthony, E. James, and Therese Benedek. *Parenthood: Its Psychology and Psychopathology.* Boston: Little, Brown, 1970.

Belsky, Jay, and John Kelly. *The Transition to Parenthood: How a First Child Changes a Marriage: Why Some Couples Grow Closer and Others Apart.* New York: Delacorte, 1994.

Galinsky, Ellen. *The Six Stages of Parenthood.* Reading, Mass: Addison-Wesley, 1987.

Group for the Advancement of Psychiatry. *The Joys and Sorrows of Parenthood.* New York: Scribner, 1973.

Hart, Holly Madeleine. "Generativity and Social Involvement." Ph.D. diss., Northwestern University, 1998.

McBride, Angela Barron. *The Growth and Development of Mothers.* New York: Harper and Row, 1973.

Palkowitz, Rob. *Involved Fathering and Men's Adult Development: Provisional Balances.* Mahawah, N. J.: Erlbaum, 2002.

Palkovitz, Rob, Marcella A. Copes, and Tara N. Woolfolk. " 'It's Like . . . You Discover a New Sense of Being': Involved Fathering as an Evoker of Adult Development." *Men and Masculinities* 4, no. 1 (2001): 49–69.

Rapoport, Rona, and Robert Rapoport. *Fathers, Mothers, and Society: Perspectives on Parenting.* New York: Vintage, 1980.

Robinson, Bryan E., and Robert L. Barret. *The Developing Father: Emerging Roles in Contemporary Society.* New York: Guilford Press, 1986.

Schoen, Elin. *Growing with Your Child: Reflections on Parent Development.* New York: Doubleday, 1995.

Unell, Barbara, and Jerry L. Wykoff. *The Eight Seasons of Parenthood: How the Stages of Parenting Constantly Reshape our Adult Identities.* New York: Random House, 2000.

Articles

Seltzer, Marsha Mailick, and Carol D. Ryff, "Parenting across the Life Span: The Normative and Nonnormative Cases." In *Life-Span Development and Behavior,* edited by David L. Featherman and Richard M. Lerner, vol. 12. Hillsdale, N. J.: Erlbaum, 1994.

PRETEENS, TEENS, AND YOUNG ADULTS
Books

Bradley, Michael. *Yes, Your Teen Is Crazy.* Gig Harbor, Wash.: Harbor Press, 2002.

Gianetti, Charlene, and Margaret Sagarese. *The Roller Coaster Years: Raising Your Child through the Maddening yet Magical Middle School Years.* New York: Broadway Books, 1997.

Henkart, Andrea Frank, and Journey Henkart. *Cool Communication.* New York: Perigee, 1998.

Hymowitz, Kay. *Ready or Not*. New York: Free Press, 1999.

Kuczmarski, Susan Smith. *The Sacred Flight of the Teenager: A Parent's Guide to Stepping Back and Letting Go*. Chicago: Book Ends, 2002.

Riera, Michael, and Joseph Di Prisco. *Field Guide to the American Teenager*. Cambridge, Mass.: Perseus, 2000.

Articles: Preteens, Teens

Abma, Joyce, Anne Driscoll, and Kristin Moore. "Young Women's Degree of Control over First Intercourse: An Exploratory Analysis." *Family Planning Perspectives* 30 (January–February 1998): 12–18.

Gallagher, Richard. "Teenagers in Trouble: Understanding and Preventing Tragic Outcomes." 2000. *http://www. pbs. org/wgbh/front/shows/georgia/isolated/gallagher. html.*

Shedler, Jonathan, and Jack Block. "Adolescent Drug Use and Psychological Health: A Longitudinal Inquiry." *American Psychologist*, May 1990, p. 612.

Wilks, J., V. J. Callan, and D. A. Austin. "Parent, Peer, and Personal Determinants of Adolescent Drinking." *British Journal of Addiction* 84, no. 6 (1989): 619–30.

Brook, Judith S., R. E. Adams, E. B. Balka, and E. Johnson. "Early Adolescent Marijuana Use: Risks for the Transition to Young Adulthood." *Psychological Medicine* 32, no. 1 (2002): 79–91.

Johnson, Monica Kirkpatrick. "Social Origins, Adolescent Experiences, and Work Value Trajectories during the Transition to Adulthood." *Social Forces* 80, no. 4 (2002): 1307–41.

Mark A. Schuster et al. "The Sexual Practices of Adolescent Virgins: Genital Sexual Activities of High School Students Who Have Never Had Vaginal Intercourse." *American Journal of Public Health* 86, no. 11 (1996): 1570–76.

Articles: Young Adults

Kasdin, Karin. *Watsamatta U: A Get-a-Grip Guide to Staying Sane through Your Child's College Application Process*. Worcester, Mass.: Chandler House Press, 2002.

Kastner, Laura, and Jennifer Wyatt. *The Launching Years: Strategies for Parenting from Senior Year to College Life*. New York: Three Rivers, 2002.

Zhu Xiao Di, Yi Yang, and Xiaodong Liu. "Young American Adults Living in Parental Homes." Paper W02-3, Joint Center for Housing Studies, Harvard University, 2002.

Glick, Paul C., and Sung-ling Lin. "More Young Adults Are Living with Their Parents: Who Are They?" *Journal of Marriage and the Family* 48, no. 1 (1986): 107–12.

SEPARATION, DIVORCE, AND SINGLE PARENTING

Aquilino, William S. "Later Life Parental Divorce and Widowhood: Impact on Young Adults' Assessment of Parent-Child Relations." *Journal of Marriage and the Family* 56, no. 4 (1994): 908–22.

Brott, Armin. *The Single Father: A Dad's Guide to Parenting without a Partner*. New York: Abbeville Press, 1999.

Cooney, Teresa M., and Peter Uhlenberg. "The Role of Divorce in Men's Relations with Their Adult Children after Mid-life." *Journal of Marriage and the Family* 52, no. 3 (1990): 677–88.

Guidabaldi, J., H. K. Cleminshaw, J. D. Perry, B. K. Natasi, and J. Lightel. "The Role of Selected Family Environment Factors in Children's Post-Divorce Adjustment." *Family Relations* 35 (1986): 141–51.

Kalter, Neil. "Long-Term Effects of Divorce on Children: A Developmental Vulnerability Mode." *American Journal of Orthopsychiatry* 57 (1987): 587–600.

McLanahan, S., and G. Sandefur. *Growing Up with a Single Parent*. Cambridge, Mass.: Harvard University Press, 1994.

Orbuch, Terri, Arland Thornton, and Jennifer Cancio. "The Impact of Divorce, Remarriage, and Marital Quality on the Relationships between Parents and Their Children." Paper presented at the NICHD Conference on Father Involvement, Washington, D. C., October 10–11, 1996.

White, L., and D. Peterson. "The Retreat from Marriage: Its Effect on Unmarried Children's Exchange with Parents." *Journal of Marriage and the Family* 57 (1995): 428–34.

STEPFAMILIES

Booth, A. , and J. Dunn, eds. *Stepfamilies: Who Benefits, Who Does Not?* Hillsdale, N. J.: Erlbaum, 1994. Heatherington, M. E., and K. M. Jodl. "Stepfamilies as Settings for Child Development." In *Stepfamilies: Who Benefits, Who Does Not?* edited by A. Booth and J. Dunn, 55–70. Hillsdale, N. J.: Erlbaum, 1994.

Lauer, Robert H, Ph.D. and Jeanette C. Lauer, Ph.D. *Becoming Family: How to Build a Stepfamily That Really Works*. Minneapolis, Minn.: Augsburg Fortress Publishers, February 1999.

Moseley, Douglas and Naomi Moseley. *Making Your Second Marriage a First-Class Success*. Roseville, Calif.: Prima Publishing. 1998.

Nelsen, Jane. *Positive Discipline for Blended Families: Nurturing Harmony, Respect, and Unity in Your New Stepfamily*. Roseville, Calif.: Prima Publishing. 1997.

Pickhardt, Carl E. . *Keys to Successful Stepfathering* (Barron's Parenting Key). New York: Barron's Educational Series, 1997.

Wisdom, Susan and Jennifer Green. *Stepcoupling: Creating and Sustaining a Strong Marriage in Today's Blended Family.* New York: Three Rivers Press, 2002.

Ziegahn, Suzen. *7 Steps to Bonding With Your Stepchild.* New York: Griffin Trade Paperback, 2001.

—— *The Stepparent's Survival Guide.* Oakland, Calif.: New Harbinger, 2002.

MISCELLANEOUS
Books

Greenspan, Stanley, and Nancy Thorndike Greenspan. *First Feelings: Milestones in the Emotional Development of Your Baby and Child.* New York: Penguin, 1985.

Heatherington, E. Mavis, et al., eds. *Child Development in Life-Span Perspective.* Hillsdale, N. J.: Erlbaum, 1988.

Heller, Joseph. *Something Happened.* New York: Ballantine, 1974.

Jones, Gerard. *Killing Monsters: Why Children Need Fantasy, Super Heroes, and Make-Believe Violence.* New York: Basic Books, 2002.

Lamb, M. E., *Nontraditional Families: Parenting and Child Development.* Hillsdale, N. J.: Erlbaum, 1982.

Larson, Reed, and Maryse H. Richards. *Divergent Realities: The Emotional Lives of Mothers, Fathers, and Adolescents.* New York: Basic Books, 1994.

Miller, Warren, and Lucile Newman, eds. *The First Child and Family Formation.* Chapel Hill, N.C.: Carolina Population Center, 1978.

Murdock, Maureen. *The Hero's Daughter.* New York: Fawcett Columbine, 1994.

Olson, D., and J. DeFrain. *Marriage and Family: Diversity and Strengths.* Mountain View, Calif.: Mayfield, 1997.

Sears, Robert, Eleanor E. Maccoby, and Harry Levin. *Patterns of Childrearing.* Evanston, Ill.: Row Peterson, 1957.

Yarrow, Leon, Judy Rubinstein, and Frank Pedersen. *Infant and Environment: Early Cognitive and Motivational Development.* New York: Halsted Press, 1975.

Articles

Cohler, Bertram J., Justin L. Weiss, and Henry V. Grunebaum. "Child Care Attitudes and Emotional Disturbances among Mothers of Young Children." *Genetic Psychology Monographs* 82 (August 1970): 33.

Cunningham, M. R., A. R. Roberts, A. P. Barbee, P. B. Druen, and C. H. Wu. "'Their Ideas of Beauty Are, on the Whole, the Same as Ours': Consistency and Variability in the Cross-Cultural Perception of Female Physical Attractiveness." *Journal of Personality and Social Psychology* 68 (1995): 261–79.

Fishman, Elizabeth A., and Steven A. Meyers. "Marital Satisfaction and Child Adjustment: Direct and Mediated Pathways." *Contemporary Family Therapy* 22, no. 4 (2000): 437–52.

Gordon, Richard. "Factors in Postpartum Emotional Adjustment." *Obstetrics and Gynecology* 25 (1965): 158–64.

Ishii-Kuntz, and Karen Seccombe Masako. "The Impact of Children upon Social Support Networks throughout the Life Course." *Journal of Marriage and the Family* 51, no. 3 (1989): 777–90.

Koestner, R., C. E. Franz, and J. Weinberger. "The Family Origins of Empathic Concern: A Twenty-six-Year Longitudinal Study." *Journal of Personality and Social Psychology* 58 (1990): 7089–117.

Melges, F. T. "Postpartum Psychiatric Syndromes." *Psychosomatic Medicine* 23 (1968): 520–25.

Reinke, Barbara. "The Timing of Psychosocial Changes in Women's Lives: The Years 25 to 45." *Journal of Personality and Social Psychology* 48 (1985): 1353–64.

Sadeh, Avi, Amiram Raviv, and Reut Gruber. "Sleep Patterns and Sleep Disruptions in School-Age Children," *Developmental Psychology* 36, no. 3 (2000): 291–301.

Acknowledgments

Although mine is the only name on the cover, this book wouldn't have been possible without the substantial contributions of literally hundreds of people, including: Bob Abrams, for his confidence and passion for these issues over the years; Jimmy Boyd and Stuart Miller, for their moral and research support; Susan Costello, for her vision and guidance; Jackie Decter, for her continued insights; Celia Fuller, for making it all look so good; Stanley Cohen, for his idea that this book should be written and for his marketing expertise; Mary Lamia, for taking so much time to tinker with the manuscript; Jim Levine and Arielle Eckstut, for launching me on a journey that none of us had any idea would last so long and be so much fun; Rob Palkovitz, Ross Parke, Michael Lamb, and Phil and Carolyn Cowan, for inspiring me and paving the way; Melissa Rowland, for keeping the wheels turning; Miranda Ottewell, for skillfully copyediting the text; Misha Beletsky, for contributing to the design; and Louise Kurtz, for handling the book production. My parents, Gene and June Brott, for reading and contributing to the early drafts; my sisters Tamar, for her editing and humor, and Rachel, for helping me brush up on my kid-wrestling skills by letting me borrow Solomon; and to Liz, for the eyes, patience, hugs, warmth, prodding, being my best friend, and for keeping me laughing. But the biggest thanks of all goes to the hundreds of men I've relied on over the years—the expecting, first time, old, young, experienced, inexperienced, widowed, gay, step, renewed, and adoptive dads—all of whom selflessly shared their insights, thoughts, fears, worries, advice, concerns, and wisdom.

Index

CARTOON CREDITS